About the Authors

Janet Gabriel Townsend is a geographer from the University of Durham, UK, who teaches Geography, Gender and Change. She came to gender issues through many years of work with pioneer families in the rainforests of Latin America, and to the work of non-governmental organisations through the women in *Women's Voices from the Rainforest*. She is also a co-author of the *Atlas of Women and Men in India*.

Emma Zapata Martelo grew up in Colombia, studied sociology at the University of Texas and has long worked with poor rural women in Mexico. She is a Professor at the Postgraduate College in Agricultural and Forestry Sciences at Montecillo, Mexico, where she has built up a group of staff and postgraduates engaged in action research in gender and development. She has published widely in Spanish and English, including *Mujeres Rurales ante el Nuevo Milenio* and *Desarrollo Rural y Genero*.

Pilar Alberti Manzanares is a Spanish anthropologist engaged in parallel work at the same College. Her specialization has been in work with indigenous women (whose first language is not Spanish), in their production of crafts and their struggles with domestic violence. She has published widely in Spanish on gender and ethnicity, and on rural women, as in *Estrategias de Sobrevivencia de Mujeres Campesinas e Indigenas ante la Crisis*; she is a co-author of *Desarrollo Rural y Genero*.

Jo Rowlands is evaluation adviser for Voluntary Service Overseas, London, UK and has lectured at the University of Durham. From her work with non-governmental organisations in the UK and Ecuador and her doctoral research in Honduras for the University of Durham, she has developed a new analysis of women's self-empowerment, published in *Questioning Empowerment: Women in Honduras* and other work in English and Spanish.

Marta Mercado Gonzalez is on leave from the Postgraduate College to research for her doctorate at the University of Guelph, Ontario, Canada, on gender, sustainable development and globalisation in Mexico.. Marta came to work with rural women from a training as a veterinary adviser and subsequent extensive field experience. She shares with Emma Zapata and Pilar Alberti a commitment to action research, and is a co-author of *Mujeres Rurales ante el Nuevo Milenio*.

(See also the Introductions to Chapters Four, Five, Six and Seven, where the authors introduce themselves.)

Women and Power: Fighting Patriarchies and Poverty

Janet Gabriel Townsend, Emma Zapata, Joanna Rowlands, Pilar Alberti and Marta Mercado

Zed Books

LONDON • NEW YORK

Women and Power: Fighting Patriarchies and Poverty was first
published by Zed Books Ltd, 7 Cynthia Street, London N1 9JF, UK,
and Room 400, 175 Fifth Avenue, New York, NY 10010, USA, in
1999.

Distributed in the USA exclusively by St Martin's Press, Inc.,
175 Fifth Avenue, New York, NY 10010, USA.

Cover designed by Andrew Corbett.
Set in Monotype Ehrhardt and Franklin Gothic by Ewan Smith.
Printed and bound in the United Kingdom by Biddles Ltd,
Guildford and King's Lynn.

A catalogue record for this book is available from the British
Library.

US CIP data is available from the Library of Congress.

ISBN 1 85649 803 4 cased
ISBN 1 85649 804 2 limp

Contents

Acknowledgements

It is to Mexican rural women and to field workers and activists that we owe this book. We feel that they have much to say to a wider world.

This book derives from many years of work with poor rural women, culminating in a project funded by the United Kingdom's Economic and Social Research Council on women's self-empowerment in rural Mexico. This funding enabled Janet Townsend and Jo Rowlands from the University of Durham (UK) to collaborate with Emma Zapata, Pilar Alberti and Marta Mercado from the Colegio de Postgraduados en Ciencias Agrícolas (Mexico) in exploring the self-empowerment of poor rural women in Mexico. We visited eight local, non-governmental organisations in eight states of Mexico in 1995, and invited all of them to a workshop at Tapalehui, Morelos. Our deepest thanks are due to the women who came to Tapalehui and to all the organisations and activists who gave us so much. All our thanks are also due to the Colegio, the University of Durham and the British Council (Mexico City). We thank in particular Josefina López, for so much listening to the recorded voices, and Silvia Alemán, Elsa Chavez, Blanca López and Beatríz Martinez for their contributions to the workshop. We are grateful to Angelika Sherp for translation. Our children, partners and friends have given us much encouragement, inspiration and patient support. Emma Zapata, Pilar Alberti and Marta Mercado thank Janet Townsend for her work on the translation of their chapters and all authors thank her for her editorial work on the book.

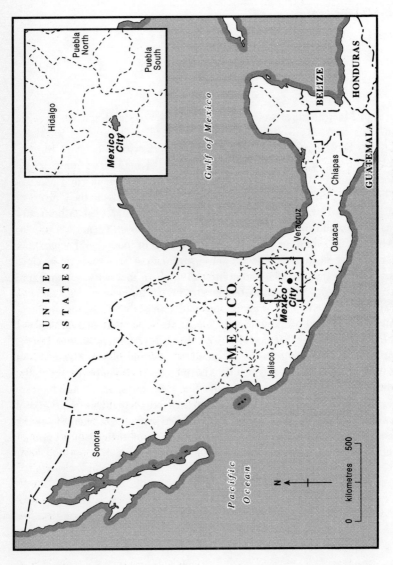

Mexico: Locations of the organisations discussed in this book

1

Introduction

Janet Gabriel Townsend and Emma Zapata

Women and Power

> I'm going to say, 'Yes, I can!' Well, I can do it, even though they tell me, 'No! No, you can't do it!' (Citlali, 1995, translated from the Spanish)

Citlali can say and can do because she has embraced the power to say and do, has empowered herself. Citlali was born poor and powerless in the sweltering lowlands in the middle of the Isthmus of Tehuantepec, in Mexico. She grew up almost excluded from Mexican society, rejected and oppressed not only as an Indian,[1] speaking Mixe (pronounced *mee-hay*) while the national language is Spanish, but as a woman. Citlali has built up the powers to work for the betterment of her people and to transform her own consciousness and her own life: to be elected secretary of the land committee in her village, to farm a plot of land, to build new, happy relationships with her husband and children and, recently, to represent the Mixe at a conference in Spain of 'indigenous' peoples from around the world. We can all learn from Citlali.

This is a book on the self-empowerment of women, intended for a wide audience. At the turn of this millennium, it seems to be poor women in poor countries who are celebrating new powers and setting out to change their own lives and those of their peoples, rather than the more obvious, Western, beneficiaries of women's liberation. 'Development',[2] as we shall see, is too often seen as a technical matter. We want to put power back into 'development', for activists, for workers in non-governmental organisations and for women's-studies scholars, in rich as well as poor countries. We have set out to deal with power in everyday terms. Although the book uses the words and experiences of specific women in Mexico, the country is merely a case study for workers and students around the world. We believe very strongly that discussions about power have become inaccessible; they tend to be limited to difficult, academic studies, as if understanding power was not everyone's business. We want to learn from Citlali by looking at her words in the context of her life and experiences, set against writings on women's empowerment from India to Peru.

Empowerment Empowerment is a word much used in 'development', but its meaning has become devalued; it can mean whatever the user wants it to mean, not what the audience understands by it. Yet the self-empowerment which Citlali has achieved is a real practical change which we can all aspire to, men as well as women. There are already good books on empowerment (Chapter Two), but here we want to put more flesh on the idea of self-empowerment, illustrating it from the talk of Mexican rural women and Mexican academics on issues of power. This is talk we have found to be meaningful to activists in Ghana, India and the Philippines and to students in the UK, India and Mexico.

About This Book

The structure of the book In Chapter Two, we tell of self-empowerment and our own understanding of it (Rowlands 1995a, b, 1997a, b) with evidence from many countries. We argue that we must each empower ourselves, that it is not helpful to speak of empowering other people. It is possible to enable another person to do this or that, but only they can empower themselves to do it, only they can take, can embrace the powers to do it. In Chapter Three, we tell of the context in which poor women in most poorer countries are facing new poverty and ever reduced services and yet at the same time are being offered new opportunities to work in groups, some of which have gone beyond the struggle to make money to work in self-empowerment.

We take a wider definition of *power* than many writers, and we structure the book around this understanding. Many define empowerment merely as gaining a place in decision-making, as a share in 'power over' other people (Chapter Seven). To us, power is more than 'power over', which is the power of those who once had the power to convince Citlali 'No! No, you can't do it!' Power is also Gandhi's 'power from within' which Citlali had to build to say, 'Yes, I can!' (Chapter Four). And power is the 'power with' other women, the power of collaboration, of the group, which gives her force (Chapter Five). Power is also the 'power to do' which Citlali is claiming (Chapter Six), and which she interprets very much in terms of new skills, of the power to earn, the power to make money. Citlali, we shall see, welcomes these ways of talking about power, and uses them to empower herself further, to take on struggles such as few of the authors or readers of this book will ever know in their own lives.

Power is seen at different levels, as discussed in Chapter Eight. There is power in a woman's idea of herself and in her personal relationships. There is power in groups, from one women's group to alliances at the regional, national or international level. Chapter Three examines the new scale and role of organisations in most societies, from women's groups through social movements to non-governmental/non-profit organisations. In the last fifteen years, the state has withdrawn from many activities in Mexico and thousands of organisations have sprouted up both to fill its place and to take on new roles. This is almost a worldwide phenomenon. We ask, first, what is the role of these new groupings of people in the world and in Mexico? And, second, what is it possible for such groups to do to support women in empowering themselves?

Chapter Nine concludes by asking how we put the power back into empowerment. The World Bank likes to present 'development' and what organisations can achieve as apolitical, technical issues (Paul Nelson 1990). For us, these are nothing of the sort, but always issues of power, so – where next? 'What is important and revealing ... is not what metropolitan intellectuals think ... but what the actors in the situation think' (Mary Louise Pratt 1997: 432).

This is our belief. Although we are 'metropolitan intellectuals', we are also deeply involved, so we cannot stand outside what is said.[3] We are 'consciously partial' in that we are taking sides because of what we have learned. We shall try to explain our views, sometimes using what other metropolitan intellectuals say – but what really matters is 'what the actors in the situation think'.

Where the book began Rural women have something special to say to academics and practitioners about empowerment. In rural areas, women are physically and often socially more isolated from each other and from global fashions. They are not exposed to the concentrated urban shock of consumerism. Yet some set out to change their lives. Empowerment is not about abstractions but about real feelings in real people and real changes in real lives. To listen to rural women is to put the power back into development, to learn from the traditionally powerless about changes in which they pride themselves.

The story begins at Tapalehui, Mexico, where an exceptional group of women met for a week in 1995. Each had her own life story of work with women, some as members of grassroots groups, others as their supporters. Across divides of class, nation, culture and ethnicity, they met in the course of their searches for new ways to build a better world for everyone. They came together to discuss women's power and to compare the many roads by which they had become activists, the way each group had worked. Do poor women have power? Do they want it? Do they use it? Or is it something remote, beyond their reach, owned and enjoyed by others, which only poststructuralist academics can fathom or debate? Behind the talk lay the experience of many years of struggle in different places, different cultures, different lifeworlds. All the women work in rural areas, but some speak Nahuatl, some Mixe, some Tzotzil, some Tzeltal, some Spanish, some even English; they came to Tapalehui (pronounced Tapal*ay*wee) from the northern deserts, the high mountains, the tropical rainforests of Mexico, from villages, towns and universities, wearing traditional embroidered dresses, jeans or Bermuda shorts.

These women's talk, their images, are of action and movement, 'waking up', 'getting out of the house', 'joining a group', 'getting to decide', 'trying to be another woman'. As the grassroots women say, 'Women were always inside the house, we went on waiting for ever in the house' (Araceli, Nahuatl-speaking woman from *Puebla North*).[4] Linaloe is an Indian woman who also speaks Nahuatl; she sounds stilted in Spanish but her meaning and conviction are clear:

> Before joining the group, the truth is, we were just ignorant. And since we got into the group we've learned so much, we get more and more aware of everything. Because, before, only the men had groups, organisations. They got organised, in the co-operative and everything, and the women went on waiting in the house. And now women go to meetings, join in, get organised. Now *we* know what we're going to do: to make our communities matter. (Linaloe, *Puebla North*)

Teresa is Spanish-speaking and comes from near the frontier with the USA, but she talks in much the same way about the time 'before' the group. She is more familiar with international feminist language:

> I used to feel so lonely, so sad, with no friends, without knowing any other women, shut up, in my house ... because before, well, the men just had you shut up. So I couldn't go out, not even to go shopping and run errands ... We've always talked about the struggle to make women equal to men ... I love trying to change, trying to be a different woman, looking for a different kind of man – I don't mean physically different, but a new kind of man who's looking for change too ... We don't want to boss everyone. One thing that worries me is, men aren't so perfect that you want to be like them.

Who are the women who say these things? What have their lives been like? How have they struggled? Why did they agree to come to Tapalehui? And how could this possibly matter to the rest of us?

The meeting First, how did we come to be at Tapalehui? We, the authors, are all feminist academics who want to know: how are poor women getting more say in their own lives?[5] We came to Tapalehui to learn from these experts, both peasant women[6] and activists, about rural women tackling issues of power. The issues are not only about making decisions or managing men's violence, but about a new, critical awareness which gives women more self-esteem and a new capacity to draw on their own inner strengths, to work with other women to achieve what they could not do alone, and to acquire and use new skills.

How do women gain different kinds of power for themselves? In many lower-income countries today, women's groups have been created by governments or charities. In some groups, the women have grown greatly in self-confidence and self-esteem, both as individuals and as groups. They have come to see themselves as agents in their own lives, as people who can make a difference. We came to learn how, in some of the very different cultures of Mexico, women achieve this. How can we understand the processes? How do they talk about them? This last is very important: women have undergone a transformation, a conversion to a new belief in themselves. How do they express the experience? They are building a new way of talking about themselves, their society and their future. They are not just parroting the opinions of middle-class feminists, Mexican or foreign, or there would have been no fundamental change. They are shaping new ways of living in the often grim realities of rural Mexico. How?

In 1995, eight Mexican organisations agreed to work with us. As we shall see, they knew us, and trusted us to help them think more about power and put their conclusions into practice. We visited each organisation, in eight states of Mexico, to learn from both peasant women and activists. Then we arranged to meet at Tapalehui, near Mexico City, to talk for five days. We went on to publish a report on the workshop, in Spanish, which has been widely read in Mexico (Alberti *et al.* 1995).

Tapalehui, at Xoxocotla, near Cuernavaca, Morelos, was once a market garden growing fruit and is now a small subtropical paradise of river and greenery. Here, a family built a cheap, simple centre for groups to meet for plain living and high thinking. (As this is backed by comforts far more reliable than in many a hotel with several stars – cleanliness, hot water, drains, electricity and simple vegetarian food – the plain living is luxury of a high order.) The idyllic surroundings gave us all pleasure, and space to explore our cultural differences.

The authors First of all, who are we, the authors? Marta Mercado is a Mexican sociologist, Pilar Alberti a Spanish anthropologist, Emma Zapata a sociologist born in Colombia. All three had worked for years with poor rural women, in action research and publication, while teaching at the Postgraduate College for Agricultural and Forestry Sciences at Montecillo,

Mexico.[7] Two of us are British: Jo Rowlands had worked with women's groups in England, Ulster, Ecuador and Honduras and wrote *Questioning Empowerment: Women in Honduras* (1997a); Janet Townsend's experience was more academic, but included work in rural Mexico (1994, 1995). (We five authors will describe ourselves in our individual chapters.) The British Economic and Social Research Council had given us funds to learn more about power with Mexican organisations working with rural women, about which there is a real gap in the literature.

Rural Women in Mexico

In 1994, when each Mexican had an average income of some US$3,000, Mexico joined NAFTA (the North American Free Trade Area) and the OECD (Organisation for Economic Co-operation and Development, which is a group of richer countries). Also in 1994, according to *Fortune* magazine, 24 Mexican men were dollar billionaires, each owning over US$1,000 million; two were among the world's ten richest men. At the same time, calculated *Fortune*, if the income of these 24 were subtracted from the 'average' US$3,000, only US$2,000 a year was left for each of the remaining ninety million or so Mexicans. (Many of these in reality had only a few hundred dollars a year.) Mexico is an 'upper middle-income economy' (*World Development Report* 1998) with spectacular gulfs between rich and poor, gulfs which deepen as the economy grows. Sadly, also in 1994, in order to win the election, the government failed to devalue the Mexican peso when necessary and caused an appalling crash in 1995 which wiped off half the value of the peso and cost millions of jobs. Economic crises had been familiar from the early 1980s. 'By 1985, to match the buying power of the father's wage in 1975, father, mother and child had to be in work' (Lourdes Arizpe *et al.* 1989).

At least 70 per cent of Mexicans live in towns and cities, and have most of the national wealth. Most poor Mexicans live in rural areas where 90 per cent have no basic services: no electricity, no running water (certainly no water fit to drink), no drains and very often not only no flush lavatory but no hole in the ground. In Mexico, rural women can expect to live three years less than urban women, and women who work as day-labourers on the land can expect sixteen years less than urban women. Most rural people are undernourished (Rosario Robles *et al.* 1993, Vania Salles 1994). Mexican 'Indians' (people whose first language is not Spanish) are mostly rural and usually even poorer.[8] Even slum-dwellers in the city are usually better off, and likely to have better access to schools and health care. Given the wealth in Mexico, rural conditions are unbelievable.

Rural Mexico is shot through with contrasts, and often there is wealth close to the poverty. Migrant workers on prosperous coffee plantations in Chiapas must accept miserable wages and conditions, because migrants from Guatemala will work for even less. In Sonora, some growing of luxury crops for export is very profitable, and again depends on hungry migrant labour (often of women and children) from near and far. Across Mexico, a myriad tiny farms provide less than subsistence, and millions must find farm work by the day, often barely getting 200 days in a year. Survival strategies dominate life in rural Mexico.

The tradition is that rural women do not 'work' on the land, but only 'help' in weeding and harvest on the family farm. Now, many women must work family land while the men are away looking for jobs, or find day labour, perhaps moving round the country with the seasons. A survey in 1990–91 of casual labourers in agriculture found more than half to be women and girls, including 15 per cent who were girls under fourteen.[9] There had always been many who made a little money by trading, selling cooked food or making handicrafts, but the economic crises of the last two decades have made millions of rural families desperate for more income. For some women, the struggles have awakened a new interest in power.

Eight Organisations

Emma Zapata had set out in 1986 to advance thinking about rural women, looking at everything from economic issues to ways of living and feeling in Mexican society – asking always what can be done to achieve change for the better. Emma Zapata and Marta Mercado worked with groups across Mexico and developed ways of working with rural women (Zapata *et al.* 1994). They were able to persuade eight of the groups to work with us.

Women came to Tapalehui from a great range of cultures, climates and ways of working: women are gaining ground in many different environments, which is one basis for our excitement. What differences do their organisations make? We must introduce the organisations here, but readers may wish to refer back to this section as they meet particular women and organisations in the chapters that follow.

Names of women other than the authors have been changed throughout. Each organisation is called by the name of its state, the two in Puebla being referred to as *Puebla North* and *Puebla South* (see map facing p. 1). This anonymity is at the women's request, as they and their organisations could suffer for what they said at Tapalehui.

Chiapas If we were to enter Mexico from Guatemala, the first of these eight organisations we would reach would be *Chiapas*, based in San

Cristóbal de las Casas. Chiapas is a poor, mountainous state where speakers of Chol, Tzetzal and Tzotzil still undergo severe discrimination and exclusion. Politics in the state are particularly corrupt and the lives of the poor, mostly Indian, are grim. Few rural people have the 'everyday' services of clean running water, electricity or even a latrine. Life expectancy is the shortest in Mexico and nutrition and health are poor. On 1 January 1994, the Zapatista rebels took up arms on their behalf; the Zapatistas are still seeking dialogue with the Mexican government, struggling to secure more rights, minimal basic needs and a little democracy for the peoples of Chiapas.[10] Most rural people are suffering horribly from the government's military occupation, and the government is at the time of writing not standing by the promises it made. Tens of thousands have fled to the towns as refugees.

Chiapas is an organisation of 873 women whose first language is Tzotzil or Tzeltal. Its members live in 23 villages and 9 municipalities, but cooperate to sell their textiles and embroidery. They do more than that: they have a team of seven paid staff, two engaged in sales, one translator and four advisers who help the members organise their own learning and other projects for their own social and economic benefit. The rural women take great pride in their cultures and languages and in their traditional dress. They are committed, like Linaloe, to reshape their cultures but to keep what they value in the face of the Westernised national life. In the end, no peasant woman could come to Tapalehui, but they sent a paid adviser, Ana. Ana is not local but a Spanish-speaking graduate (in engineering!) from Venezuela, who has found her life in Chiapas. Ana is decided, independent, cosmopolitan, no respecter of important persons, and she is strongly identified with the women with whom she works. (Several organisations who had welcomed our visits and promised to send peasant women to Tapalehui were unable in the end to do so.)

Oaxaca *Oaxaca* is a membership organisation set up by a very poor, Mixe-speaking group who live in the hot, humid lands of the Isthmus of Tehuantepec, on small plots of poor, eroded land. Living conditions are much like Chiapas, and the Mixe suffer similar discrimination. Seeking to build a new autonomy for the Mixe, their elected Council (all men) supervises six areas of work: agriculture, law, women, planning, housing and forests. *Oaxaca* actually created their women's section under pressure from a European funding agency. Three women came to Tapalehui: Isabel is a paid adviser, whose first language is Spanish; she is quick, penetrating, thoughtful – and fun. Citlali and Xochitl are peasant women who have become change-agents or leaders in the 'women's section'. For them, Spanish is very much a second language and it is vital to carry forward their culture as a living way of life. However, appearance is less important and Western dress is usual. Their position in a men's organisation is hard.

In Mexico between 1917 and 1991, half the country's agricultural land was given to peasant communities as *ejidos*, which are village lands which peasants can use and inherit but not sell.[11] Citlali holds such a plot of land, and had been elected by her community to be their Secretary, an important office which attracts respect. A tiny minority of the peasants holding office in land-reform communities in Mexico are women. Xochitl, like Citlali, was active in the women's section of *Oaxaca*, organising the production and sale of *totopos* (big, thin, local pancakes of maize flour), of blouses they embroider, of chickens and vegetables. Both promote literacy in Mixe and work in health issues and human rights. Few women in their villages will ever have seen a city, but Citlali and Xochitl have learned to respond warmly and openly to outsiders (like the rest of us at Tapalehui) who treat them with respect. Citlali is older and more experienced than Xochitl. Both have a vivid sense of humour and are extremely competent; both have families.

Veracruz North-west of Tehuantepec, in the coffee zone of Veracruz, high on the slopes above the Atlantic coast, works *Veracruz*. This is a small, non-governmental organisation (NGO) of three paid staff, set up to learn from the people of the coffee zone and understand their experiences. *Veracruz* was helpful and exciting to visit, and planned to send Esteban to Tapalehui. He was the one man coming to join the workshop, but at the last minute he could not.

Puebla North Three of our groups come from the central mountains of Mexico, because Emma, Marta and Pilar knew them through their work on gender in rural change and had often drawn on the skills of their colleagues from the agricultural departments of the university to train women in new kinds of production (as we shall see for *Puebla South* and *Hidalgo*).

High in the mountains west of *Veracruz*, is *Puebla North*. This, like *Chiapas*, is an organisation of women artisans, some 200 in this case, working together to sell their embroidery and textiles. These are Nahuatl-speaking women, deeply proud of their traditional dresses, their language and culture. Like the peoples of Chiapas, they have known bitter oppression since colonial days and suffer exclusion and discrimination today.[12] These Nahua women belonged earlier to a mixed Nahuatl-speaking co-operative, but, finding great hostility from the men even to their selling handicrafts, let alone their search to develop themselves as women, broke away and formed a separate organisation. 'We tried everything to get the men to understand,' they told us, 'but we were just talking on different levels' (Rigoberta, Nahua change-agent). The organisation has always had outside advisers, including Pilar who has worked with them on domestic violence. Linaloe and Araceli came to Tapalehui, both Nahua and proud, in fine traditional dress. They are aunt and niece; both are single, choosing to be spinsters rather than settle for the marriage and children they would like but which would force them to conform and prevent them leaving their village. Marriage would also mean acceptance of a violence they refuse. Partners who would support their new independence of body and mind are not to be found.[13] Araceli and Linaloe, like the other Indian women, want to rebuild their culture, to wipe out the acceptance of male violence to women and the restrictions on women's mobility, and to take their culture forward to show those urban Spanish-speakers how to live. Linaloe is older, experienced, determined. She sometimes looks closed and watchful but opens into laughter with other women who share the same goals. For a Nahua woman not to have married by her age is an act of courage and determination. Araceli was the youngest and perhaps the most optimistic woman to come to Tapalehui. Guadalupe and María, both academics, had worked here as advisers.

Puebla South María and Margarita (both academics) work as advisers with Nahuatl- and Spanish-speaking women's groups in a desperately dry, poor part of Puebla South.[14] People cannot make a living from their tiny, arid plots of land, so many men travel out to work in the cities, by the day, week or month. Again, no peasant women came from *Puebla South*, but Margarita and María were vigorous participants. These women's groups also seek to generate income from crafts, and have local projects in water supply, vegetable production and appropriate technology. (The main vegetable, given the aridity, is *nopales*, an edible cactus.) The women of one Spanish-speaking village were granted a government pig-rearing project: they were given the breeding stock and material for the buildings, so that they could breed pigs on agricultural and kitchen waste. Life here being so marginal that there is little waste, this had to be a commercial venture based on bought feed, for which the women had no relevant skills. It was María and Margarita who persuaded university experts to come and train the women to make it work. The Mexican government has had such schemes since the 1970s, but the misfit between project and community skills and resources is all too common and the country is peppered with failed projects.[15] Mexican agricultural scientists were in the vanguard of the Green Revolution and see themselves as a technical elite, rarely considering social or even economic feasibility; many bureaucrats imitate them.

Hidalgo In Hidalgo, also in the highlands of central Mexico, Emma and Marta had helped women set up groups. Sadly, none of the peasant women managed to come, but Felipa and Catalina, academics who had begun to work as advisers, were at the workshop. *Hidalgo* is in what was the barley belt of Mexico until disease ended barley production. As in *Puebla South*, many men commute out to work, but living conditions are far better than in Chiapas or for the Mixe or Nahua women. Although daily needs are still hard to meet, rural people here own more goods, enjoy more facilities and are more touched by urban life. They know how poor their standards of living are by comparison with many even in the local towns, especially in terms of schools and health, which are of central importance to the mothers. *Hidalgo*'s experiences illustrate the grim realities of the Mexican countryside, and not only with the failure of the barley. In the mid-1980s, an international agency funded cow breeding and milk production for one *Hidalgo* group. Again, the funding did not cover the necessary training, given in the end by colleagues of Emma and Marta. The women learned to produce the calves and milk, but prices dropped, so that there was little gain. Several groups learned how to raise sheep, but Mexico's entry into NAFTA means that neither meat nor wool produced in highland Mexico can compete with that from more suitable climates in the USA. Every group of peasant women in Mexico wants to make an income in the face of rural economic crisis, but conditions are against them.

Jalisco *Jalisco* works in the very different agricultural area of the hot, rich lowlands around Guadalajara. Poor people here have poor land or no land, and many men and some women migrate regularly to find work, often to the United States. Like *Oaxaca*, *Jalisco* is a mixed organisation of women and men, but *Jalisco* concentrates on income-generation and services. For instance, they buy fertilisers and pesticides cheaply in bulk for their members, and sell maize in bulk to wholesalers for a better price. Sadly, they were unable to send anyone to Tapalehui.

Sonora *Sonora*, in the far north-west of Mexico, is different again. *Sonora* is a Society for Social Solidarity with some 600 women in 29 groups, from a very different culture, also much influenced by men's temporary migration, in this case migration to the United States. All speak Spanish. *Sonora* are exceptional in many ways. First, they have a Council of Advisers entirely elected from among themselves. For specific tasks, they contract professional advisers, perhaps to give a training course so that the women can develop new skills, but they do their own day-to-day management, planning and fundraising. Only *Sonora* has ventured into savings. *Microcredit* is widespread in rural Mexico (see next chapter, pp. 24–5), but savings have historically been difficult to develop. Savings-and-loan organisations other than commercial banks used not to be allowed, as the banks saw them as competition. If *Sonora* can develop a successful savings-and-loan system for their members, they will achieve an independence from funding agencies that will make them the envy of organisations in Mexico. Teresa and Carmen were at Tapalehui; Elisa came as far as Mexico City, but turned back because she was worried about one of her children. Teresa was the first elected president of the organisation and is indeed an inspiration to others, someone who can encourage and enable, not command or control. She is lively, ebullient, vigorous, outspoken. Carmen, another elected leader, is quieter, thoughtful. They and the women speaking Spanish as a second language should have been worlds apart, but met and related easily in the common cause, laughing and arguing.

Sonora is also exceptional in not having worked from the beginning on their relationships with men: although a women's organisation, they took no interest in gender issues until the year of the workshop, when they realised how much domestic violence and divorce was arising as a result of their success. *Sonora* is exceptional too in their achievement in making money. Generally, the philosophy of advisers to women's groups in Mexico is that the women should develop income-generating projects out of their own skills. Unfortunately, these skills are by definition common; the *Oaxaca* women sell *totopos* but at a very low price, for all Mixe women make *totopos*. Factory farming of chickens and pigs in Mexico produces cheap eggs, chicken and pork. It may pay women to raise a few chickens and pigs for their own use, if they simply cannot afford to buy them, but they cannot compete in price with the factory farms in selling to anyone but their neighbours, who also have chickens and pigs ...

Agriculture itself in Mexico is now rarely a secure or even moderately profitable proposition, and the agriculture which the poor can afford is unlikely to earn them much. Similarly, farm wages are low and, worse, seasonal and unpredictable. Very few 'income-generating projects' for poor men or women pay even as much as a farm wage; their saving grace is that some of them are year-round. Only organic coffee and fair-trade coffee yield more than the farm wage for men, while women have had some success producing chocolate. Handicrafts, even the superb weaving and embroidery of the groups we worked with, simply do not command a price which pays even half a farm wage for the time they take. *Sonora* has innovated: they tried hiring out bicycles (not profitable), selling ice (profitable), installing photocopying machines in centrally placed villages (very profitable, given the interminable demand for paper by the Mexican bureaucracy) and they also have a wonderful mobile washing machine which women hire by the hour.

Some projects run by women's groups make little money but provide great services (Ana María Fernández *et al.* 1994). The central milling of maize, in place of interminable grinding or milling by hand, saves an immense amount of work. So does a *tortillería* where maize dough can be shaped into *tortillas*, a staple food for much of rural Mexico, and baked centrally in bulk. So do many community services. Often, the man in the family has the family money and would not pay much for such services, but even if the returns are low the whole group can gain through saving time and effort. From Chiapas to Sonora, these activities are important to women's groups and to whole communities. It is actually making the money to live which proves so difficult.

A diverse gathering Some of us at Tapalehui, then, came from the poorest, most outcast, most rejected rural groups: people whose first language is not Spanish. One came from the battlefield of Chiapas, which the Mexican government seeks to hide from the world. Others were merely poor, from much more prosperous areas. Others were academics, poorly paid by Mexican or British standards, but rich indeed by the standards of the rest. Our cultures ranged from the Nahua through the Mixe and the relatively urbanised cultures of *Jalisco* or slightly Americanised *Sonora* to the much more urban, international academics and the foreigners. We were married, widowed and single, young and old ... Tapalehui has a small swimming pool: academics, advisers, change agents and foreigners splashed happily, eventually persuading the Mixe women to join us; Nahua women sat on the side in crisp, white, embroidered dresses and laughed at us. The porter on night duty kindly lent us some taped music to dance to in the evenings. Of course, the shortness of our time together protected us from friction, but issues of women's power not only brought us together but sparked a togetherness, a sisterhood, such as we may not all know again.

Although only half the women from grassroots organisations who had promised to come were able to do so, we were lucky to have Luisa, an adviser from another NGO working with peasant women's groups in northern Puebla, and Lucía from Mexico City, who is an adviser in savings-and-loan and works with women's groups around the country. Luisa has long experience with peasant women and a relaxed, bubbly charm; Lucía is younger, forceful, ebullient, talkative.

Putting the Book Together

Definitions The world of 'voluntary' organisations has grown so much in scale and importance that it has a whole new language, often obscure.

For one thing, the organisations are rarely staffed by volunteers. We shall use *non-governmental organisations (NGOs)* for professional organisations with paid staff, the users or clients of which have no say in the NGO. Funding is primarily from '*donors*': from the state, from private 'donors' or international agencies, and the NGO is accountable to the 'donors' rather than to its clients. (We use quotation marks for 'donors', because the word implies giving and 'donors' not only give but lend at interest.) *Membership organisations (MOs)*, have members, not users, who set their own priorities and pay staff to raise funds from similar sources; the members may even contribute themselves. In Mexico these are often 'popular organisations'[16] or formal Societies for Social Solidarity (SSS), as we shall see in Chapter Three.

Mexican women speak of the *levels* of women in organisations, which has an unfortunate suggestion of hierarchy but is difficult to translate in other words. At the most important, grassroots level are *group members*. Group members who have had special training to support the group are *change-agents*. At Tapalehui, only Araceli was a group member not trained as a change-agent, so we shall sometimes refer to all the *peasant women* together to include Araceli with the change-agents. For the outside, professional advisers, we shall use *advisers*. Of course there is complex overlap: Teresa and Carmen are members of *Sonora* elected from inside the organisation to be its advisers, whereas Ana has been appointed from outside by *Chiapas* as a paid adviser. Their roles are in many ways similar but they have very different backgrounds as Teresa and Carmen are peasant women, Ana a graduate. Luisa and Lucía are highly skilled and experienced, as are Emma, Marta and Pilar, who are not members of the organisations nor paid by them nor by an NGO, but give their work as a part of their academic action research.

Our methods The most important foundation for the research was trust. All the rural women who came to Tapalehui knew some of the academics already, and had known them for up to fifteen years. Some also knew each other. There had been a long history of projects and workshops and of involvement in the National Network of Advisers Working with Rural Women, so that many people had worked closely together over the years. Neither the visits to the organisations nor the meeting at Tapalehui would have been fruitful without this foundation of mutual trust. These years of learning together were also years when we observed the work and changes of the organisations, so that the interpretations which we offer in this book are rooted not only in the visits and the meeting but in years of experience.

Marta Mercado, Blanca Lopez and Jo Rowlands spent two months visiting all the eight organisations, to learn from their understandings of power and of group projects and to report on them at the workshop. At Tapalehui, we all talked for two days about the work and achievements of each organisation. Then we introduced the ideas of Srilatha Batliwala (1993, 1994, 1997) from South Asia and Jo Rowlands (1995a, 1997b) from Honduras, and spent two more days talking about these.

At Tapalehui, we met each day in 'focus groups' for a couple of hours. Focus groups are so fashionable now in politics, retailing and legal work that they have become a little embarrassing, but they taught us a great deal. We divided into two groups, one for the peasant women and the staff of the organisations, one for the more academic women, who had been more exposed to urban, national and international influences. This was a division for convenience, because we all still work with the same problems and the same themes, and with both real people and ideas. But we wanted to stop the 'global' talk from drowning the 'local', and to give the rural women a space to speak out and communicate their own ideas. In practice, the more 'local' group depended on drawing images on flip charts almost as much as on words to communicate, while the more 'global' group was highly verbal. This division into focus groups was only for two hours each day and strong links appeared between the groups at other times. The themes of the focus groups were planned in advance by the authors and the facilitators of the groups, as will appear. After each, we met for general discussion, and at other times of day we met in spontaneous groups to talk about topics as they came up. We did a great deal of talking, recorded all the sessions for later analysis,[17] and reported back to the organisations afterwards (Alberti *et al.* 1995). In this book, we shall refer to the focus group with grassroots women and advisers as *rural women* and the other as *academic*, but there is no sharp division and it would be more exact to call the groups 'rather more rural' and 'rather more academic'.

A collective project In order to advance understanding of empowerment, this book sets out to show others how some poor, rural Mexican women have taken more power into their own lives. General themes on empowerment are being increasingly well developed, but what women make of this trend is not the same from Sonora to Chiapas, let alone Andhra Pradesh in India. What are specific cultures, specific groups, specific women building?

The book is a collective project. The organisations participated as equals in the project and have rights in the material. On the basis of the report by Marta, Jo and Blanca, and in discussion with Luisa and Lucía, the authors designed the meeting at Tapalehui and wrote the subsequent account (Alberti *et al.* 1995). Then the authors met to plan the computer

analysis. We agreed how to code the discussions, coded half on each side
of the Atlantic, collaborating by email, planned the book and decided which
codes belonged primarily in each chapter. Some chapters are collective or
joint, while others are written from the perspectives of their authors. All
chapters were nevertheless read and discussed by all of us. As an example,
several quotes from what was said were naturally used by more than one
author (including one used by four of us). We decided that each should be
used in the place where it was most effective, and came to an agreement
on the final placement of each. We hope that the book will reflect both the
agreement and the diversity among the authors as well as the speakers.

Above all, all the authors want to celebrate the achievements of poor
rural women, which seems to us to happen too rarely nowadays. Thirty
years ago, too many people thought of poor rural women as passive,
submissive, compliant sufferers who sounded rather dull. Ten years ago,
women became the answer to every 'development' problem (Caroline Moser
1989): more efficient, more caring, more responsible. More recently, writers
rejecting these simplicities have often thrown out the baby with the bath
water, minimising the achievements of millions by arguing either that the
changes are not real or that they can be shown to be not gains but losses.
Academics, too often, think that our understanding is privileged, that we
can see from our eyries how others are deluding themselves. Even feminist
academics can forget that we do not know better than our subjects, that
there really are multiple truths. We can all learn from listening more
respectfully to the joys as well as the sorrows of others.

In Santiago Tangamandapio in Western Mexico, local people have built
successful home industries making sweaters under contract for the world
market. They run sweatshops in their homes, where most workers are
women and girls. To workers and local bosses, this a triumph over both
the transnational corporations and the national bureaucracy, while the
women think they have improved their position under patriarchy. To many
Western feminists, all this is an illusion: the women are exploited by
international capital and face new kinds of subordination. Fiona Wilson
(1990, 1991) argues that there are many truths here. For us, the authors,
there is an exact parallel in the way Western women triumph over their
escape from the home into the labour market, and celebrate the increases
in women in paid work in each country as successes in the women's
struggle. Yet in every richer country in the world, as the number of workers
in services goes up and the numbers in agriculture and industry go down,
so more and more women enter the labour market (Alan Townsend 1997).
When it was suggested to an audience of (mainly Western) academic
feminists in Washington DC that women have entered the labour force less
through their own struggles than through the needs of the market, the

audience was very angry.[18] Western women, of course, are also exploited by international capital and face new kinds of subordination (Sylvia Walby 1990). The women of Santiago Tangamandapio have the same rights as Western academic feminists.

At Tapalehui, all delighted in the changes being made, even though all knew how small these changes are. That delight is a truth from which others can learn. Joy is not, at the turn of the millennium, a very respectable emotion; feminist social scientists in rich countries seem to discount, to trivialise delight or even pleasure. These can only be, it seems, illusions to be deconstructed. We beg to disagree. Joy matters in itself. Women's pleasure in changes they are making will recur throughout the book: please respect it![19] We are all experts in our own lives.

Notes

1. The politically correct term in Mexico for an 'Indian' (one whose first language is not Spanish) is 'indigenous', as 'Indian' can be a term of abuse. We, however, find that this causes confusion among non-Mexicans and shall mainly use 'Indian' in this book.

2. The word 'development' has been much discredited. Everybody uses it to refer to some positive change which they want to see. For a transnational corporation, 'development' might mean growth regardless of the human consequences; for some governments it might mean prestige projects which harm the poor. The women of whom we are writing, as we shall see, want to build societies where they can meet their basic needs without becoming enslaved to capitalist consumerism.

3. We admire Álvarez, Dagnino and Escobar (eds) 1998, for their efforts to prioritise what the actors think. These authors avoid taking sides with or against the movements they discuss, in order not to stand above them. We take sides openly, because we are involved, but not because we want to claim, as academics, a higher authority than the actors who are living the situation.

4. All quotations with no date in this book are from the research described in this Introduction, from 1995. All are translated from the Spanish.

5. In much policy writing on women in lower-income countries, writers refer to 'a gender perspective' rather than 'a feminist perspective' because of widespread hostility to feminism. This is common in Mexico.

6. We shall use 'peasant' to refer to people in poor families working part-time or full-time on the land, whether as labourers, tenants or holders of the land, as Mexicans use *campesino*. Neither Araceli nor Linaloe work on the land themselves, but their families do.

7. Zapata *et al.* 1994, Alberti and Zapata eds 1997, Mercado 1997, Zapata 1997.

8. In Mexico, it is language and culture which define an individual far more than apparent physical characteristics. (See Alberti 1997, Bonfil 1997, Bartolomé 1997, Salles 1994).

9. Unpublished survey by Antonietta Barrón, cited in Robles *et al.* 1993.

10. For an account of women's experiences with the Zapatistas, see Rovira 1997,

Lovera and Palomo (eds) 1997 or the earlier Rojas (ed.) 1994. For the struggle in general, see Gilly 1997 and, for a negative account, Le Bot 1997.

11. In 1991, the process was discontinued and the holders of such land were given the right, by agreement, to privatise and sell their plots.

12. Claudio Lomnitz-Adler (1992: 234–41) has explored difficulties of other Nahua Indian leaders (all male, and residing further north-west, in the Huasteca) in living between 'Nahua', 'Mexican Indian' and 'Mexican' cultures.

13. We do not know what sexual choices they have (see pp. 66–8).

14. Beatríz Martínez and Susana Mejía (1997b) describe the area.

15. Lynn Stephen, 1997, confirms this for government women's projects in Nayarit, where 'even the "successful" projects ... do not appear to be economically empowering women in any significant way' (p. 187) as pay for two or three hours' work a day may total only US$10–15 per month, or a cent or two an hour.

16. *Organizaciones Populares.*

17. All the meetings were recorded and transcribed for later computer analysis with the software HyperResearch which enabled us to code sections of text. We used one set of codes for ideas which, on reading and re-reading the text, were clearly important to the participants, such as self-esteem, fear, shame, the organisation, the house and violence, and another set for the things we wanted to learn about, such as the different forms of power and aspects of self-empowerment.

18. For the paper given, see A.R. Townsend, 1992; for the argument, see A.R. Townsend 1997: 101–2.

19. We are willing to be chided for 'romantically listening to the movements' (Slater 1998: 396).

2

Empowerment Matters: Understanding Power

Janet Gabriel Townsend with other authors

Power, the Rich and the Poor

The rich countries plan to halve world poverty by the year 2015. To have any chance of doing this, the concept of power would have to be at the centre of all their theory, practice and methods, which it is not. For us, the authors, world poverty has been created and is kept going chiefly (though not only) by the abuse of power: abuse of power in international trade, debt, investment and aid, as well as in national and local politics, and abuse of power in the treatment of poor people by rich and of women by men. These abuses are possible because poor countries, poor people and women do not have the power to stop them.[1] As Clare Short has said, as British Minister for International Development, 'Governments are not going to be pro-poor.' The global systems of inequalities in power begin at the bottom. 'The relations of domination and subordination at the micro, local levels of society make possible the global systems of inequalities in power' (Dianne Otto 1996: 134). 'The goal of women's empowerment is not just to change hierarchical gender relations but to change all hierarchical relations in society, class, caste, race, ethnic, North–South relations' (Kamla Bhasin 1995: 13). In our project, we wanted to learn about one kind of change, to learn from poor peasant women in Mexico who are gaining the power to help themselves. Because the top priority of these women is poverty, poverty looms large in our thinking about power.

Empowerment   The gaining of power by the vulnerable is now often called *empowerment*. From work with the 'powerless' (or the 'socially excluded') came the idea that what the destitute, the hungry or the homeless really need is the power to solve their own problems. This outlook has developed over the last two decades in rather different groups in poor and rich countries. In poor countries, many of those working with the very poor, from feminist activists in India to liberation theologians in Brazil, came to see the central problem as what a Brazilian bishop called 'the assistance mentality' (Helder Camara 1969: 44). Naila Kabeer has written of 'the disempowering and infantilizing ways in which policymakers have frequently treated the poor, particularly poor women' (1994: 230). For a long time, many Western thinkers had argued that a transformation in the nature and distribution of power was necessary for a better world, but a new wave of concern about power arose in the 1960s, in civil rights movements in the United States, which influenced much of Western activism and social science. Later, more specific ideas of empowerment were developed in social work, health, counselling, education, youth work, training and 'community development',[2] and studies of the process of gaining power appeared in these fields long before they did in 'development studies', at least in English (G. W. Albee *et al.* 1988). In the United States in particular, an important body of empowerment theory and practice has been developed and published in and around 'community development'. (Unexpectedly, writers on 'development' and American 'community development' seem rarely to read each other's work. This has important theoretical implications which we discuss in the Appendix.) More recently, empowerment has become a key term in neoliberalism (see p. 48), as we shall see, while students in business schools are taught that workers who feel themselves to be more powerful will work better. 'Empowerment is a force of reform developed primarily in business management to devolve more power down the management hierarchy' (Robert Bennett *et al.* 1994: 1).

Feminists in poor countries developed very bottom-up approaches to empowerment by different routes. In Latin America, Paulo Freire's concept of *conscientisation* (1973), the idea that the poor needed to develop a critical awareness of their own society in order to take more command over their own lives, was widely adopted in 'popular education' but with no gender awareness (Chapter Three). In the 1970s, Latin American feminists learned much from popular education and critical awareness.[3] At the same time, activists in India were learning from very different struggles around the rights of self-employed women (J. Sebstadt 1982). Interest grew in the 1980s as structural adjustment policies greatly increased the sufferings of poor women, particularly in Africa and Latin America. Many groups of poor women in Brazil discovered for themselves the links between their bodies and the state of the economy (Saskia Wieringa 1997: 153). 'The strength of Third World feminism lies in its insistence on the materiality of power relations, not only in cultural practices, but in all aspects of daily life' (Saskia Wieringa 1995: 19). For the United Women's Conference in Nairobi in 1985, Gita Sen and Caren Grown of the Third World feminist group Development Alternatives for Women in the New Era (DAWN) wrote vital discussion documents on empowerment which swept round women activists in poor countries (Sen and Grown 1987). In a classic article, Caroline Moser (1989) described 'aid' to poor women in poor countries in terms of a succession of types: welfare, equity, anti-poverty, efficiency and empowerment, the last having arisen from the struggles of poor women.

At the next United Nations Women's Conference in Beijing, 1995, empowerment was adopted as a requirement for a better world for women. But while more and more people working with the vulnerable were wanting to put power at the centre of the search for a better world,[4] other very different groups also adopted the word empowerment, made it part of development-speak and emptied it of meaning. Power is being pushed back out of the language of 'development' by the powerful, who have taken a bundle of words, such as *empowerment, participation, emancipation, democratisation* and *development*, and turned them into words which mean whatever the user chooses them to mean. In the 1970s, different schools of thought in 'development' used different words for their conflicting understandings of desirable change, such as *growth, modernisation, dependency, underdevelopment*. In the 1990s they all use the same words to mean different things, which is extremely confusing. So, in rich countries and poor, the *participation* of local people in a project can mean involvement in all design and implementation, or merely a show of consultation which is never intended to be allowed to change anything. *Development* can refer to better nutrition, health and education, or to economic growth for the rich with increased poverty for the poor. Similarly, *empowerment* can be used to describe poor people finding the power to help themselves, or a government privatising health or pensions so that it can cut taxes in order to 'empower' citizens to decide whether to spend their income on health or pensions or conspicuous consumption. Or, at a more local level, it now seems to refer to promoting entrepreneurial confidence among poor women rather than any need for the powerful to change, as if the only problem is the lack of drive among poor women! (See Kate Young 1997.) President Clinton's 'community development' policy was called the Empowerment Zone Initiative, but Douglas Perkins (1995) reports that it related mainly to community investment banks, with little in the legislation that was enabling or new. The word has been emptied of content. Terry Pratchett, in a comic fantasy novel (1996), refers to 'the town of Empowerment in California' to satirise impractical dreams.

'Development'? The meaning of the word development is too often reduced to welfare or to poverty alleviation, or even to free trade and foreign investment. Poor people need fundamental changes in power relations, at all levels from the global to the local. Poor women also need a transformation of structures which hold them down; they need radical changes in law, property rights and other institutions that perpetuate men's control over them (Srilatha Batliwala 1994). Power remains central both to keeping people poor, and to poor people changing their condition, but power keeps slipping back out of the debates, for men as well as for women.

A whole school of thought, Gender and Development or GAD, was created to stress the importance of power relations between women and men. We hoped that this line of thought would open the door to exposing power relations in 'development', but many projects and programmes with this label pay only lip-service to power or empowerment. In 'development planning', as in business studies, people talk instead of capacity-building, a more specific and also very useful concept, but without the embarrassing associations of power. Or they emphasise the complexities and political difficulties of power until no one can speak about power at all. The body of specialists working in development for local, national and international agencies may be seen as the 'development industry'. We, the authors, are obviously a part of this industry but seek to change it, for the industry as a whole has always sought to avoid talk of power and to present itself as professional and technical, which we see as defeating much positive change.

Arturo Escobar, from Colombia, argues that the international development industry has never been about reducing world poverty and shows no sign of being so now (1995). Perhaps the development industry should not be held accountable for the unfairness of international trade or debt or the arms trade, but if the 'aid' given each year since World War II had really been aid, rather than serving the political and economic interests of the 'donor' countries, it would have been enough almost to end absolute poverty. 'Development' agencies, international, government and non-governmental (NGOs), are all very good at employing the middle classes but often have minimal impact on poverty. There are many valuable exceptions among NGOs, and governments can do a great deal about poverty given political will, whether in revolutionary China, racist Malaysia or repressive Taiwan. But trade, debt, investment, aid and the development industry have together established the control of poor countries by international capitalism.

Arturo Escobar urges that in response to this sad truth, academics should study what people are making of global capitalism, what new realities and hybrid cultures they are creating out of old traditions and new influences, how poor people are subverting global pressures to their own ends. We worked with eight non-governmental and membership organisations (NGOs and MOs) which were already seeking to enable rural women to help themselves. These are indeed hybrid cultures, as peasant women try to get what they want out of a new international community of funding agencies (non-profit and government), foreign

NGOs and national NGOs (see Chapter Three). We came to listen to the peasant women and learn what they are making of this international community for themselves. Most writings on empowerment in low income countries are about women, and in this book we are writing about one small group of women. Many of the issues, however, apply to all vulnerable people.

Power   In this book, we use the word *power* mainly in its traditional sense as 'a force exercised by individuals or groups'. Today, however, many workers in the social sciences and humanities prefer Michel Foucault's interpretations of power. Pilar Alberti, in Chapter Seven, will draw on Foucault to understand 'power over', showing *power as constituted through discourses*, and people being constructed as subjects in discourses. There are three reasons for the substantial use we make of the traditional under-standing in this book:

- The understandings which Mexican rural women have of power are much closer to the traditional Western interpretation than to Foucault's, and this, naturally, was what they talked about at Tapalehui. In Spanish, 'power' has two meanings, one of strength/worth/authority and one of skills/capacities (Soledad Dueñas *et al.* 1997). Both are more readily understood as a force exercised by individuals or groups than as con-stituted through discourses.
- Foucault, for most of his life and writings, failed to identify the cen-trality of gender in the power relations he analysed. Most feminists see fundamental conflicts between Foucault and feminism, but many still find much to learn from his writings, and there is a substantial literature.[5]
- 'Traditional' notions of power developed in Western, male-dominated, hierarchical societies; they grew out of and expressed the social relations of expanding market/capitalist societies in Europe. This understanding of power is so central to the languages of Western Europe that it is a part of them, and Foucault had to create a new, difficult language to express his innovations, which discourages most readers outside an exclusive group of specialists. For Foucault, power is everywhere and ultimately nowhere.

Nevertheless, we (the authors) are all interested in *postliberal* analyses of power, which derive from Foucault. We share their basic dislike of institutional structures, because these tend to centralise power, to control participants and force them into a standard mould. We hope that network-ing, which operates horizontally and co-operatively, may be an alternative to hierarchical institutional structures (Marc Nerfin 1986). *Neoliberalism* (see p. 48) regards Western democracy as the best support for economic growth, despite academic evidence to the contrary (Deepak Lal 1996), and it defines politics in terms of national states which concentrate power through the 'highly artificial notion of consent through the ballot box' (Dianne Otto 1996: 134). Neoliberalism speaks of 'empowerment', but with reference to the electoral rights of the individual in the nation state and the rights of the entrepreneur, not empowerment of the community or the group, let alone a right to critical awareness. Postliberals, on the other hand, understand power as dispersed throughout human society. The micromechanisms of power at the local level produce local criticisms which, if organised politically, develop into strategies to resist the mechanisms of power.

Self-empowerment We do not think that anyone can empower another person, and to us this understanding is the key to success in changing power relations. In English this is a new concept, for which we have no word, and we are using *self-empowerment* until a better word evolves. We think that it is possible to enable other people to do something, but not to empower them, not to give them power. If you give someone power, you can take it away: it is only if they take that power for themselves that it is theirs. In the proverb, you can lead a horse to water, but you cannot make it drink. For us, true empowerment is self-empowerment.[6] For many other feminist writers, only a part of empowerment may be self-empowerment, as for Naila Kabeer.[7] In this book, we want to argue that world poverty will not be reduced unless power and self-empowerment are at the head of the agenda.

Self-empowerment is a process, not a result. Professional advisers or facilitators in self-empowerment seek to enable awareness and choice, but cannot control any outcomes because the choices rest with the people who must empower themselves, as Srilatha Batliwala argues (1993). Self-empowerment is therefore very difficult for an outsider to evaluate, especially in the short term, and no measures of it are widely accepted (Linda Mayoux 1998).[8] As we shall now describe, this makes it increasingly difficult to obtain funding for empowerment activities. 'By its very nature, the process of empowerment is uncertain: although it is possible to initiate the journey in a structured way (using particular techniques and methods, for example) *the ultimate destination is always unknown*' (Mike Edwards and David Hulme 1995: 12, our emphasis).

Very reasonably, the development industry seeks to concentrate expenditure on projects and programmes which, unlike those devoted to the process of self-empowerment, give measurable results. The fashion is to escape out of issues of power, of land ownership and rights, into *microcredit*. The latter, which gives poor people access to very small amounts of credit, both answers this demand for quantifiable indicators of success and tackles one issue of power, which has always been the denial of credit to the poor. But this elixir ignores other problems of power and therefore cannot lift many out of poverty and often does not even improve standards of living. Around the world, millions of poor people (a majority of them thought to be women) are borrowing small amounts of money and repaying the money with interest. This is claimed to mean that credit is an answer to poverty which poor people welcome. On closer examination it proves that the very poorest cannot use credit, and that although the less poor do welcome credit and often achieve a small but stable rise in income, credit does not place them on a ladder out of poverty which they can then proceed to climb but just helps them to take one step up (David Hulme and Paul Mosley 1997). On top of this, their slightly higher income may not pay for any improvement in their standard of living, for in many places prices and taxes are rising and subsidies are being cut, so that poor people are working hard to use the newly available credit just to stay in the same place (Mayoux 1998). As we can see, the worldwide enthusiasm of the poor for borrowing means that microcredit does meet a need but does not necessarily mean that they are better off. Microcredit does help some of the poor take one step up, but is certainly no solution to poverty.

Self-empowerment is no solution either unless it is achieved very widely, but it can bring fundamental change. Unlike microcredit, however, self-empowerment does not offer results that are predictable or readily measurable, because the outcomes are not possible to predict in advance. People who become aware of more choices and take their own decisions are free to do as they choose. In India, low-caste women have been known to choose to work for a cemetery for their caste so that their loved ones may be decently buried, rather than to work for income or education (Batliwala 1994). That is their choice and their right.

It all sounds very abstract and academic, precisely because we talk so little about power. Self-empowerment also sounds ineffective when we think about it in terms of individuals, of a strictly secluded woman in Afghanistan or a sex-worker in the Philippines. What has made self-empowerment real for millions of women around the world has been the almost worldwide emphasis on women's groups. This is yet another global fashion, but it has enabled some remarkable changes through two very important processes: the bringing together of women away from their men, and the creating of a space for women to set their own priorities, two processes which have proved to be closely interlinked. We shall see why later in the chapter.

This book will describe and analyse empowerment in terms of Jo Rowlands's account in *Questioning Empowerment: Working with Women in*

Honduras (1997a).[9] At the workshop, her ideas appealed to peasant women and academics alike. To repeat, we identify four forms of power: 'power over', 'power from within', 'power to' and 'power with', around which we shall organise Chapters Four to Seven, and three levels of power relations, to be discussed in Chapter Eight: personal empowerment, power in close relationships and collective power. These are not distinct, separate kinds of power, for each form merges and overlaps with the others and empowerment is fluid and unpredictable. The language simply gives us a way to think more positively and specifically about power. We shall try to describe it here by drawing both on what was said at the workshop and what the authors wrote for each other in 1997, after analysing the workshop.

Power over

'Power over' (Chapter Seven) is the obvious power, and is what we usually think of first in imagining power. It is the power of one person or group to get another person or group to do something against their will (Rowlands 1995, 1997). 'Power over' is plain to us in decision-making by individuals or groups, or in who wins in a conflict, whether between countries over territory or between husband and wife over her/his pay packet. 'Power over' may be enforced through violence or fear, or there may simply be social rules which force the weaker to accept the will of the stronger. Only in the 1990s did it become legally a crime in England for a man to rape the wife with whom he was living; in India or Nigeria, it is still not a crime to rape even a divorced or separated wife.[10] 'Power over' can be a matter of strength and even force, physical, economic or social. Poorer countries had to agree to the rules of the World Trade Organisation which are often to their disadvantage, because rich countries forced them to do so. Most of us will give what we have to a mugger with a knife.

'Power over' is exercised particularly (but not only) by men and groups of men. Men's power over women is the great motor which achieves and maintains the subjugation and exclusion of women found in so many societies.[11] In some cases, the power is established through force or threats, but often it is more subtle. Throughout the workshop, peasant women talked of their own fearfulness as the great obstacle they face. But in most cases this is not a direct fear of male violence or male strength being used against them. Not all 'power over' comes from people giving in to the threats of others or even to the customs of their society. The fears expressed by peasant women and academics at Tapalehui are those we have learned to impose on ourselves.

According to one view of power and politics, which is shared by some Mexican feminists (Anna M. Fernández Poncela [ed.] 1995), power is about having a say in decisions made in the public sphere.[12] As we shall see, getting access to power is then a matter of 'participation' in decision-making.[13] We disagree with this view in three ways:

- Like many Western feminists, we argue that 'power over' is diffused throughout society and that 'feminist politics may take place anywhere' (Joni Lovenduski and Vicky Randall 1993: 5), from the home to the United Nations. The 'notion that men alone are the political actors, that state and civil society have been established by men who act on behalf of the population as a whole' (Lovenduski and Randall 1993: 172) simply defines women out.
- So does the notion that power is most visible – or only visible – in terms of decision-making in public space. 'Power is exercised over the cornflakes packet, in the supermarket, in darkened streets, in school-rooms, between the sheets and through the remote control of the television set' (Anna Coote and Polly Pattullo 1990: 19).[14]
- We think that power, even 'power over', is about far more than decision-making, for the most efficient forms of oppression are hidden and unconscious, and 'the most effective and insidious use of power is to prevent … conflict arising in the first place' (Steven Lukes 1974: 23–4).

As Steven Lukes argued, power goes far beyond decision-making and even beyond observable conflicts of interests, for the exercise of power not only prevents people from doing things but sometimes even from thinking them. Political science has to explain quiescence and rebellion as well as decision-making.[15] (As we shall see in Chapter Three, these two arguments are important in the understanding of social movements in Latin America today.)

For instance, children or minority groups or women or men with learning difficulties may not even see themselves as fit to have a say in decisions that affect them greatly. They may have been taught that, for them, submission, sacrifice and silent suffering are virtues. For Srilatha Batliwala (1994), power is about control, not only over human bodies and physical and financial resources, but over the ideology which sets rules and ideals. Much 'power over' is oppressive, divisive and destructive. So is patriarchy, under which men make the rules by which women live (Sylvia Walby 1990). Patriarchy takes many forms, and too often pervades not only the legal system and social and economic custom but ideology and ideals of femininity as well. As Monique Devaux writes (1996: 224), 'Feminists need to look at the *inner* processes that condition women's sense of freedom and choice … Addressing women's freedom requires that we look at internal impediments to choice as well as tangible obstacles to its realization.'[16] Patriarchies commonly pervade daily life. In rural

Mexico, even the layout of her own kitchen is often not seen as a woman's business.

> We have a project to improve housing. The women say, 'Before, *we had no ideas about how the house should be built*. Why? Because it was the man who paid for everything to be done in the house. So, now that we are the ones who get the credit, now we decide how we want the floor, how we want the window, how we want the kitchen.' (Teresa, *Sonora*, emphasis added)

> The other women in my village *don't have the power to speak, to answer, to say* anything. And all the men, as only they ever speak, feel very powerful, very big. (Araceli, Nahua woman, *Puebla North*, emphasis added)

'Power over' other people may easily seem thoroughly unattractive and undesirable, but in today's societies everyone needs some share in 'power over'. (In a 'postliberal' society, the emphasis would be on respect, tolerance, open debate and the promotion of egalitarian values that embrace participation and diversity, rather than on the tyranny of the majority through the ballot box.) In our societies, sharing in 'power over' may still be our best protection, from the collective powers that guarantee human rights, elect governments and decide disputes between neighbours to an individual's entitlement to a fair share of the family's food. But this is a zero-sum game, because the more of this kind of power one person has, the less others have (Rowlands 1997a). In Mexico, women usually need their husband's permission to go out to work. When a woman can go without permission, her husband has less power over her. Men in many societies see gains in power by women as threatening, and in terms of men's power over women they are quite right. If women empower themselves, men's power over them will be reduced. Men will also be freed from the roles of oppressor and exploiter, and will lose not only traditional privileges but traditional burdens (Batliwala 1994).

In Mexico since the mid-1980s, millions of women have responded to the national economic crisis by earning something somehow, which has undermined the notion of the man of the household as provider, as breadwinner. In Mexico, the average real wage dropped by 40 per cent in the 1980s and most wages are still lower than in 1979. In addition, government support was withdrawn from rural areas on a large scale, so that by the early 1990s very little agriculture was still profitable and rural Mexico suffered badly. Often, grassroots women who had seen their work as only 'help', no matter how long the hours in the fields, came to see themselves as compensating for the wages the men had lost. Men who had valued their women's place in the home came to welcome their women going out and joining groups to earn even a little. On the downside, many women were 'liberated' into a double day of work, while the loss of breadwinner status was hard for men.

Deniz Kandiyoti (1988a) describes the gendered struggle for 'power over' as a 'patriarchal bargain', in which men dominate but women secure specific perceived advantages. This is a bargain in that the 'rules' as to how women and men should behave are constantly contested and renegotiated in daily life. In Mexico, the stereotype was that a manly man had to be a good provider for his family (as well as a heavy drinker, socialising mainly with his mates when not engaged in vigorous promiscuity). A womanly woman, on the other hand, was chaste and pure, the bearer of her husband's honour; she stayed in the home, cared well for him and their children, and had an unending capacity for endurance, for suffering. In the 1980s, many men lost the possibility of being a good provider, and lost much of their power and status outside the home. The patriarchal bargain came under threat. Women could still go on suffering (not a virtue in a man): men could no longer be real men, but women were still real women. In both urban and rural areas, many men took out their frustrations and loss of power outside the home in violence within it, with appalling consequences for women and children (Mercedes González de la Rocha 1986, 1994, Janet Townsend *et al.* 1995). Patriarchal bargains may change slowly, or they may be damaged by other changes, for instance when women are drawn into the labour market.

> Shamefully, the Power Over is felt brutally every day. We feel this Power above all through sheer economic deprivation. This sometimes weighs so heavily that it paralyses us, when we analyse world economic structures and we see how this system moves step by step towards greater inequality much emphasised by gender. (Marta Mercado 1997)

Marta Mercado is an academic, but bitterly aware of the recent economic vicissitudes through which rural Mexicans have become desperately aware of other people's power over them and women have formed groups which have led some of them to new visions.

In Mexico, the Zapatistas also define power as much broader than 'power over':

> When we say we don't want to take power, we don't mean we will remain neutral about power. When we talk of organizing society, we are talking of power, but a different kind of power. We have a different conception of power; it is more a social kind of power. It does not have to be represented in government. (Zapatista representative Priscilla Pacheco Castillo, cited in George Yudice 1997)

We agree with the Zapatistas and with Monique Devaux (1996: 224) that Foucault is too much concerned with 'a dynamic of acting upon' others and too little with other forms of power to help us 'understand empowerment and disempowerment, freedom and nonfreedom'.

Power from Within

'Power from within' arises from a recognition that one is not helpless, not the source of all one's own problems, that one is restricted in part by structures outside oneself. In the *Oxfam Gender Training Manual*, it is 'the spiritual strength and uniqueness that resides in each one of us and makes us truly human. Its basis is self-acceptance and self-respect which extend, in turn, to respect for and acceptance of others as equals,' (Suzanne Williams *et al.* 1994: 233). This power is central to empowerment.[17] 'The empowerment approach ... seeks to identify power less in terms of domination over others ... and more in terms of the capacity of women to increase their own self-reliance and internal strength' (Caroline Moser 1989: 107–8).

The 'power from within' must, it is agreed, be self-generated,[18] and is the fundamental power on which women must build, the beginning of an answer to the powers of patriarchy and capitalism over them.[19] Women have to realise both what they can do and what is holding them down and back. Most Mexican rural women have learned from childhood a world view which leads them to take part in their own oppression by men. It seems natural to be isolated in the home and family, controlled by their husband, needing his permission to go out to visit their mother (Janet Townsend *et al.* 1995). To them, this is disagreeable but natural, like a cold, wet day against which rebellion is irrelevant. Srilatha Batliwala notes that in South Asia most self-empowerment begins not with a woman rebelling against traditional structures but with some novelty from outside, perhaps an event, perhaps an activist. Thousands of women in southern India waged a war on alcoholic drink, sparked off not by any external, professional adviser but by a story in a literacy primer (Batliwala 1994).

'[T]o be empowered is to discover when the problem is outside you, to stop feeling guilty but still learn from your mistakes, to accept responsibility' (Emma Zapata, 1997). For Emma Zapata, to recognise one's own powers is to admit and accept responsibility. Many women, crippled by their experiences, shrink from the recognition and withdraw into continued oppression or, as Linaloe, a change-agent from *Puebla North* put it, 'hide in the house'. Emma makes a severe comment on Mexican society with which not all Mexican women would agree, but which all would recognise, arguing that only empowerment permits Mexican women to enjoy their 'own sexuality, without repression or guilt, to feel pleasure, to be able to delight in fun, friendship, love or youth'.

For Pilar Alberti, to be more aware of the structures of oppression is to see through the illusions to the even more real obstacles behind them. At the workshop, a big and unexpected difference appeared between the 'more academic' and the 'more rural' women (see pp. 80–81). It was the academic women who expressed more anguish and frustration, although, as they agree, they suffer so much less than the rural and particularly the peasant women in everyday life. The peasant women endure frequent hunger, deprivation, disease and violence but seemed far more able to revel in a small advance. Pilar has worked with foreign experts in women's rights, with government officials and with academics engaged in research and activism with women. Her research has brought her into close contact with 'peasants, women and men, with the leaders of co-operatives of women and of men, with government agricultural promoters, with social workers, doctors, traditional healers, midwives, bonesetters, teachers and government officials who work in the countryside' (Pilar Alberti 1997). All these people operating at different levels of action, including powerful outsiders working with women (whether urban, rural, Spanish-speaking, Indian, old, young or girls) have shown her the dimensions and complexity of the problem of empowerment. 'Being a feminist, an academic who teaches and researches gender and works with peasant and non-Spanish-speaking women, I am only more aware of the restrictions which I face and the obstacles which I cannot overcome, because I am a woman.' Perhaps this awareness, this frustration, these large goals, explain why talk of power caused so much more distress to the academics than the peasant women or the NGO workers at our workshop.

Power with

'Power with', the capacity to achieve with others what one could not achieve alone, is too often dismissed as an impractical socialist ideal in this competitive world. At the end of the twentieth century, however, we realise that capitalism cannot exist without this 'power with' either, and Francis Fukuyama's *Trust: The Social Virtues and the Creation of Prosperity* has been a best-seller spawning dozens of followers in business studies and economics. Fukuyama is an analyst at the Rand Corporation who argues that capitalism depends on social capital, or the ability to work together in groups and organisations. People's ability to associate with each other becomes critical to economic life.

'Power with', then, is present in all societies and expressed in all actions by more than one person. For Jo Rowlands, it is not only a capacity but an awareness, 'a sense of the whole being greater than the sum of the individuals, especially when a group tackles a problem together' (Rowlands, 1997a: 13). The PAEM women with whom Jo worked in Honduras had achieved a sense of group agency, so that 'there was an implicit assumption that the women had the capacity to achieve great things and to take charge of their own empowerment processes' (Rowlands 1997a: 134). Such a sense is rarely met with, but PAEM has unusual features. The initiative and ideas came from Maria Esther, a local peasant woman with some years of experience as a worker and leader with the Catholic Church, the national union of rural workers and radio schools. Under her influence, PAEM was organised, very radically:

- in a way that did not immediately fill an economic, income-generating purpose;
- beginning with the sense of self and accepting slow progress;
- working with materials the women designed themselves;
- with the women identifying their own needs and ways of satisfying these from the beginning;
- seeking to create a new style of leadership from within the groups, so that Maria Esther would cease to be needed.

PAEM is led by an elected council and both change-agents and advisers come from within the groups. External advisers are hired in for specific tasks, but there are no regular paid staff, inside or outside the groups. For Maria Esther, 'It's obvious that NGOs and the church don't strengthen the self-management of women, because then they won't be able to take the decisions' (Rowlands 1997a: 99).

Among the groups we worked with in Mexico, only *Sonora* approaches this model, which is that proposed by Srilatha Batliwala for South Asia and by Jane Stein for the improvement of women's health worldwide. This model places participation at the centre of the empowerment process, particularly in terms of 'power with', as we shall see in Chapter Five. In all the groups with which we worked, women revel in their participation in decision-making. The degree of co-partnership from the very beginning was highest in *Sonora*, while others seemed rather to seek to increase the level of participation as time went on.

No form of power is an undiluted good. The psychological sense of communion which made us all feel good at Tapalehui presumably has its counterpart for members of American and British right-wing groups; Stephanie Riger quotes Jack Kemp's 'Empower America' as an example.[20] (This champions entrepreneurship, lower taxes, less government spending/regulation and more international free market capitalism.) Similarly, local empowerment may be a goal for conservatives as well as those in search of change. Or, in Mexico, the land reform which created community holdings in land did much to keep the present governing party in power from the 1930s until today (Chapter Three), by creating a small feeling of local power. But a feeling of empowerment can be illusory when all is controlled at the macrolevel (Riger 1997), as all at Tapalehui were well aware.

Power to

'Empowerment that is based on the "power to" involves gaining access to a full range of human abilities and potential' (Rowlands 1995b: 22). The 'power to' is creative and enabling as women reconstruct and reinvent themselves. At our workshop, fear and blame seemed very important in the way women limit themselves.

> To be empowered is to rise above all the barriers, to do things you've never imagined. Above all, it is to overcome the fear of doing things. But this fear is defeated when you feel capable of doing things. For this, you need the power from within, that is to say you need a positive reinforcement and to realise that you really can do them, can learn, can take charge of yourself and can go forward. This is a dialectical process because you never get back to the same point, to where you started. To live empowerment is to go on changing yourself every day, and this is what happens in the women in the groups of which we speak. (Marta Mercado 1997)

Of the authors, it is Marta Mercado who best catches the flavour of what the peasant women say themselves. For them, *the conquest of fear and the recognition of their 'power to', of themselves as agents in their own lives*, are central.[21]

At the workshop, the 'power to' generated real excitement, as if the label 'power' was new but the excitement longstanding. In Mexico, people whose first language is not Spanish are poor and suffer a great deal of discrimination. Linaloe is a Nahua Indian; if only we could supply a video to convey the force and conviction with which she spoke:

LINALOE: I can plan a project for the community, you see, getting ideas which we women can put into practice. And I've also learned, you see, to take on a duty and sell our embroidery, and learned how to be in charge, the accounts and the management and the paperwork.

ARACELI (Linaloe's niece): And the computer.

LINALOE: Oh, yes, the computer too, we can use it well!

The power to do new things, and pride in what they can do, are a liberation for these women. To an outsider this is extraordinary, when they already had a great deal to do and much of the new work, we shall see, is additional to a heavy workload and a long working day. In the literature, the 'power to' is often used to mean a political power, a power to influence others, to have a say in decisions, but at the workshop it was captured to celebrate pride in women's skills (Chapter Six). All the powers overflow into each other and relate strongly to each other; the power to may be an expression of the power from within, it may nourish the power from within, or both.

Power as Resistance

Resistance is the complement to 'power over': neither is found alone.[22] 'When the great lord passes the wise peasant bows deeply and silently farts' (Ethiopian proverb, cited on the front page of James C. Scott *Domination and the Arts of Resistance*). Oppressed people have their own powers of resistance, one of which is manipulation (also used by the powerful as an alternative to coercion). Sarah Hrdy writes (1981) that the females of all primate species are manipulative in their behaviour and, whether from choice or instinct, humans are certainly no exception. The power of a woman to persuade her husband that he wants what she wants and it was his idea in the first place is an old power. Acting stupid, acting ignorant, conniving, colluding, doing bad work deliberately: these are all powers of the 'powerless'. We need to think about resistance in its less elegant forms: perhaps a minimal 'power from within', 'power to', 'power with', even 'power over'. How may we understand the powers of secluded Hausa women in Northern Nigeria, who run profitable trading activities through their children without ever leaving their husbands' compounds? Or the powers of secluded women in the extreme case of Patricia Jeffrey's *Frogs in a Well*, where the Muslim families who staff a shrine close to Delhi seclude their women to a very unusual degree. (This is a fascinating study of one small group, but of course is not and does not claim to be representative of Islam, in India or anywhere else.) Yet these women not only live in a world 'where valued relationships with other women can grow relatively undisturbed by men's intrusions' (Patricia Jeffrey 1979: 171) but have the 'power to' socialise their children, and 'power over' their children and daughters-in-law. Above all, they and they only have access to the women of other households. 'Through networks of gossip and friendship from which men are excluded, the women can build up banks of information about suitable marriage partners [for their children]' (Patricia Jeffrey 1979: 171). Marriages are arranged, often with strangers, and mothers often determine the partners.

Women to whom we have listened in rural Mexico are not powerless, nor do they 'stay in the house', although they say they do! When Jennie Bain and Janet Townsend first arrived in La Laguna, Los Tuxtlas (Janet Townsend with Bain de Corcuera 1993) all the women said they never went out, and some claimed that they went to the stream to do the washing at times when no others would be there, to avoid the gossip. No woman made a living for herself and few engaged in any economic activity at all. Yet within a few hours, every woman in the village knew all about us; either they had been going out after all or the children had borne the news. Some women seemed appallingly oppressed. Although pre-teen girls were very lively and forthcoming, and many older women were confident and impressive, most young married women were fearful of us and presented themselves as unable to speak for themselves. (This is common in rural Mexico.) The village has no women's group and the women have none of the experiences or the language of the peasant women at Tapalehui. Yet some older women have built a world in which they do know they can get things done.

Isolated women may direct resistance against an individual; women in groups often use the 'power with' against larger targets, whether groups or customs. The impact on women's lives in Mexico of joining any women's group has been widely documented. In Diaz Ordaz, near La Laguna, the Seventh Day Adventist temple has contributed greatly to women's confidence: those who joined in their Saturday women's discussions had striking self-assurance. In Diaz Ordaz, when our research team met to select the women who would be asked to tell their life histories, we could, as usual, only select them from the women we had met, either from our random sample for questionnaires or from being introduced to them as key informants. We wanted to approach for life histories women who felt relaxed with us, were forthcoming and could express themselves. When we checked the list we had made for variety in lives and personalities, we found that they were nearly all Seventh Day Adventists, and had to start again. But not only the Adventists have developed their own powers; Dona Mariana, a very confident mother of eight, speaking of domestic violence in the village, told the team that the first time her husband raised his hand to her after they were married, she stopped him in such terms that he never did it again.

A more open awareness of women's power may close off their traditional manipulative avenues for getting their own way. In Colombia, Dona Carmen was explicit, lucid and convincing on the powerlessness of women in her co-operative: of their economic weakness and lack of status (Janet Townsend *et al.* 1995: 48–9). These women do indeed lack formal power. But at all co-operative meetings, Dona Carmen was one of the main and most respected speakers. Of her six children, four had land in the co-operative, which she could never have achieved through open, formal routes. Dona Carmen had informal power in abundance. Informal power can be crucial. Dorien Brunt (1992) has shown that women in a community in Western Mexico were severely disadvantaged because they only had access to formal mechanisms for negotiations with the bureaucracy. The men of the community had, over many decades, developed very strong informal links with officials; they were able to transform official plans for their community. The informal links operated through routes closed to women: the men, as individuals and elected village representatives, went to the city (not acceptable for women) and built up very positive relationships with the officials, taking them drinking, dining and whoring. In disputes between women and men, it was the men who could influence the officials. Of course, women's informal power can be exaggerated. Jane K. Cowan argues (1996) that this happened in Greece and was used there to discredit feminism, on the (contested) argument that if informal power were taken into account, women were more powerful than men. Yet to us, the (discredited?) powers of the oppressed are important. It is very easy for well-meaning outsiders to 'give' them new formal powers, but destroy the old power base on which they have always depended. We cannot empower other people, but we can disempower them.

Women and Power

Rural women and power at Tapalehui   Empowerment is a foreign word imported into Spanish as *empoderamiento*.[23] In Mexico, those who finance women's projects have adopted the term and often demand empowerment as a part of projects, usually leaving the meaning very vague. All the more formally educated women at the workshop had met the specially created word which sounds very strange in Spanish, but the peasant women and change-agents either had not heard it or did not like the sound of it at all. It made them think of power, which to them was power over others.

> We didn't like the word much, because in the first place it sounded very aggressive, being a very literal translation, and because you generally have the idea that anything to do with power is negative, has a suggestion of harm – not harm – yes, harm in the end for us women, us poor people. (Citlali, Mixe change-agent, *Oaxaca*)

'Those who have power are the men, or the community bosses, or him in the shop' (Xochitl, Mixe change-agent, *Oaxaca*). 'What's empowerment? Some said they saw it as very much like the people in public positions in political terms, and at the family level too, like the men, who, well, have more power' (Ana, paid adviser, *Chiapas*). At the beginning of the workshop, power was seen as something men have which is necessary to women as a means, but not attractive as an end. Once Jo had talked about different forms of power, on the third day of the meeting, the idea appealed greatly to the rural women. The 'power to do' this or that, and the power to achieve with others what one could not achieve alone, these are powers that women want to take, to have and to celebrate and that they describe vigorously. 'The power from within', in Gandhi's terms, which enables them to leave the house and begin to act outside, is one they describe with immense pride, as we shall see. Very quickly, the word 'power' was a word to claim and proclaim, as one good way of describing the changes between people that they want and have achieved or still seek to achieve.

Academic women and power at Tapalehui   Academic women proved to have much more abstract notions of power, and more familiarity with international discussions. Academics too have doubts about the word. 'It gets repudiated, because we normally reject what comes from other cultures' (Catalina, adviser and academic, *Hidalgo*). 'Because power for me is "power over" others, I asked myself what would happen with the poor and with non-Spanish-speaking groups if this power were given to them, so I still had my doubts' (María, adviser and academic, *Puebla North* and *South*). 'I associate power with oppression, with using "power over" others and controlling others. I prefer the concept of autonomy, of self-motivation, which suggests to me an equality of rights, of respect for the individual' (Margarita, adviser and academic, *Puebla South*). Male academics seem suspicious of women's power. 'They tell you, "OK, go and have your autonomy," but you just say the word empowerment and the next thing is, the men's hair falls out with fright' (Felipa, adviser and academic, *Hidalgo*). Academic women, like the peasant women, have no doubt of women's needs and the importance of power relations to women's advance. 'I believe the crux of the question of gender is the search for power ... because the vital thing is unequal power relations – is the taking of power' (Emma Zapata 1997). But, unlike Batliwala, Kabeer or Jo Rowlands, they do not see the notion as very saleable to rural women or as a good theme on which to begin work, and they expect the process to take not years but decades.[24]

> Obviously, when it comes to the women we work with, we are not going to talk about empowerment, because they could see it as taking the power from the men (as indeed it is), but you can't say this at the beginning because the women are going to believe that now they will be the oppressors. (Felipa, adviser and academic, *Hidalgo*)

Mexico has a very unusual political system. The same political party, the PRI, the Institutional Revolutionary Party, has been in power since the 1930s: every six years, there are multiparty elections, but the outgoing PRI president recommends the new PRI presidential candidate, who has always been elected. Although electoral fraud has been one reason for this, the PRI has quite exceptional power and has, over the decades, made rural people extremely dependent on the state. This dependence is readily transferred to NGOs or to the paid staff of MOs, and presents change-agents and advisers wishing to promote self-empowerment with severe difficulties. As we shall see, the experience of *Sonora* is intriguing in this context.

Each woman at the workshop came from a specific context and specific personal experience. Context and experience strongly influence personal empowerment, as will appear from the following chapters.

The Zapatista Revolutionary Law of Women On 1 January 1994, when the North American Free Trade Area came into effect, the Zapatistas rose against the government of Mexico. On the same day, they published their Revolutionary Law of Women (translated into English in Lynn Stephen, 1997: 14). The Revolutionary Law details the rights of women to work for a fair wage, to decide on their sexual partners and numbers of children, to participate in democracy and the revolutionary struggle, to receive health care and education, to be free from rape and violence and to hold leadership positions. The Law (revolutionary indeed) is important in its own right, and known to women activists across Mexico and to the urban, middle-class, educated readers of the newspaper *La Jornada* which published the Law.[25] On 1 March 1994, the Zapatistas made their first list of demands of the government (of which few had to any degree been met at the time of writing in 1999, when Chiapas had tens of thousands of internal refugees and some 50,000 troops instead). Sara Lovera and Nellys Palomo (1997: 37), who have worked with the Zapatista women, identify Article 29 of these demands as that contributed by the non-Spanish-speaking women, and listing their 'urgent necessities, to which the government has never offered any solution'. This can give us insights into the context of the uprising, and the living conditions of most rural women in Mexico. Article 29 calls for:

> Maternity clinics, with gynaecologists, so that rural women receive the necessary medical attention.
> Creches and playgroups to be built in the villages.
> We ask the government to send us enough food for the children, in all rural areas, such as milk, maize flour, rice, maize, soya, oil, beans, cheese, eggs, sugar, pasta, oatmeal, etc.
> That kitchens and canteens be built for the children in rural areas, with all services.
> That maize mills and *tortillerías* be placed in all villages, depending on the number of families.

That we be given projects to raise chickens, rabbits, sheep, pigs etc., supported by technical advisers and vets.

We ask for projects for bread shops with ovens and construction materials.

We want workshops to be built for crafts with equipment and raw materials.

For crafts for which there is a market where they can be sold at a fair price.

That schools be built where women can get technical training.

That there be pre-school centres in the villages where the children can play
and grow healthy, morally and physically.

As women, we want to have adequate transport to get around ourselves and
to transport our products from the various projects.

(Sara Lovera and Nellys Palomo 1997: 37–8)

The women, then, added to the Zapatista list demands which are a
mixture of basic needs and of opportunities to add to their incomes. Lynn
Stephen (1997: 55) has a vital insight here (although she is referring to a
women's movement in El Salvador), that 'to identify motherhood with
child-rearing, personal sacrifice for one's children, persistent confrontation
with the authorities, and campaigns to end rape and promote sex education
may appear contradictory to people outside the movement', but the experiences of specific women have made these ideals consistent.

Questions about Empowerment

At the end of the millennium, a fashion in the development industry
for bringing women together to work in groups for self-improvement,
whether in income, education or empowerment, has changed the daily
lives, the lifeworlds, the activity space of millions of women. At the same
time, neoliberal discourse has brought great Western and World Bank
support for notions of citizenship and democracy. New forms of resistance
and participation have become possible, if still severely restricted: there are
new spaces for action. Peasants, men and women, who would have risked
death had they tried to claim their needs in the past, may now have
legitimacy as a co-operative or perhaps an 'indigenous'[26] organisation. Many
women in Mexico who would never have been allowed by their parents or
husbands or mothers-in-law to associate freely with other women are now
encouraged to do so.

Our concern in this book is to explore the talk of rural women in
Mexico on self-empowerment. Comparison between places will be important in the future. For Kamla Bhasin, for instance:

Empowerment for us cannot mean power over others, power to control more
than our share; it means *power to be*, power to control one's own greed,
avarice, violence; power to nurture, heal, care for others; power to fight for

justice, ethics, morality; power to achieve inner growth leading to wisdom and compassion ... Empowerment for women *is not just a one-way process* – in which some activists can go and empower others. It is a two-way process in which we empower and get empowered. This is an *ongoing journey for all* of us. No one can be empowered for good and then become an expert in empowering others. (Bhasin 1995: 13–14)

How far are the apparent differences between Bhasin's formulations and ours real, and how far a matter of expression? We emphasise the need for self-empowerment, she the interactive nature of empowerment.

Similarly, for Naila Kabeer (1994) or Magdalena León (1997), the 'power to' is the power to mobilise for change (after Lukes 1974); at Tapalehui, 'power to' was the person's recognition of their power to do this or that. Naila Kabeer comes from Bangladesh and has extensive experience of women's organisations in South Asia. She too writes of the 'power with' and the 'power from within' but her 'power to' influence and mobilise for change replaces 'power over'. Srilatha Batliwala (1993, 1994), from India, reported on a workshop of South Asian NGOs on empowerment and concluded that 'the process of challenging existing power relations, and of gaining greater control over the sources of power, may be termed *empowerment*' (Batliwala, 1994: 130). Batliwala takes power far beyond the formal, political sphere. She writes of a spiral of empowerment, in which 'empowerment really begins in the mind', in a process where 'women find a time and space of their own and begin to re-examine their lives critically and collectively' (1993: 10). For Batliwala, empowerment begins at the beginning, through awareness-building and organising women in a non-directive, open-ended strategy, so that they choose their own priorities, rather than being incorporated in integrated rural development, education or income-generation. Later in the process, they must develop mass movements, but without accepting existing definitions of power. 'In the ultimate analysis, women's empowerment cannot transform society unless it becomes a political force ... The need is for a new understanding for power itself' (Batliwala, 1993: 12). PAEM in Honduras had taken the non-directive, open-ended strategy (Rowlands 1995b). Jane Stein's model (1997), in her *Empowerment and Women's Health: Theory, Methods and Practice*, works with a more restricted definition of empowerment (achieving power so as to affect change) and applies it in the field of health, but still emphasises the importance of participation and choice.

Our own thinking was much influenced by Srilatha Batliwala and Naila Kabeer, and by the earlier work of Gita Sen and Caren Grown (1987), which emphasised the importance in women's empowerment of struggle for everyday needs. Magdalena León's edited collection (1997), *Poder y empoderamiento de las mujeres*, presents an array of understandings which disagree yet have a great deal in common. (All chapters but Magdalena's had been previously published in English.) In one sense, the empowerment process responds strongly to the conditions of one place and time, perhaps even one woman's life, but groups willing to explore issues of power can benefit from discussing a range of ideas.

Caution is also in order. Fuzzy, utopian visions of empowerment that fail to recognise difference can clearly be dangerous, as Nira Yuval-Davis (1998) has shown.[27] In the North, empowerment of the oppressed and powerless can be presented as a simple solution, as if the excluded all have the same interests and goals and will easily fall into agreement. 'Community' may also be idealised, as if communities were somehow naturally in accord and naturally good; in the UK today, we talk of social exclusion as a problem and the community as an answer, without recognising that communities exclude people in the first place. Empowerment is not a panacea; both increased empowerment and increased subordination of women are taking place in Latin America. In New York and Philadelphia, black women domestic servants strive for a feeling of self-worth and a sense of agency merely to live with their 'low status, low paid and dirtiest of women's jobs', not to seek radical change (Bonnie Thornton Dill 1988: 51). Empowerment does not of itself resolve conflicts and may indeed bring them to the surface. It is necessary to work at building coalitions between groups and across communities, as at Tapalehui.

New forms of self-empowerment are a reality in a diversity of places. What are the burning questions now?

- We need to know more of the psychology of the process, particularly in a range of cultures.

  Most of the work to date on psychologies of empowerment has been done in the USA. Stephanie Riger (1997) argues that empowerment is the leading concept in American community psychology today (see Appendix). Yet, she points out, the individual defined as 'sane' in psychology now is a product of Western culture at this moment in time and might be regarded very differently at other times or in other cultures. Our cognitive psychology puts the individual above the context in understanding human behaviour (Riger 1997: 58). We can lose sight of inescapable hunger, deprivation, discrimination. Our societies rank personal autonomy above communion with others and the power to do far above the power to feel or communicate. In American community psychology, argues Riger, empowerment has driven out the concept of sense of community. In our world now, neoliberalism tends to give primacy to individual rights, not community or group rights.

- We need a stronger relationship between the empowerment literature and academic writing on power.
- We need more studies of what specific groups are making of self-empowerment, and in this book we seek to supply one, as we now explain.

New opportunities have arisen for the poor and powerless, but how similar are the responses? Studies of social movements around the world have found immense differences. Economic crisis and fashion have produced movements in many societies, but they are created so much by local people in local circumstances that they can be difficult to compare or to theorise from in any general sense. Similarly, from Mysore to Mexico City, millions of women are getting into groups, but again the groups vary enormously. Some are hierarchical, repressive and/or corrupt. In others, women have had experiences described by the women at Tapalehui in terms almost of a religious conversion, as experiences of a total transformation of life and being. This is happening cross-culturally on a remarkable scale, but how similar are the outcomes? We have studies looking for features of the process which are similar in different places.[28] We need to look more closely at what individuals, groups and communities are making, out of their very different cultures and experiences, of the new opportunities. Strategies for empowerment cannot be taken out of their historical context, but we can still learn from each other.

So, what of women's groups involved with issues around power? How are women in Chiapas and Coimbatore taking up the new discourses, the new opportunities and making new lives? What new lives do they build and how do they speak of them? How are concepts and practices transmuted? From the work of Srilatha Batliwala, Naila Kabeer and Jo Rowlands in English, with the work published in Spanish in Magdalena León's edited *Poder y empoderamiento de las mujeres*, we have important general themes. What do these mean in different cultures? Haleh Afshar's edited *Women and Empowerment: Illustrations from the Third World* (1988) develops this theme. We cannot hope to construct rules, only to build a body of experience which others can use to explore their own situation and possibilities. We need to learn from many varieties of experience about the empowerment process, its satisfactions and the risks that attend it. Academics will want to be able to compare, to evaluate; as Jane Stein writes (1997), this calls for 'indigenization', for 'contextualizing research approaches and empowerment concepts such as self-esteem in the local setting'.

Above all, women need to learn from each other, to network, to build their own new realities, for 'feminist writings on empowerment suggest the need to place the subject's interpretation and mediation of her experiences at the center of our enquiries into the hows and whys of power' (Monique Devaux 1996: 233).

Summary of Chapter 2

We want to see questions of power in discussion of 'development', including attention to empowerment.

For us, empowerment is self-empowerment: we can each empower ourselves and no one else, although we may support the self-empowerment of others. Empowerment is about building our own powers, taking new powers. It is a process, not an end result.

We speak of four forms of power, which overlap, combine and interact. We organise this book around them:

- 'Power over' is the power of one person or group to get another person or group to do (or not do) something, against their will. This may be through open force, or through hidden, even unconscious processes. 'Power over' is everywhere, not only in formal politics and international capitalism, but in homes and beds and at the breakfast table. Resistance is created by 'power over', so that the two are inseparable (Chapter Seven).
- 'Power from within' builds on strengths within each of us, based on self-acceptance and self-respect which lead us to respect and accept others and enable us to combat fear (Chapter Four).
- 'Power with' is the capacity to achieve with others what one could not do alone (Chapter Five).
- 'Power to' involves gaining access to a full range of human abilities and potential. Within the 'power to', this book emphasises the 'power to do' (Chapter Six).

We also explore levels of power (Chapter Eight) including 'personal power', 'relational power' and 'group power'.

Notes

1. We are not suggesting that all abuses of power are one-way – that, for instance, no woman ever abuses her power against a man or another woman or a child. We can all be simultaneously oppressors and oppressed, but some structures are bigger and more consistent.

2. Rowlands 1995b, 1997a, 1998; Stein 1997.

3. See also Sen and Grown 1987, Batliwala 1993, Kabeer 1994, León (ed.) 1997.

4. Bookman and Morgen (1988) have a general definition of empowerment as a

process directed towards changing the nature and distribution of power within a particular cultural context. See also Schuler 1997.

5. See for example Nicholson (ed.) 1990, Ramazanoglu (ed.) 1993, Hekman (ed.) 1996. Foucault's thinking is referred to in most recent feminist discussions of power, except those defining power as present only when explicit in decision-making.

6. For Jane Stein (1997), the consensus is that 'to give empowerment' is a contradiction in terms. See Stromquist 1997: 81 and also Wieringa 1997: 162. See also 'The theoretical and practical bases of empowerment', pp. 13–22 in Carolyn Medel-Añonuevo (ed.) 1995, and 'Women's literacy and the quest for empowerment' in Jeannette Claessen and Lillian Van Wesemal-Smit (eds) 1992.

7. Kabeer 1994. In Kabeer 1998, Kabeer argues that government or non-governmental programmes may be designed to 'empower' people in ways they do not want. This is to us a contradiction in terms.

8. Zimmerman (1995) argues that no universal, global measures of psychological empowerment are feasible or appropriate. But see review in Stein 1997: 68–70.

9. See also Rowlands 1995b, 1998.

10. Rape of a divorced or separated wife was already a crime in England; rape of a live-in wife was already a crime in Scotland.

11. Women's subordination is neither simple or universal: see Sanday and Goodenough 1990.

12. Dennis Wrong (1979: 2) defines power as 'the capacity of some persons to produce intended and foreseen effects on others'. For Stuart Clegg (1989: 208) 'power always involves power over others'.

13. As in Karl 1995.

14. Although the book deals with the public sphere, the authors state that this is only a part of politics.

15. Bachrach and Baratz (1970) had already argued that 'to the extent that a person or group – consciously or unconsciously – creates or reinforces barriers to the public airing of policy conflicts, that person has power,' (p. 8), and that 'organization is the mobilization of bias'. Latin American political scientists such as Nestor García Canclini take the same understanding today.

16. See also Devaux 1996: 232, 'Foucault's power analysis allows little room for an account of the processes involved in developing personal and collective capacities for political activism; empowerment is not about actions upon agents in a relationship of power and so cannot be undersood within the confines of this analysis.'

17. Friedmann (1992) writes of an individual sense of potency as 'psychological empowerment', alongside political and social power. But his sense of potency comes from success rather than merely awareness.

18. Batliwala 1993, Kabeer 1994, Rowlands 1995a, 1995b, 1997a, b, 1998.

19. See also Collins 1991: 111 for this theme as central to Black feminist thought in the United States.

20. Riger 1997. First presented as 'What's wrong with empowerment?' at the Convention of the American Institute of Psychology, Toronto, 1993.

21. David Slater (1994) explores 'the capacity to act, the power to' in writing of new social movements (Chapter Three).

22. To this degree, we agree with Michel Foucault (1980). See Chapter Eight.

23. Other words such as *potenciar* have been suggested. Sara Lovera and Nellys Palomo, writing of the Zapatista women, prefer *formación de poderío* or *autoafirmación*.

24. Nelly Stromquist (1997: 92) also argues from experience in other Latin American countries that there is no hope for rapid, massive response.

25. *Doble Jornada* 1994: 8. Newspapers in Mexico have a mainly urban readership with a bias to the middle classes; *La Jornada* is read mainly by the educated, left of centre middle class.

The Law was published first in *El Despertador Mexicano*, the newsheet of the Zapatistas, with the first *Declaración de la Selva Lacandona*, dated 1 December 1993. It appears again in Lovera and Palomo 1997: 40–41.

26. 'Indigenous' is an important official category in Mexico for peoples whose first language is not Spanish.

27. See also Stein 1997: 46–9.

28. Batliwala 1993, 1994; Kabeer 1994; Rowlands 1995b, 1997a; Afshar 1998.

3

Outsiders and Self-empowerment

Emma Zapata and Janet Gabriel Townsend

The 'Associational Revolution'

To understand the talk at Tapalehui, it is important to understand the environment in which this handful of small, local organisations in rural Mexico is working. The emphasis of later chapters will be very much on the women themselves as co-partners in their groups, using the resources of outside organisations to build new lives and plan new worlds. In this chapter we want to ask, what can the outside organisations contribute, and how? And we want to bring to life the strange context which the rural women at Tapalehui are seeking to turn to their advantage.

First we need to understand the organisations. One puzzle for these rural women is the 'associational revolution', the sheer numbers of new organisations that have sprung up (David Hulme and Mike Edwards 1997: 3). Since the 1980s and their crises for both market and state, associations outside both have mushroomed, some offering new kinds of support to rural women. This sudden appearance of new opportunities came just as economic crisis was confronting them with new challenges. Although the most common response to crisis is individualisation,[1] non-governmental and membership organisations (NGOs and MOs) have sprouted up all over Mexico, even in remote rural areas and among minority groups. They are of all kinds, from highly didactic and even exploitative organisations (see Ana's experience, Chapter Five, pp. 85–6) to a few like *Sonora* which work in real co-partnership. We saw in Chapter Two that women's groups have become a leading official 'solution' to social and economic problems. In fact, women's groups are only a part of the 1990s trend among international 'development' agencies towards promoting new kinds of association. (The great exception to the associational revolution is China, where only organisations under the control of the state are acceptable; see Jude Howell 1997.) As we said in Chapter Two, we seek in this book to learn what the groups who came to Tapalehui are making of the new transnational community of 'international development' from which suddenly, sometimes, they can get a little funding. 'Out there' are sources of money and training, both government and non-governmental, which exist to support (acceptable) MOs and NGOs. Why?

Economic crisis In Mexico and most of the South (particularly Africa and Latin America), the 1980s brought harsh economic crisis which bore heavily on the poor. (Basically, the North had a recession which it exported to the South in greatly magnified form, but that is another story.) International lending agencies then moved away from the 'myth of the state' (Hulme and Edwards 1997) as the leading actor in 'development', and imposed programmes of 'adjustment' and 'stabilisation' which forced drastic cuts in state expenditure. The main achievement of these programmes was to enable poor countries to continue to pay interest to rich countries on the money they had borrowed. This produced a new pattern for, since 1982, far more resources have moved every year from poor countries to rich than the other way round, since poor countries are paying rich ones much more in interest on the debt than they receive in 'aid', loans and investment combined. In Mexico and everywhere else, the programmes hurt the poor through cuts in education, health and social services. In Mexico, programmes to support agriculture and rural areas were cut by 60 per cent, and the real wage has still not recovered. The poor in Mexico have less now than the inadequate wages, services and government support they had twenty years ago. As it says in the Bible 'From him that hath not, even that which he hath shall be taken away' (Luke 19: 26).

In Latin America in this crisis, there was little experience of any democracy through which the poor could pressure the government to act differently.[2] Mexico was an extreme example: in the 1930s, the governing Institutional Revolutionary Party (PRI) built support networks among peasants, urban workers, the women's movement and the elite which are so strong that, at the time of writing, the PRI is still in power, outdoing any other political party on earth, and still in tight control of its networks. The government's human rights record is bloody but its abuses, through government control of television, are largely invisible, even in 1999 (Luis Hernández and Jonathan Fox 1995). Although elections are held every six years, bribery of supporting groups and electoral fraud have together been so effective that Mexico has been called 'the perfect dictatorship' in a speech by Mario Vargas Llosa 1991 (cited in Hernández and Fox 1995).

Even before the crisis of the 1980s, economic growth in Latin America had failed to reach the poor, who had begun to develop grassroots organisations, while thinkers such as Paulo Freire (1973) and Ivan Illich (1971) had sought new forms of education for a new society. The hunt was already up for routes to new and different goals (Orlando Fals Borda 1979). A range of opportunities had opened up for grassroots involvement, such as 'popular education'[3] (of enormous importance in Mexico), the women's movement (Ibarrola 1991, Pedersen 1989) and Catholic base communities. New social movements arose. For decades, there had been enormous differences between rich and poor in Latin America, and Mexico had been seen as having 'the richest rich and the poorest poor' of all. As 'adjustment' increased this polarisation, new social movements became more active in the 1980s (Slater 1991, 1994).

Neoliberalism The International Monetary Fund and the World Bank, for their part, have had the power to respond to the debt crisis by enforcing a list of economic responses which promote the role of the market. Their policies are often referred to as *neoliberalism*. This tends to lead to the reduction of services on the one hand, by slashing of public expenditure, and of wages on the other, by currency devaluations and the promotion of 'flexibility' in the labour market. Financial deregulation, in Mexico's case, allowed the crash of 1995 (p. 6). These policies have contributed to the opening of Latin America, including Mexico, to global forces. We prefer not to enter the discussion as to what 'globalisation' is and whether it is increasing, but certainly Mexico is far more open to the world economy and international capitalism than it was twenty years ago.[4]

The 'new aid agenda' In the 1990s, pressure from Washington for greater 'democracy' has come while the gulf between rich and poor is still widening. Although 'democracy' in Washington tends to mean multiparty elections and the tyranny of the ballot box rather than real participation, a new myth that 'the market plus civil society' (Hulme and Edwards 1997) will solve both poverty and oppression has meant that international funding has become available not only for organisations working on poverty or welfare, but also for those working on citizenship and rights. (The idea is that a strong 'civil society', made up of many, diverse organisations, can bring pressure to bear on the state to work more for the people and to regulate the market more fairly, as some think happened in Europe.)[5] In Latin America, a mosaic of organisations works with many sorts of groups on a variety of themes.

The associational revolution is large and complex. In Mexico, membership organisations (MOs, also known as grassroots organisations) such as Oaxaca exist in theory to serve their members, while non-governmental organisations (NGOs) like Luisa's provide services to clients or client organisations. There are also many shades in between. Then there are much looser groupings, new social movements where many supporters are neither members nor clients. Other groups are less formal still. All these organisations have seized opportunities as the state has withdrawn, not merely taking over some welfare activities, but opening up whole new areas of work, with and without outside funding. The opportunities have been remarkable.

At the same time, the real agenda of 'international development' still fails to put the needs of the poor first. On the contrary, the poor lose to the North more than they gain, and 'there is an emerging system of global governance with methods and instruments geared to containing and managing symptoms rather than removing causes' (Ankie Hoogvelt 1997: 177). An increase in numbers and forms of formal associations is not always a change for the better, for such associations can contribute to hierarchy and oppression as well as to equality and liberation. Organisations of the elite may well act to prevent governments from promoting demo- cracy or redistribution (Laura Macdonald 1997).

At the same time, 'the new aid agenda moves from incorporating the periphery to managing and containing it' (Mark Duffield 1996: 42) while the faith in NGOs marginalises attempts to understand poverty and depriva- tion in terms of power and violence (Duffield 1996: 3). The question remains, as with all resistance, how far the poor can subvert the new aid agenda towards some of their own ends.

Microcredit As we saw in Chapter Two, microcredit, or giving poor people access to small amounts of credit to be used to make a little money ('generate income'), is a leading fashion in the development industry, although no solution to poverty (see pp. 24–5). Worldwide, such credit is most often made available to groups, and particularly to women's groups, which is perhaps the most important incentive for women to form such groups in Mexico and many other countries. We shall see in Chapter Six that peasant women at Tapalehui warmly celebrated the 'power to do' which they had developed (partly but not only) through getting such credit, managing it, learning new skills for income generation and using the credit either to make money or to reduce their workloads. In fact, they tend to celebrate the credit. We would celebrate instead their taking hold of the opportunity and using it to their own ends. The tendency of microcredit is to institute new controls, to bring such women further into the market, even to proletarianise them; it is to us part of Ankie Hoogvelt's 'emerging system of global governance', above. It can be argued that NGOs are a leading edge of capitalism, creating jobs for their (middle-class) staff to teach the poor and dispossessed how to enter the world of production for profit. We think that they are exactly this, but for poor women the question is whether they can turn these events to their advantage. The question for us is, are the women with whom we worked using the credit for self-empowerment?

New Organisations and Work for a Better World

Mexican academics are not all equally enthusiastic about the recent upsurge of new organisations.

New social movements 'New social movements' are the loosest of these groupings, and are often not formally organised at all; they may rather be people seeking to change their daily lives in roughly the same direction, perhaps linked by networks. Such movements, including the women's movement, are seen by some as opening the way to democracy, being in the vanguard of an alternative to 'development', another way to a better world, completely different from the neoliberalism we have today. This is Virginia Vargas's 'democracy of the intimate ... in countries, homes and beds' (Vargas Valente and Olea Mauleon 1997: 27). Such movements 'announce to society that something "else" is possible' (Alberto Melucci 1989: 812). For instance, at the United Nations International Women's Conference in Nairobi in 1985, women indeed called for something `else':

> We want a world where inequality based on class, gender and race is absent from every country, and from the relationships among countries. We want a world where basic needs become basic rights and where poverty and all forms of violence are eliminated. (Gita Sen and Caren Grown 1987: 80)

These ideas may now be encountered from Chiapas to Laos, each locally adopted and adapted. Such movements seek to connect everyday life with new possibilities at all levels of human organisation; their message is that politics is about human relations, from inside the family to the global level (B. Falk 1987). They commonly reject violence as a means, and state power as the principal objective; they reject the market, obsession with economic growth, consumerism and, in some cases, patriarchy. In short, many new social movements reject capitalism as we know it and seek Arturo Escobar's 'alternatives to development'. María Luisa Tarres (1996) includes the women in the Zapatista army (see pp. 38–9) among the new associations.

Ideally, social movements are networks, not hierarchies, and networks work horizontally, with centres everywhere and peripheries nowhere, in contrast to the hierarchical pyramids of conventional institutions (Marc Nerfin 1986). Traditional institutions represent 'power over', while networks use 'power with' to enable genuine participation and self-empowerment. In the 1980s, many academics attached great hope to the movements, but not all were equally enthusiastic. For pessimists such as Abby Peterson (1989), such movements help sustain today's world, rather than transforming it, by channelling effort into ineffective action. Today, many analysts prefer to try to understand rather than to judge. The movements have become accepted as leading features of Latin America, struggling to develop alternative blueprints for democracy. Some see the movements as working to change cultures to make these alternatives possible: power resides not in government nor even in institutions but in the dominant political culture. The language is far from that of Steven Lukes (p. 27), but seeks to explain the same problems (Sonia E. Álvarez, Evelina Dagnino and Arturo Escobar 1988).

Taking on democracy implies much more than rebuilding institutions and dismantling undemocratic uses of power, be they authoritarian, corporative or coercive. Democracy demands new approaches to the distribution of 'power over' and the recognition of individual rights and of new social actors. In this context, one of the main feminist contributions has been criticism of the Western concept of 'development' as patriarchal and Eurocentric, rooted in the belief that men are the universal point of reference and women or 'others' are different and unseen. Women have demanded, on the one hand, rights equal to men's and, on the other, recognition of their difference from men, a recognition that favours creativity but avoids dogmatism. In Latin America, the women's movement has played a fundamental role in the struggle for democracy. The rise of NGOs coincided with the fall of the dictatorships and the visible presence of women as social agents. At the same time, new social movements have changed many women. 'Women's awareness of gender-subordination is gained through their participation in social movements' (Elizabeth Jelin 1997: 57). 'Women [in Mexico] were beaten up just for going to meetings. There was a real need to deal with these types of issues. That's why we decided to have the first national meeting just for women' (Elizabeth Jelin 1997).

NGOs NGOs in practice overlap to some degree both with new social movements and with MOs. It is NGOs, the professional organisations, which most belong to international circuits and which have the strongest links to the international 'development' community and, often, to government. Although they make some use of volunteers, most of their staff are paid. In Latin America, many professionals who lost their jobs through state cuts either set up NGOs or are employed by them. It may be an overstatement to say, 'no middle-class, no NGOs', but this has often been the case (see Lester Salamon and Helmut Anheier 1997: 499). Again, there is a division of opinion. Some see NGOs as a vital alternative to the state. Others accept the 'myth of the market and civil society' and expect NGOs to improve both state and market; David Korten (1990) celebrated the great potential of NGOs in the fight against poverty – if only they would be democratic and transparent as most, sadly, are not. Many people have repeated his optimism without his warnings. For others, NGOs serve to deepen the gulf between rich and poor already amplified by neoliberalism (Farrington *et al.* 1993). Initially, NGOs expanded as substitutes for the state, but since the impact of structural adjustment, some have argued that they could also substitute for the market (Alain de Janvry 1995). For other authors, the nature of NGOs is defined by the social services they provide, not by the interests of their clients (Vera Giannotten and Tom de Witt 1995). In Bangladesh, for instance, huge NGOs provide services to millions. These NGOs managed at first to be egalitarian both within the NGO and with clients, but as they have grown they have reverted to the surrounding hierarchical, authoritarian culture which defers strongly to status and leadership. A narrow NGO leadership now monopolises contact with government and donors.

There is no consensus on the origins of NGOs in Latin America. Some writers place this in the 1950s with the work of the Catholic Church through CARITAS, which served to postpone the feared revolt of the poor and in some places to control them (Laura Macdonald 1997). The concept of the Mutual Support Fund (Foro de Apoyo Mutuo or FAM) came from the United Nations itself fifty years ago. Luís Lopezllera (1988: 31) sees NGOs differently, saying that the term 'has been imposed on us from different realities and defines us by what we are not rather than by all the immense riches and great potential of what we are: civil organisations, organisations for social action, alternative organisations, a civil society which seeks profound changes'.

In recent years, some NGOs have become intermediaries or links between state and people by contracting to provide cheap welfare services. Others have opened up space for groups that were simply shut out of national life. They have enabled excluded groups to relate to each other and in some cases not only brought resources to the impoverished but set out to change who gets them and how they are used. Some have become representatives of the urban and rural poor, to the point that they are themselves a channel through which these groups have managed to increase their bargaining power and promote democracy, which would have been almost unimaginable without the NGOs. This rapid development of NGOs, created by citizens, has made some of them vital elements of civil society and of processes of change. New social movements, NGOs and MOs have gained ground in such a way that the few, scattered organisations of early years have today become a great structure that gives them a presence and legitimates their work.

NGOs in Mexico The power of the state and the limited access of Mexican NGOs to external funding have kept them weak by comparison with, say, NGOs in Chile, Brazil or Peru (Hernández and Fox 1995). Mexico has been seen too widely as a democratic, middle-income country to appeal to the 'donors'. Numbers of NGOs and MOs are always very difficult to determine, and, on top of this, they vary in size and their impact is not always related to the numbers involved. Some are more dynamic, some have regional influence, others have national coverage. NGOs have proliferated in many contexts, representing local, regional, national and transnational interests. Support has come from international organisations, private foundations, religious groups and national govern-ments. Each organisation is strongly influenced not only by the specific needs of its country but by the socio-political, economic and ideological position of other NGOs. It is possible to identify a 'non-profit sector' of organisations that are neither part of the state nor make profits in the market. Lester Salamon and Helmut Anheier (1997) set out to define this sector and compare it across a range of countries, but found this difficult. In each, state, market and non-profit sectors have been shaped by their struggles with each other so that non-profit sectors are very different. In rural Mexico, NGOs have been seen as a new option in rural development, especially in sustainable development, democracy and political resistance. In Mexico as elsewhere, organisations grew from the economic crisis and the cuts in state provision, but here they also received a great impulse from the events of the earthquake in Mexico City in 1985, when citizens, not the state, took nearly all the effective action in rescue and early reconstruction.[6]

One directory of NGOs in Mexico lists 2,800 (Foro de Apoyo Mutuo 1995); the Mexican Centre of Philanthropy reports more than 2,600; SEDESOL (Ministry for Social Development) thinks 3,500. The FAM thinks that 5,000 might be a reasonable estimate, while the Civic Alliance in San Cristóbal de las Casas estimates 7,500 (*La Jornada* 1996: 9). Lorena Parada (1995) classifies Mexican NGOs into three groups:

- the 'traditional' (like the Lions' Club), created to assist the needy;
- the 'historic', which came out of grassroots groups in search of a better world and have humanitarian and/or religious and/or political roots;
- the 'phantom', designed to channel funds from the state or from inter-national agencies to a range of social groups. These last have usually been set up by ex-civil servants who lost their jobs through the privat-isation and modernisation of the state.

Recently, much funding from North America and some from Europe has been redirected from Latin America to Eastern Europe, so that Latin

American NGOs have become increasingly dependent on support from their own governments.

The value of NGOs is much debated. Can they revitalise civil society, give voices to the poor, the minorities, the excluded? For Lopezlleras (1995: Separata 7), those in Mexico are 'a reflection of the richness of social variety. Given their diversity, they instigate interaction, ideas, representation and the direction of their efforts.' NGOs are coming into their own where policies are made and programmes decided at regional, national and international levels. But even the best NGOs may duplicate work and waste resources, or compete among themselves, or be divided and/or marginalised, due primarily to the financial resources that they seek and on which they depend. Others are more concerned to finance their staff than deliver services, let alone facilitate change. In some cases, the groups in need of 'help' become the livelihoods of the paid staff, so perpetuating dependency and preventing autonomy. The government encourages NGOs to become contractors for public services, which may reduce costs and decentralise social security but will in no way challenge international capitalism or promote the search for new options. With David Hulme and Michael Edwards (1997), we fear that there may be a simple division in future between well-funded NGOs that provide services and poorly-funded NGOs that facilitate change.

Many NGOs and MOs get funding to help poor people increase their incomes by making or selling goods or services. However, in the context of the restructuring of capital (Lopezllera 1995), the funding available to encourage people to share in enterprises that they themselves develop and manage is insignificant, trivial, marginal when compared with the huge profits to be made from speculation in the name of the free market. It is equally trivial compared to repayments on the debt: the funding of the associational revolution is tiny compared to the activities of state and market.

Overall, we would argue that it is a mistake to generalise about NGOs against the state. First, no empirical study has ever demonstrated that NGOs are 'better' than the state, however often this is said. Rather, so far as the poor and excluded are concerned, there are 'good' NGOs and 'bad' NGOs, just as there are 'good' and 'bad' states. Compared to Costa Rica, Cuba or Sri Lanka, which provide much better for their poor citizens, Mexico has a 'bad' state from the point of view of the poor. (All three provide better with far fewer resources per head than Mexico.) Second, NGOs can be most effective where they can support the poor in demanding services of the state. All too often in Africa, and to a lesser degree in Mexico, the local NGO has vehicles and telephones that work and the resources to keep them running, while local government only has staff, who cannot repair, fuel or use their vehicles and simply cannot fulfil most of their supposed duties.

For NGOs in the South, including Mexico, upward accountability has become the norm. That is, they are accountable to those who finance them, whether the World Bank, a private foundation or the government, and not to their clients. To some degree, this gives an advantage to MOs that are in theory accountable to their members. In practice, the paid staff determine the policies of too many MOs (Chapter Seven). (Several kinds of MOs exist that are legally different, including co-operatives and Societies for Social Solidarity. The latter tend to be project-oriented.) MOs also contract with NGOs for services and projects, and the details of the agreement are often crucial to the relationship.

'Indigenous' peoples Soledad Dueñas *et al.* (1997) write of the experience of minority groups in Cotopaxi, Ecuador. They have experienced transitions from exclusion and disempowerment, through works of mercy, to external ideologies of 'indigenous cosmovision' which 'guarantee that our formula for development will guarantee the recovery of your culture and rebuild your identity'. These ideologies, argue Dueñas *et al.*, internalise a discourse of devaluation and legitimate authority figures. Many Mexican minority communities have had similar experiences, others more positive ones.

The Zapatistas have brought a new world to Indians in Mexico. Formal organisations already existed, but after the uprising new alliances were set up in many parts of Mexico and sympathy with the Zapatistas is widespread. As we write, the Mexican government thinks of Mexican Indians in terms of the Zapatistas. Indigenous peoples are represented on government-controlled television channels in picture-postcard terms. They 'have only appeared as images in museums, tourist guidebooks, crafts advertising … The eye of the camera seeks them out as an anthropological curiosity or a colorful detail of a remote past' (Marco Barrera Bassols *et al.* 1995).[7] New laws relating to 'indigenous' peoples have been proposed, but without prior consultation, so that they have been fiercely challenged. Previous agreements signed with the Zapatistas about Indian rights have not been honoured. The long struggle of Mexican Indians for territorial autonomy within the country continues.

The women's movement Sonia Álvarez (1997) sees radical change taking place in the Latin American women's movement. On the one hand, the movement itself has become 'ever more heterogeneous, spatially and organisationally dispersed, and polycentric' (p. 316) while, on the other, there has been a 'relatively rapid appropriation or absorption of some new and historic feminist ideas and issues by the mainstream of contemporary Latin American states and societies' (p. 302). There are gains and losses from the institutionalisation of a gender perspective. Many feminists have entered traditionally male-dominated institutions with a view to changing them and may now be called `femocrats', or 'a new gender technocracy', while 'feminist NGOs sometimes act like "neo-" rather than non-governmental organisations' (p. 307).

We agree strongly with this last point. In all these new complexities, Álvarez argues that advances have been made in policies and rights (1997), but that the movement 'is increasingly mined by uneven power relations between women'.

In Mexico, the women's movement is longstanding, but leading sections were co-opted by the PRI in the 1930s. In the 1970s, small consciousness-raising groups were the main activity, but again the 1985 earthquake had a central role in the formation and strengthening of groups of working-class women (Esperanza Tuñón 1992). As elsewhere in Latin America, the movement has become 'NGOised' in the 1990s as significant material resources were put into the more professionalised sectors of the movement (Álvarez 1997) to implement new public policies. Again, the movement is highly diverse. The Inclusive Women's Movement (MAM) has an important public presence, representing three groups in particular, feminists, working-class women and women active in the political parties, who may be in considerable conflict (E. Tuñón 1997). One important concern of MAM is democracy and women's place in the political process. Around the movement, the greatest activity is again among these three groups; as with NGOs, there is a strong concentration in Mexico City and state capitals, with little work on democracy or rights in rural areas and less still on power. Historically, rural women have been outside the movement and even now play a very minor role. An important social actor in rural areas is the Network of Advisers Working with Rural Women, around which a whole array of workshops and training courses has developed which enable rural women to see themselves as having a new and different collective identity which they themselves are defining. The wider movement has provided more resources on which they can call, using ideas which others have defined. Some rural women have become Melucci's 'networks of small groups submerged in everyday life ... [engaged in] daily production of alternative frameworks of meaning' (1989: 800) – in Melucci's terms, a movement.

NGOs working with women NGOs that work with women have proliferated in Mexico in the last few years but suffer from much the same limitations as other NGOs. At least they give women the chance to get out

TABLE 3.1 Eighty-six organisations registered in Mexico between 1986–91 as working specifically to improve the lives of women and bring about change in gender relations

Types of organisation	per cent
NGOs	52
Unions, Church or business	22
University-based	14
State-run	11
Unspecified	1

Objectives	per cent
Welfare of poor women	22
Academic research	19
Against domestic violence	8
National education on women's problems	8
Human rights, older women, union objectives, political and cultural	4

Women are involved	per cent
Rural and urban poor	35
Researchers and students	17
Battered women	9
Union women, older women, single mothers, refugees	29
Unspecified	9

Area served	per cent
Local	40
National	37
Regional	9
Unspecified	2

Source: Parada 1995.

into a group, provide services previously the responsibility of the state (such as health education) and increase women's negotiating power. Apart from service provision, they are active in education/training, alternative technologies and work against domestic violence. Some work for an alternative society where gender relations are equal. Their staff, however, are drawn from the educated middle class (María Luisa Tarres 1996). NGOs for women have the same weaknesses as other NGOs, since they too depend on outside resources to survive and have to meet the requirements of (often the same) funding agencies. They too are accountable to their 'donors'. These NGOs cover a broad spectrum, from the highly traditional to a few seeking a different democracy for a better world. NGOs for women at one

extreme take neoliberal positions (such as 'integrating women into development') while others advocate 'anti-poverty' programmes, 'redistribution
with growth' or 'basic needs' (Moser 1989). Yet others place particular
emphasis on the unequal relations of power between women and men.[8]

Parada (1995: 1) recognises two types of institutions:

- the welfarist, which do not encourage the women to organise but merely
  to reproduce their existing social roles;
- organisations that work with women as a gender. One objective is to
  transform the condition of women, be this by integrating them into
  society or by subverting the power relationships between women and
  men.

Not all women's NGOs understand gender in the same way. Some use it
as a descriptive, empty word and keep gender relations intact. Others
dynamise their whole organisation and change their entire scope. '[P]olicies
related to gender in Latin America date back only fifteen years. We must
create terms and theory from a very weak, little studied experience'
(Montaño 1996). It is among NGOs working exclusively with women that
ideas are developing rapidly for the radical transformation of gender
relations within a newly democratised society. María Luisa Tarres (1996)
found organisations working with women to be highly concentrated in
Mexico City, which has nearly half, most of the rest being in state capitals
or other leading cities. In rural areas, few NGOs or MOs seek to change
gender relations. Technically, thousands of MOs have been set up by or
for rural women to borrow money or generate income, but these almost
never have wider interests (Tarres 1996).

Such are women's NGOs in Mexico. They may take on the idea of
gender as a dynamic concept, or use it as a backdrop to secure funds while
keeping gender inequalities unchanged.

Outsiders and Self-empowerment

The place of outsiders in the self-empowerment of rural women As
we have seen, rural women who are taking new powers to themselves do
so mainly in the context of national and international women's movements
which offer them alternative ways of being. Most institutions, of course,
work the other way. Television companies support the PRI and shut out
other truths, maintaining a high degree of political ignorance among the
electorate. Women who take new powers are accused of destroying the
family, of betraying their husbands and children. Powerful campaigns work
against many rights that are taken for granted in other countries. They
work to stop sex education in schools, they overturned a ruling that legalised

abortion and they object to any teaching or advertisement that promotes any protection againt AIDS other than chastity. Rural women know that neither police nor doctors will support them over domestic violence, and that their human rights will not be recognised, particularly in Chiapas.

NGOs are often a source of change for rural women, perhaps under contract to an MO. In terms of empowerment, both Srilatha Batliwala (1993) and Naila Kabeer (1994), working in South Asia, argue that the empowerment process usually starts with outside advisers. These cannot impose or control the process, but can support it. In *The Myth of Community* (1998) Irene Guijt and Meera Kaul Shah explore gender issues (not empowerment) in participatory development but raise many relevant issues of attitude, behaviour, values and ethics which also apply in work in empowerment. In Mexico, as in South Asia, there is a significant number of NGOs that enable real change, even though others are didactic and disabling.

Outsiders seen from Tapalehui Women at Tapalehui saw organisations as the beginning of change for them. Some had set up groups and sought outside help; in other cases, outside organisations set up the groups. Outside organisations get a great deal of credit, deserved and undeserved (Chapter Six). 'I think the other thing that can give us power is just belonging to an organisation' (Carmen, elected adviser, *Sonora*). 'If it wasn't for *Oaxaca*, well, no, it wouldn't have happened – if all the women, all the men, hadn't organised, we'd just have the same as before' (Citlali, Mixe change-agent, *Oaxaca*). 'Sometimes we don't have the skills, the knowledge, the training we need. We may be set on changing the world, changing what it is to be a woman – and for us that means minority women, rural women – but it's really difficult to find ways to do it' (Xochitl, Mixe change-agent, *Oaxaca*).

> Before we had the meetings, we were very, well, very downtrodden by all our people, because before, the organisation didn't come here. Because when we heard there was an organisation, from then on, we got together little by little, all the villages, men and women, and looked for the right way to fight. Then, *Oaxaca* woke us up and from there – How can I tell you about Oaxaca? We were right at the bottom, we had nothing, not even credit – only the rich had that, in the bank, then, well, by getting organised we got the clinic, then credit for the chickens, then for housing too, and I've seen my people advance a bit. (Citlali, Mixe change-agent, *Oaxaca*)

Outsiders can help rural women use their rights under the law. Women's rights in the Mexican constitution may not be fully feminist, but they are far better than most women in Mexico know. 'Well, we've had workshops on our rights through the projects, because the truth is we had no idea what our rights were, but now I'm getting to understand that we have a right to freedom, and to be ourselves, that's it' (Linaloe, Nahua change-agent, *Puebla North*). Not a good word was said about state agencies set up to help women or Indian peoples (see Ana's tale on pp. 85–6). 'Government agencies – well, yes, we say they interfere, and usually we try to get out from under, because they're very bossy, not like other people we've worked with' (Teresa, elected adviser, *Sonora*).

Feelings on foreign agencies were more divided. For the women's section of *Oaxaca*, the experience has been positive.

> We get most of our money from a European agency, and they do interfere. But it's helped us, really, because the agency is keen to strengthen the position of women inside organisations – women's place in taking decisions, women's place in development itself. So, in this sense, I think it's gone well for us. (Xochitl, Mixe change-agent, *Oaxaca*)

But for *Sonora*, 'Well, as to what was said about foreign agencies, it's true that some are there to help, but others interfere and stop development so that they can hang on to the power' (Teresa, elected adviser).

Outsiders could have a great deal to offer, but to us, the authors, most seem neocolonial and few of the others have the motivation or the under-standing of power relations and empowerment to enable self-empowerment. This is a hard task that takes years: it is not a matter of a single workshop, but of the whole comportment of outside change-agents, advisers and specialists in all work that is done with the group, whether in infant care or income-generation.

Summary of Chapter 3

The world is seeing an 'associational revolution' in which organ-isations outside state and market are multiplying rapidly, some filling niches vacated by the state. Local groups seek to use the organisations for their own ends. Women's groups have become a 'solution' to problems of 'development'. Yet the 'new aid agenda' leaves aside questions of power and violence.

Both neoliberalism and economic crisis are the context in which these organisations sprang up. Neoliberalism promoted first 'the myth of the market' as the solution to 'development' and now 'the myth of the market and civil society', civil society being com-posed largely of the organisations.

Three main forms of organisation appear in this book:

- New social movements have arisen to seek new possibilities for everyday life and many see power as about all human relations, from the personal to the global. They include the women's movement.
- Non-governmental organisations (NGOs) are more formal, more professional and depend largely or wholly on paid staff to secure funding to work for clients. Some see them as a vital alternative to the state, others as advancing capitalism. They are controlled by their staff and their sources of funding, not their clients.
- Membership organisations (MOs) are set up and, in theory, controlled by their members, who may hire paid staff.

In Mexico, some NGOs and MOs working with women do so to improve basic needs but keep society as it is. Others are radical and seek to enable real change. Individual women and groups of women in search of livelihoods and/or change have to find their way in this global, national and local framework.

Notes

1. Stephen (1997), writing of the Women's Regional Council of the National Council of the Urban Popular Movement in Mexico.

2. Not that the poor have been more successful with the governments in the USA or the UK in the last two decades.

3. Education for adults which increased political awareness at the same time as imparting useful skills (Nuñez 1985, Schmelkes 1990).

4. For a recent discussion, see Gwynne and Kay 1999a.

5. Strong civil societies, however, can equally be organised to exclude and oppress the poor.

6. J. Tuñon 1992, Hernández and Fox 1995, Tarres 1996.

7. Cited by Yudice 1998: 372.

8. Welfare, equity, antipoverty, efficiency and empowerment: Moser 1989.

4

'Power from Within': Getting Out of That House!

Janet Gabriel Townsend

Who is Writing?

First, so that the reader may read more critically, who am I? I write as an outsider, a foreigner from a British university, who has worked with peasant women in rural Mexico who only dream of groups such as these we were studying (Janet Townsend *et al.* 1995). I am a feminist geographer, much influenced by Haleh Afshar, Mike Crang, Arturo Escobar, Nina Laurie and Doreen Massey: an old Marxist influenced by poststructuralism. Like four Mexican women at Tapalehui, I speak Spanish imperfectly, as a second language. My working life has been as an academic, with some privileged spells of research in rural Latin America, but I have not learned what it is to be a poor rural woman. I have had the joys of travel, of living in the rainforest, and the discomforts of typhoid, hepatitis and military ambush, but most researchers have well-nourished bodies, healthy immune systems (strengthened by vaccinations), medical kits, insurance, education and money. We may have to camp, or sling hammocks in one-roomed huts with the family; we may have to carry the water and boil it on an open fire, but we do not experience rural life unprotected. We see without sharing the poverty, hunger and malnutrition. We are 'rural development tourists' (Robert Chambers 1984), voyeurs who do not have to watch our own children die or even suffer.[1] I have enjoyed rural development tourism in Nigeria, visiting women's farming groups; in India, I have admired Rayalaseema Sewa Samiti, a local NGO in Andhra Pradesh working very successfully in the welfare of poor women, children and disabled people; above all, Indian feminists have taken me to groups of poor rural women engaged in self-empowerment around Hyderabad – groups which really give me hope for the future of the world. But in India and Nigeria I speak no local languages and am even more of a tourist.

Working in remote villages in the forests of south-east Mexico (Janet Townsend *et al.* 1995), I was deeply impressed by the work of local women in the face of economic crisis. All want to find a way to earn, and see women's groups as a means (see Chapter Five). Many have bad experiences, for the government programme that supports women's groups sets impossible conditions and trains one or two people: if they manage to make any money, the trained people come to control the group and part or all of the profits. But the demand for training for whole groups is here, there and everywhere, so that training and groups were local women's solution for the problems of deforestation and poverty (Townsend *et al.* 1995, Townsend 1997).

Peasant women at Tapalehui had also wanted to find in their groups better ways to combat poverty, and had found limited answers (pp. 11–13, 115–17). But their groups worked in more than making money, and the women celebrated a new world they had found and meant to build.

The Power from Within

The core of the empowerment process involves fundamental psychological and psycho-social processes and changes ... Central to these are the development of self-confidence and self-esteem, and a sense of agency ... a sense of self within a wider context. (Jo Rowlands, 1997a: 111–13)

In the international literature, the *power from within* is grounded both in self-esteem and in an awareness of external reality. It is knowing who you are, that you have a right to exist; it is self-respect. The Spanish word *dignidad*, used much by the PAEM women in Honduras (Rowlands 1997a), encapsulates the basis of the power from within. This is more than the English meaning of dignity: it is self-respect linked to the expectation of respect and the right to respect. A sense of agency is immensely important, coupled to an awareness of some limitations on the agency (see pp. 72–4). The references to a sense of agency by peasant women at Tapalehui were indirect; *dignidad* was mentioned, but not often nor with great emphasis. Their talk is more practical. 'The thing is, we can decide and we can move on, so that the men won't tell us what to do any more. We women can decide and we've got to do the things we want' (Citlali, Mixe change-agent, *Oaxaca*). As we shall see, the peasant women speak of the 'power from within' in terms of the capacity it gives them to overcome obstacles, so that their talk is crowded with negative words such as fear, lack of confidence, restriction. Oddly enough, the peasant women at Tapalehui talk a great deal more about escaping from the house and joining the group than about self-esteem or agency. Tales told at Tapalehui of dragons slain tell us a great deal about the oppression of women in rural Mexico and something about Mexican universities.

The obstacles On our last day at Tapalehui, when we asked ourselves,

'What powers do women want?', we talked and talked about the defeat of fear, about self-empowerment as the conquest of obstacles. Above all, everyone agreed that the self-empowerment of peasant women in Mexico depends on women shaking off their fears. Fear, men and fear of men came up in all discussions, and domestic violence is a daily reality (see Chapter Seven). Power from within is about strength, valour, courage, throwing off fear. Peasant women use it in 'daring to do so many things which they used not to dare' (Elena, academic, *Hidalgo*). The same feelings were expressed again and again. When we talked about our achievements, Lucía, a very articulate graduate who works to help peasant women set up local credit organisations, said, 'I feel a bit stronger than I was.' Peasant women, advisers and academics all felt that they had taken a small step in combating fears, a small step which takes them towards undreamed-of possibilities.

New Consciousness

Everyone at Tapalehui talked of a new consciousness, but the peasant women drew it on paper while the academics spun words (p. 15). 'She's learned to dream, don't you see, to dream on a grand scale,' said Margarita (academic and adviser, *Puebla South*).[2] For the academic women, the potential is there in all peasant women, waiting for them to release it; for María, 'Each one of us is a store of wisdom ... [and has only to] become aware of her own reality.' But the academic goal is not to preach what they see as Western feminism. They do not want women to throw aside their 'traditional' roles: each must value the work she does, each must set 'a greater value on yourself and your activities', says Felipa (adviser and academic, *Hidalgo*) and 'appreciate the role she's been playing in her family' (Guadalupe, adviser and academic, *Puebla North*).

For Sara (adviser and academic, *Hidalgo*):

> If you ask them who they are and how they define themselves, many women say 'workers', that's the first way they measure themselves. But also, they can be really hard on themselves, because they sometimes say, 'We don't do anything.' At one and the same time, they don't recognise the work they do and they know they're hard at it all day.

Throwing off fear The biggest part of this new consciousness is women's new power to recognise that they can do things, have choices, can throw off the old fears. 'I said, "Right, well, why can't I? I can do it too. If I want, I can do it." Then I was scared, scared to speak, to give an opinion, to do anything' (Carmen, elected adviser, *Sonora*; for her full account, see the end of this chapter). In academic terms, Carmen is describing the breaking down of internalised oppression, of controls so effective that women themselves thought themselves incapable. 'Empowerment ... has to include the processes that lead the individual or group being enabled to *perceive themselves as able to occupy that decision-making space*' (emphasis added, from Jo Rowlands, 1997a: 23).

The academic group talking at Tapalehui about this new consciousness were excited by peasant women's new capacities 'to break down, to destroy a fear or a guilt' (María, adviser and academic, *Puebla South*), 'to feel safe in front of others' (Lucía, credit adviser) and, more positively, 'to be able to explain what they think' (Catalina, adviser and academic, *Hidalgo*). 'We want to get to a point where the women know themselves and lose the fear of joining in' (Lucía). Academics agree that there is a stereotype, an ideology in Latin America that sees the ideal woman as the Virgin Mary, capable of infinite suffering. The capacity to endure, for ever and without question, is an important part of traditional femininity but not of masculinity (Janet Townsend *et al.* 1994, 1995).[3] Even women who do not conform still have to live with the idea. 'So success is not to suffer, not to accept this suffering, no, not to accept it as a beautiful thing' (Janet, academic).

A process of rebuilding Peasant women's groups do 'exercises' (often invented by urban, middle-class women), exercises in trying to talk positively about themselves. They have learned to belittle themselves and do not find this easy.

> At first, when I did this exercise, I also felt I was showing off a bit, you see. Because they said we had to make claims about what we had done, and flatter ourselves and I don't know what, but when you have to give yourself flowers (because not everybody does) yes, you feel good, don't you, yes, you feel good. (Carmen, elected adviser, *Sonora*)

Liberating the 'power from within' is going to mean, said the advisers, 'they begin to question some parts of their culture which have been very thankless for them' (Ana, paid adviser, *Chiapas*), but the advisers' objective is not a breaking through from tradition to some kind of modernity. 'They [the peasant women] have to think through their culture, setting a value on all the things they feel they need to keep' (Ana).

At the individual level, says Lucía (credit adviser) of herself:

> This is a process of rebuilding, don't you see, through the contradiction between my needs to be feminine and my new needs. Not new needs, but the needs that as women we're not allowed to have – the need to know, for example, the needs for power which are a part of us but denied by society.

This is 'power over' oneself as well as with or against others, and it always calls for more development. So, Lucía again, being very abstract:

> I have some 'power from within', but it's limited. I'd like to have more 'power over' myself, to rebuild myself. That is, there are things in which I've been rebuilding myself, to which I'm really paying attention, which are part of my gendered self which has been socially constructed and which I want to reconstruct. But I'd like to have more power to make it all happen quicker. I have the power of knowledge, the power of analysis, the 'power over' my sexuality. And, well, the powers which I do have don't include the public powers, because as a woman in this society I'm not allowed to have them. That's to say, well, the political powers.
>
> I have to think every day who I am, what I have accomplished. It's as if you exercise the mind and get to know yourself ... When they tell us to change, we do things almost automatically, don't we? But soon we lose the idea. But when you yourself set out to make a new way to live, you get keen, don't you, you get keen and you aren't afraid of anyone. Or, if you like, it gives you the strength you talk about, to go ahead. Because the objective, for me, is to change my way of life. I don't want to always do the same thing ... Don't you see, I want to swing it so that the men come in on the new level, in this new way of living. (Lucía, credit adviser)

For the advisers too, the awakening is about new wants. 'And new needs, too ... because then the needs which make up a woman change. Now it isn't only, "I want to be a mother, I want to care for my children, I want to earn more to give it to my children", but, "I want to learn too, I want to get out into the world"' (Lucía).

Not everyone agrees. Felipa (adviser and academic, *Hidalgo*) does not.

> 'Power from within'? No, I think it's the power we fear most or which it costs us most to get: economic power. Not the 'power from within'. Because I think that has more to do with oneself and the need to change. So I think that many women are terrified of economic power. I don't say that it wouldn't be the ideal one to get, no, but I think it's the most frightening because it implies a freedom to choose, and when you have freedom to choose you can make mistakes. Yes, there is a kind of power now, a personal power, to do more, to go out, to speak, but it's not from within – the inside, what's inside us, that's much further on.

Sex and sexuality There is also a downside to developing new needs, such as wanting a violence-free marriage. Several women at the workshop despaired of finding a partner who would accept their ideals. Linaloe and Araceli, the Nahua women from *Puebla North*, are unmarried, not because they do not want children, or sex with men, but because of the downside of marriage for them. They have made a positive choice to be free to be activists and to leave the community. Marriage would both deprive them of such freedom and entail submission to the beatings now seen as normal among their people. Linaloe and Araceli want to marry Nahua men, but cannot find any who can accept them as they now are.

The academics also see feminism as an obstacle to heterosexual relationships in Mexico, which is hard for the heterosexual. For single women:

> The way the relationship with men is, it's really very difficult, really amazing how we are moving towards an idea which can't be met, because you won't find a partner on this level. And not only will you not find one, but you'll find yourself harassed, rejected for having these ideas. So it seems to me that you have to give up looking. So, I'd say I'm in a position that the men don't want me because I'm a feminist. (Felipa, adviser and academic)

'I'd like to back up what you said about feminism a bit … The thing is, it's really hard to find a man who's different' (Guadalupe, adviser and academic, *Puebla North*).

What are women's choices in terms of their sexuality in rural Mexico? Marta Lamas has written bitterly of the prevailing ignorance and repression even in urban areas. 'As far as sexuality is concerned, the twentieth century did not begin until the 1970s … the explicit and implicit rules about sexuality stink of the nineteenth century … homophobia tinges much of intellectual production' (Marta Lamas, 1998: 20). For instance, although abortion in Mexico is widely seen as the business of the mother or parents, not church nor state, this is not reflected in law or availability (Rayas 1998). As a result, there are an estimated half million abortions a year, nearly all illegal, and one in four results in medical complications.[4] The Church responds by promoting sexual abstinence. Since 1992, the Catholic Church has been given legal status in Mexico and many members of the hierarchy have used this to promote a sexist and homophobic agenda. Sex education is now said to 'incite licentious behaviour and harm Mexican morals',[5] and is under attack alongside all birth control (other than by the rhythm method), abortion and the use of condoms for protection against AIDS. There are no effective government campaigns against the spread of HIV.[6] In such a climate, it is hard for women's groups to discuss even marital sexuality, and other options become a near-impossibility for debate. The feminist movement, under this pressure, struggles to keep itself from being identified with lesbianism (Marta Lamas 1998) although individual feminists are more positive. In urban Mexico, it is hard to be a lesbian, but groups exist. We do not know how many rural Mexican women enjoy lesbian relationships or how much of an option such relationships are, because they are not mentioned or, as far as we know, studied. Nearly all rural Mexicans marry, but some men, as in urban areas, also have gay relationships. Tradition has been so repressive that simply accepting and enjoying their sexuality is hard for heterosexual women; what choices others have, we do not know, and we did not raise the question at Tapalehui.

Autogestión* and *dignidad For rural women and for academics at Tapalehui, the development of *autogestión* and *dignidad* is a test of success in self-empowerment. But what do they mean? The literal translations are very inadequate. *Autogestión* is not in Spanish–English dictionaries. Nancy Sternbach *et al.* (1992: 238) say, '*Auto-gestión* (of a meeting) literally means self-gestating, that is, a free form, a spontaneous structure ...'[7] Literally, it would mean self-insemination as well as self-gestation, because *autogestión* includes the whole process from having the idea through taking the initiative to managing the action/project to completion. 'Independence' is too vague. Loosely, *autogestión* is self-determination, in the sense of self-reliance, self-direction. It is, they continue, 'thinking of things and carrying them through on one's own account' or 'if an individual or group is capable of *autogestión*, that means that if they have a free hand they can make good use of it'. (There must be a word in modern management-speak! 'Initiative' comes to mind, but *autogestión* means more than initiative. It puzzles me that, in English, the closest words turn out to apply to machines, not people: self-starting, self-propelled, autopilot.)

Dignidad is not a new word in Spanish; it has always meant dignity, but it is stronger. A person with *dignidad* is a person of high quality. *Dignidad* defines the quality of a person; it suggests independence of mind and, in the positive sense, self-respect and self-esteem (*auto-estima* is another objective). In Spanish as in English, *dignidad* can describe the way a person behaves and carries themselves, but that is not the meaning here. In this sense, *dignidad* is honour and integrity; it earns the respect of others but is independent of such respect. Both, then, are internal qualities which have to develop from within, and have long been goals of Latin American feminism and particularly of feminist work with poor women. Although they are aspects of the new concept of the 'power from within', which we brought to Tapalehui, they were already deeply rooted.

Getting Out of That House!

A language of movement As a geographer, I am fascinated by the geographical language and drawings used at Tapalehui to express liberation and self-empowerment in terms of place and space. The peasant women and advisers celebrate their achievements in a language adapted from the urban women and from international NGO-speak, but in an idiom all their own, an idiom of spaces and places and movement. In this section, these words and phrases of movement, of spaces and places and of joining, groups and organisation, will be italicised for emphasis. The house, the home, becomes restrictive, limiting, disabling. Inside is stagnation. Outside are opportunities to join with other women, to participate, to organise (see Chapter Five). Each woman has *got out*, leapt out of the house, taken off into a world of action, and *joined* other women to form *a group, an organisation* which changes their whole life. Every peasant woman at the workshop spoke of the home, of getting out, of joining an organisation. The language is of movement, escape, progress. 'One of their achievements is to have learned to *fly* towards hope, isn't it? What we are trying to find out is how to *go ahead, as far as we can get*' (Margarita, adviser, *Puebla South*).

Teresa (elected adviser, *Sonora*) explained her drawing of her own successes like this, 'I put the sun here, for the energy which *reaches* all women so that we have the strength *to go forward.*' In the UK, we use a little of the same language but with nothing like the force of meaning. In Honduras, women also spoke repeatedly to Jo of 'the isolation of the individual woman in her home' (Joanna Rowlands 1997a: 113) and re-counted obstacles similar to those described at Tapalehui.

The academic women are familiar with the talk, but it is not their talk and they said little about it and will feature little here. They did do a drawing about the situation of peasant women, and chose to feature in the middle of the picture a naked woman, triumphant in her body, surrounded by other women. To the left, the same woman is a very small figure, *leaving her house* under the rising sun, and getting bigger as she *approaches the group*; on the right, evening is falling and she is going home *under the eye of the community* and of the men, getting smaller and smaller as she goes to her house and enters it.

As we shall see in Chapter Seven, peasant women, advisers and acad-emics agree that Mexican peasant women who have joined groups and are seeking to change their lives are achieving much more in women's and other *groups* and *within themselves* than in their *close relationships* (see Chapter Two, p. 26), whether with their partners or their children. We think that this constant harping on the home as a place to get out of may reflect not only their continuing real difficulties in close relationships but a certain defeatedness in the face of trying to change these relationships. Women who accept defeat in this area are not all poor or rural. In England, Nicky Gregson and Michelle Lowe have demonstrated that there is a whole new demand for domestic workers, a 'new servant class', created to a considerable degree by women in well-paid work who would rather hire another woman to do the domestic chores than try to get their husbands to join in the housework (Gregson and Lowe, 1994).

The bad old days In Spanish, there are separate words for 'house' and 'home' (roughly *casa* and *hogar*), but they do not quite translate literally and *casa* is frequently used for either so we cannot be sure which is meant in our terms. The house/home plays a big part in accounts of the old days, usually in rather gloomy terms and with men featuring as jailers. Linaloe (Nahuatl-speaking change-agent, *Puebla North*), said early in the workshop that before the university encouraged them to set up an organisation, 'women were always *in the house*, they always *stayed in the house, waiting* ... Before, I used *not to go out*, I was always *in my house*.' Women not *in the groups* are spoken of as trapped. 'We wanted them to *join in* too, to *come out* like us from where they were *shut in*' (Teresa, elected adviser, *Sonora*).

'Internalised oppression' is not one of the peasant women's catch-phrases, but they communicate it brilliantly. 'We didn't feel up to much, even to be women, even *to go out, to take part in other places*, to talk, or even, often enough, to get to know other women' (Teresa, elected adviser, *Sonora*).

I felt so alone, really sad. Because without having any friends, without know-ing the other women, *being shut in my house*, I used to think a lot about what I could do to be able to *go out and join in, or get about*, you see, because, before, the men had you *shut in* there, didn't they? So I *couldn't go out*, not even *go out to shop*, I always had to take one of my children. (Xochitl, Mixe change-agent, *Oaxaca*)

Taking the children seemed not to count as 'going out' or 'getting out', so is 'being shut in the house' really 'being shut in the family'? For a daughter it was just as hard. 'Before I left home, I *wasn't allowed to go out*, because they said I'd be robbed. I was only *allowed to go to town* with my brothers, the men. I'm the only girl and my brothers *always went out*' (Lucía, credit adviser). Women's place clearly was – and is? – in the home. 'They give us the idea we are better *at home*,' says Lucía, but peasant women at the workshop take a dim view of their place in this home. 'If I'm only *in my house*, I'm not going to do anything,' says Araceli, Linaloe's niece and also an unmarried Nahua woman.

If I *hadn't got out* of my house, if I *hadn't been allowed out*, although I *wanted to go out*, to hear new things, but if I hadn't been allowed, where was I going to get this enthusiasm? Who would have *come to me*? Where would I have *gone to make this step* the other women were making? Because no one *would have come to my house* to say, 'Look at this!' (Citlali, Mixe change-agent, *Oaxaca*)

The home is a refuge, but not necessarily an attractive one:

> People around us, especially our husbands and the boys, they have always been the bosses, they have always been making the decisions, with us always following. Then, with all the changes and with us feeling bad, we are feeling bad and in the face of this either we leave our husbands or we *go back to the house, to seek refuge in the house*, so as not to feel bad. (Teresa, elected adviser, *Sonora*)

Taking off The house, the home, has become a place where a woman is enclosed, hemmed in, useless, and 'to get out of the house' is the crucial action. To come out of the house is to get started, to get moving, to take off. Leaving the house is the decisive moment in many of the peasant women's definitions of self-empowerment. The action is an expression of power, 'power from within'. 'I think we've got power as women by deciding *to come out of the house, to have a group*' (Teresa, elected adviser, *Sonora*). 'We've been talking about empowerment, haven't we? What I think is that there is a big change, and that really we aren't the same women as we were *when we came out of the house*, for example, do you see?' (Isabel, paid adviser, *Chiapas*). 'Talking of the word "empowerment", I understand that *when we get out of the house*, we take the "power to" learn other things. When a woman *gets out*, no-one can tell us *we can't go*, because we have the *power to go out to other places*' (Lucía, credit adviser).

> Well, for me the word 'empowerment' is new, I'd never heard it before, and I see it as if the word empowerment … is like the revolution which we women are living. As if, in this transformation, when we *come outside our houses*, then we are changing already … and I see it as if – as if when we are *in the house*, we say, 'We can't make anything happen', or, 'I can't, I'm not fit to do it, because I'm a woman' … You see, when you begin *to join in*, you realise you can, and this is the moment when you take the power. 'Yes, I can – yes, I can!' and we get it into our heads that yes, we can get a lot done. (Teresa, elected adviser, *Sonora*)

> I say that the power to argue is a 'power to', because we're doing it, aren't we? The 'power from within' would be this power we women are talking about, to keep taking part, to say 'You've kept me *in the house*. *I'm going out*, I'm *going* to the meeting.' (María, adviser and academic, *Puebla South*)

The academics reflect the same ideas in describing 'power from within' for peasant women. The 'power from within' is, to them, 'for a woman to give herself time *to go to the meeting*, and to make that a decision' (Guadalupe, adviser and academic, *Puebla North*). To them, deciding one's time or simply making decisions in general depends on the 'power from within'. Another issue seen as crucial is 'to make a break with the daily chores' (Xochitl, Mixe change-agent, *Oaxaca*) so that it's success when 'Now they've been able to let go of what they'd always thought they had to do, because it was their duty and only theirs to do it' (Teresa, elected adviser, *Sonora*).

A place of power?   But, as the peasant women themselves say, the house itself can be a place of power. 'Well, you see ... I understand "empowerment" as like now, when we decide *in our own house*, we know what we are going to do' (Citlali, Mixe change-agent, *Oaxaca*). Going out can help with the balance of power in the house:

> Or sometimes, when we have problems at home, well, *I get out of the house and go* and talk with someone about what I'm going to do with my family. Because I have problems which give me ideas like this, I think it's a power which gives me strength *to go out of the house*. (Teresa, elected adviser, *Sonora*)

But power in the home remains contested. The peasant women disagreed over whether the home is a traditional place of power for women. Some peasant women feel that, in a sense, they have the power to bring up their children in the home and to decide what the family will eat, but others were very outspoken about the limits on these powers, because the men may demand junk food and, as regards household chores, 'The weight of authority in what the men say is very strong for the boys' (Lucía, credit adviser). 'Power over' in personal relations becomes the central issue here.

Peasant women's exploits   During the first morning, spent talking about women's achievements, getting out of the house was named as an achievement 34 times in two hours by the rural women! 'I've managed to *get out of my house*!' (Araceli, Nahuatl-speaking woman). For Citlali, commenting on Araceli's drawing:

> I feel that our friend has *been in her house*, and has had some successes of knowing, of, well, *getting out of her house*, of having dared to insist on *getting out of her house, outside her house*, and has had to climb a harsh road, a really difficult road because that's how it is, and that she has managed *to get out*, and *to climb* into other spaces, and that is a success for her, isn't it, it's a success even if she does no more than *get out* and see cars on the road, perhaps.

Fear had dogged them, getting out had been a daring exploit, a breaking of barriers, of chains. (See Carmen's account at the end of this chapter.)

All of us, all of us, have said it was a great achievement *to have come out of the house*, to have dared assert ourselves. We've all met obstacles, we've all talked of obstacles of different kinds, but we all had obstacles, we all talked of learning, or, if you like, we've learned a lot, and that it's good to have learned about everything. (Xochitl, Mixe change-agent, *Oaxaca*)

For the Mixe women, getting out of the house was a step on the road to the international. (They belong to a mixed organisation which exists for the benefit of women and men whose first language is Mixe, p. 89).

[We have] the power of being there, having a say in the mixed organisations, with all the obstacles we face. But little by little – we are there, you see, and in the positions where decisions are made. Well, before, there were no women's sections and now there are, as we go working our way up the mixed organisations. I agree that at the moment when we *came out* to get organised, a women's struggle started, for resources. Because all this has given us power, you see, in institutions, Mexican and foreign institutions. (Citlali, Mixe change-agent, *Oaxaca*)

'Getting out' is not only out of the house: all movement, all travel is celebrated, beginning with the next village:

Leaving behind the fear of going to another village, like this, and making yourself strong, brave *to go to another village*, because, for instance, take me: if I hadn't decided, if I hadn't thought, if when some women said to me, '*Come along, we're going there,*' well, I'd have stayed there like a nun. I could have said, 'I'd have *to leave* my husband, I'd have *to leave* my children, and who is going to look after my little grandson?' Well, the fear has won, I don't have the strength, I don't have the courage to decide whether I'm going to hear what other women are going to hear ... Well, this thing about the power, you have to work and to find a way to, say, go to sell things somewhere else – because I sell things and I think the powers I have when *I go out to sell* things, and now I go out elsewhere to sell, and then I think this is a power too. And then the care of our children in the home, and then the 'power to' stand up for ourselves when someone criticises us. (Citlali)

And on to Mexico City, the biggest city in the world, and to the metro. Linaloe is a middle-aged Nahua woman, in charge of the sales of *Puebla North*, a peasant women's co–operative which embroiders blouses in traditional Nahua styles. Linaloe, like her niece Araceli, wore traditional embroidered dress throughout the workshop and sat on the edge of the swimming pool, laughing, rather than join the rest of us in the water. They value and seek to preserve many of their traditions.

Now I've lost the fear, now I *can go out alone, travel in the city, in the metro and in other places ...* And when you *go out*, when you *go to Mexico City* to whatever office, now you have the courage to speak, or let's say now you have the power, now you aren't *afraid to go.* Because a great many things have happened to me by now, as I'm responsible for the sales. Once they happened to ask for very large quantities of the crafts and then as soon as I arrived, they wanted to send them back. So I began to argue. I said to the señora, 'Well, you wanted to buy it,' I said, 'I'm not taking my things away, because you asked for them. I've got to leave them here because I've paid the fare to come, and how am I going to take my things back now?' I had power, and now I used it to defend my goods. So the señora now, 'Yes, yes,' because she spoke with the director and the director called us and we too began to talk. I said to the Señor Director, 'Well, we shan't take them away again, because it's difficult once we've got them to the city, we've brought them, and to get to the city again and to Cuetzalan again, if they don't pay me – .' Well, they took the consignment and later they repaid me the money. So that's how I took hold of a power and yes, this señor said, 'Leave it and I'll pay you', and they paid me when I delivered it. (Linaloe)

A new balance?   There is reflection too. For some women, as for Lucía, the credit adviser, home is regaining its place in a new life: a new home, a changed home.

Because in the changes we've made so far, it's when we *live in our home*, that we know what we are doing, when we know to ask for our rights, to demand empowerment, to know very clearly what we understand by this word when we manage the *group's* resources and decide what to do with them ... I've had the good luck to get plenty of work, but when I get home to rest a little, to read a little more, to understand more what I read, to set myself to sweep or do chores with pleasure, because I want to do them, not because it was my duty to be doing them.

Even coming out is not a complete solution.

At least, if we've decided to *take part outside*, but still inside, at least, I feel that inside I still have fears ... Oh, I don't know how to put it, but sometimes you say, 'There's this barrier, or that hurdle, how am I going to break through it?' And at times it's very difficult for us to break through. So I say that the *act of coming out* does not give us the power, but these are steps which we take very slowly but which will still take us towards breaking out. (Xochitl, Mixe change-agent, *Oaxaca*)

Pleasure!   Escape is also frankly to enjoyment. For the peasant women talking about their achievements, 'It gives me such pleasure to come out into the community' (Carmen, elected adviser, *Sonora*); 'She really likes to travel and it makes her very happy' (Teresa, elected adviser, *Sonora*); 'I just love to travel!' (Xochitl, Mixe change-agent, *Oaxaca*).

Understanding the Talk

A woman's place 'Getting out of the house' is not just a figure of speech but a real event to Mexican peasant women from very different cultures. This is familiar to anyone who has lived in Latin America. I have drawn world maps from data from the International Labour Office (ILO) of women's share in the paid labour force in agriculture, industry and services (Janet Townsend 1991). Latin America features alongside the Muslim Middle East, North Africa, Pakistan and Bangladesh for women's extremely small recorded share of agricultural work, which is much smaller than India or the rest of Asia, and tiny compared to Africa. Of course, in Latin America as in Bangladesh, the figures are too low: they are only the ILO's best guess. In Mexico, the official figure is that in 1990 only one worker in ten in rural areas was a woman,[8] but this is ridiculously low. Most of women's work on the land in Latin America is on the tiny family farm, or is seasonal or casual, or the work of minority groups, and these are all types of work often not recognised or recorded. In most Latin American societies, women still work on the land far less than men, and call it not 'work' but 'help', although the work often involves long hours and heavy labour.

In much of rural Mexico, a woman's work is very much what she can do in her home and garden; this is what makes her respectable, and she fights to sustain this state of affairs. The symbols and talk have strong roots in the colonial period. Before the conquest of Latin America by Europeans, most people worked on the land although there might be different tasks by gender, age and power. The Spanish and Portuguese conquerors, however, brought the idea that women should be 'in the house'; to some degree, the idea had come from the Muslim conquerors who had only just been driven out of Spain and Portugal when Columbus found his way to America. For Steve J. Stern (1995: 340–41), documenting bitter struggles around gender rights and obligations in late colonial Mexico, there are still 'deep continuities in gendered life and argument' under which people 'redeploy old dynamics of quarrel, claim, repression and power', using the same phrases (and the same violence) in very different circumstances today. Many writers have shown that the idea that 'women's place is in the home' still survives in much of rural Latin America. Because being 'in the home' reflects well on the woman, her husband and family, most women who do work in the fields are the very poor: most who can get out of it choose not to do it. Some Mexican women think that they are 'lucky' to be women because it is the men who have to work in the sun (Janet Townsend *et al.* 1994, 1995). Of course, women and girls still carry wood and water, sometimes as heavy loads for long distances. And where there is no piped water, it makes sense to do the washing at the stream. The stream can be a meeting-place for women, but some women avoid the meeting-place 'to avoid the gossip' of which their men disapprove. As always, there is great variety in rural Mexico between regions and cultures, but in this case the value set on the home is very widespread. In twelve villages across south-east Mexico, we found differences in the amount women did in the fields of the family farm but all women attached great importance to the home and to being in the home (Janet Townsend *et al.* 1994, 1995). Everywhere, women who go out to work as domestic servants or as paid workers on the land come from the poorest. Verónica Vasquez (1997: 189) cites a vivid example in a Nahua community in the south of Veracruz, where those women who are the only wife or the first wife seek 'to give themselves the luxury of not having to go out to work' and either leave earning to the man or earn in the home. These are the 'respectable' women who 'respect the home'. As neither second wives nor single mothers get much support from the fathers of their children, both must go out and earn, which they can do as they have no 'reputation' left to protect. The connection between being in the home and respectability is widespread even in urban Latin America, but less so for professional women whose work has its own respectability.

In towns, women do go out to work in industry, and Mexico of course has *maquiladoras* (factories producing for export), which are largely staffed by women. Most women who do paid work do so in 'services', from domestic services to offices. But across Latin America, women are associated with the home. In the very different circumstances of a poor neighbourhood in Medellín (Colombia), Kristina Bohman (1984) explored class and gender and found 'the house' to be a recurring motif. The woman belonged to the house, the man to 'the street', meaning the male domain of public life. To describe a woman as 'of the house' was very positive; she should stay inside and do the housework (work of very low status), or be in the houses of other women, mostly relatives. It is remarkable that women's lives in a big city could resonate so strongly with those of peasant women in Mexico, some more than 2,500 miles away. Mexico has enormous amounts of 'homeworking' (Wilson 1991), for both the export and the domestic market. If the reader is wearing a sweater, it may well have been made by a woman in someone's back room in Mexico, although that will not be on the label. Most of this labour force is women and girls working for the market but, respectably, in the home.

The countryside, then, is different from the towns, for in the countryside 'women's work' is in caring for others, in cooking, cleaning, childcare, caring for the sick, carrying water and wood and 'helping' on the farm – all activities given very low status and not recognised as work. As we saw, 'We didn't feel up to much, even to be women, even *to go out*, to take part *in other places*, to talk, or even, often enough, to get to know other women' (Teresa, elected adviser, *Sonora*).

For the majority of people in rural Mexico, a woman's place has always been in the home from the time of puberty, that is, from first menstruation. Before that, a girl might play with other children, carry water, sell snacks; after that, she should stay at at home and her friendships should be with girls and women in her own and later her husband's family. Traditionally, girls' contacts with boys and men were so restricted and her life at home so hard that she often ran away in her early teens with a man she hardly knew (Janet Townsend *et al.* 1994, 1995 and many other studies). Other girls and women were often no more acceptable as friends or associates than boys or men. Many married women could not visit their mothers without their husband's permission, nor meet other women to do the laundry at the stream. At first, school could just be built into this system. Girls would often be taken out of school when they began to menstruate, itself tradi-tionally very frightening as they had been kept ignorant (and often still are). Their brothers might walk to the next village to school, but the 'risk' for them would be seen as too high. Now, it seems that being at school in their teens changes the lives of urban girls, not for what they are supposed to learn at school but simply for the chance to associate with girls of their own age (Sarah Le Vine with Clara Sunderland Correa 1993). Far fewer girls elope, and roles in marriage change. This has been perhaps the biggest change in women's lives this century in Mexico, but it has still not reached many rural girls. As in much of Latin America, Mexican governments have been laggardly in achieving universal education, even at primary level.

Getting together The importance for women of simply getting together has long been established in Latin American 'popular education', as Marcy Fink observed (1992: 177). Popular education is directed primarily to the poor (women and men, boys and girls) and seeks to enable them to liberate themselves.

> Low-income women, rural and urban, often lead an isolated social existence … One outcome of women's isolation and hardship is a tendency to blame the family's hardships and socio-economic problems on oneself or one's husband. The chance to break out of the daily routine, to sit down on a regular basis with other women and community members with similar burdens helps women recognise that they are not alone, that their problems

are shared and that, upon further analysis, that the root causes go beyond individual fault or responsibility. This relieves women of a tremendous burden and allows them to move slowly from an individual to a collective perspective. (Marcy Fink 1992)[9]

The group itself, then, can be liberating. Lynn Stephen (1997) explains the process in terms of groups generating a common set, not of answers, but of questions, and at the same time developing a shared commitment to help one another improve their lives. 'The process of participating has in part transformed who they are' (p. 194), even in the Women's Council of UELC, in Nayarit (Mexico), which is a small part of a strong, very male Indian organisation. The Council has neither a gender-based ideology nor significant contacts with other women's groups, yet has ideas very similar to those of radical women's movements in Mexico. From the case of a Chilean organisation, she concludes, 'When rural women have their own political spaces – either as women's groups or as autonomous move-ments – they often begin to experience their gendered identity in a different light' (p. 259).

Public and private   We agree with Tessa Cubitt and Helen Greenslade (1997: 57) that 'any analysis [of gender] based on public and private spheres is specious'.[10] Worldwide, the 'private' sphere is often described as women's domain in an ideology that sets up a dichotomy between 'public' spaces as men's and 'private' as women's. Not only is women's supposed control of domestic space, home and family often a fiction, but, as peasant women at Tapalehui had clearly recognised, the notion of public and private is a common cornerstone of women's oppression, deeply embedded in both law and culture (Margaret Schuler 1997: 35). Britain and Brazil consider themselves to be sexually liberal, but in both cases 'a woman of the streets' means a prostitute. Feminist social scientists used to distinguish between the 'private' physical space of the home and 'public' places, but now find the real integration of the two to be much more interesting than the notional division. One important achievement for women in Mexico has been state intervention in the 'private' sphere by some legal recognition of women's rights to freedom from violence in the home. Such rights are often not supported in practice, and the Catholic Church's definition of the family as 'the sanctuary of life' perhaps explains widespread estimates that between 70 and 80 per cent of Latin American women have been subject to conjugal violence (Ricardo Cicerchia 1997).

Sylvia Walby (1990) describes Western Europe and North America as having been under two forms of patriarchy in succession. The first was 'private patriarchy', where women were ideally in the home under the rule of a father, husband or brother, the second 'public patriarchy', where women have entered the public space of politics and paid work but are still strongly controlled. Emma Zapata would extend this description to Mexico, where women have entered both paid work and formal politics with little impact on subordination.[11] Sylvia Walby describes also a change in the nature of femininity between the patriarchies. A century ago, writes Walby, femininity and womanhood were about motherhood. Now, femininity is about attracting men. This is clearly not progress; in the West, we have got out of the house but still have far to go; perhaps Mexican women will be able to do it differently. In Britain, women have got out of the house but more and more attacks on women outside the home have been reported to the police and dramatised by the media until places outside the home have become places of fear for many (Gill Valentine 1989, Rachel Pain 1991). In thirty years, there has been no increase in the UK in the number of children murdered by strangers, yet children whose parents would have travelled to school at their age must now be escorted to school and play. Many elderly people are afraid to go out, particularly after dark, which would have surprised their parents very much. Many women do not go out after dark without an escort. Many middle-class women are afraid to travel other than in their cars. Yet most attacks on children and women take place in the home.

For Mexican women too, 'home' was supposed to be a place of safety, but hid appalling violence and sexual abuse. Getting out of the home is described as escape from incapacitating control, and is expressed in terms of all forms of power. It is 'power from within' that enables a woman to come out and join with other women; 'power with', she builds with other women; new 'power to do', she acquires and celebrates with them, and she begins to share in 'power over', in decisions from the village to the nation. The past is dead, still, stagnant; present and future are about movement, about the courage, the power, to be out of the house, even out of the community, alone and unafraid. Their safety now is in the group, with their *compañeras*, and in the power that they now recognise within themselves.

The academics at Tapalehui drew a picture of woman diminished under the eye of the community (p. 69). The fear of public gaze and gossip may be what matters about 'public space'. In Cotopaxi, Ecuador, urban, Spanish-speaking women working in issues of power and identity with Quechua women describe them as at a distant remove from power, controlled by the fear of 'what people will say' and hypersensitive to mockery, resulting in low self-esteem (Dueñas *et al.* 1997). The similarity of the phrases at Tapalehui and in Cotopaxi is remarkable: fear, worth, rights, new tasks, losing fears, deciding, resisting the violence of husbands, going to the city alone, speaking, problem-solving – all recur in both. Soledad Dueñas,

Carmen Gangotena and Monica Garcés (1997: 106) write of the 'current divorce between feminine identity and the exercise of power' in Cotopaxi.

There are echoes at Tapalehui and in Cotopaxi of experiences to the north of Mexico.

In the women's movement in North America, we began with consciousness-raising. We began with a struggle with and within language. It isn't that we weren't conscious or that we ceased to be subjects when we were at home doing the work of caring and cleaning. The extraordinary moment came when we saw that this was a place from which we could speak to and of the society at large, moving into a terrain of public discourse that somewhere along the line had been appropriated by and ceded to men. (Dorothy Smith 1990: 199)

Women outside such groups In many Mexican languages, from one end of the country to the other, women in groups where awareness is raised speak of a world of liberation, of escape from the home and from men into a world of women and solidarity.

I say women in groups: other peasant women who are successful as individuals do not in my experience use this language. Clara, who ran a corn mill, overcame domestic violence and built a new relationship with her husband, did not talk about escape from the house (Janet Townsend *et al.* 1995: 167–79). Nor did Guillermina, who built up a successful business from nothing, trading in fish from her village on the Gulf of Mexico to Mexico City (Janet Townsend *et al.* 1995: 102). These are women of considerable inner strength and an acuity of vision which has enabled them to develop their 'power from within'; but this is individual power, not collective power. Many feminists see the neoliberal emphasis on individual power as dangerous. 'For the poor, self-empowerment and more control over their lives could reduce the interdependence which produces the strong sense of community' (Stephanie Riger 1997).

The emphasis on the 'empowerment' of women through internationally funded self-esteem and leadership seminars, for example, tends to further the individualism of the neoliberal agenda, while the professionalisation of NGOs channels political energies into controllable spaces. This is one aspect of what Sonia Álvarez (1997) has called the 'transnationalisation of feminist organisations, agendas and strategies in Latin America'. (Jean Franco, 1998)

At Tapalehui, peasant women did not talk of an individual power that pulled them away from the group, but of new forms of sharing experiences good and bad. Stephanie Riger (1997) is also critical of 'empowerment', arguing that there are two kinds of empowering organisations: those that contribute to personal growth or psychological empowerment, and those that are effective and sustainable in political action. Again, Tapalehui women want to link the development of the 'power from within' with that of the 'power to do' through 'the power with'. Stephanie Riger also fears that a feeling of empowerment can be illusory when all is controlled at the macro-level. We agree, but found an unexpected contrast here at Tapalehui. 'Liberated' peasant women know how limited their achievements are, but they celebrate them. They see the 'power from within' as strongly linked to awareness of the structures that oppress them, but they still delight in the power and the awareness. It was the academic women at Tapalehui, Mexican and British, who pulled back from celebration, pointed out the limitations, the new forms of control under the new ways of living (see Chapter Two, p. 31). Our ideas of self-empowerment, clearly, involve the 'power with', the 'power to' and even some forms of 'power over', alongside the 'power from within'.

Carmen's Picture

On the first day at Tapalehui, when we set out to find out what everyone saw as their own and their organisation's successes, Carmen from *Sonora* set out to draw her own achievements, her successes in life. Her sketch details a complete pilgrim's progress, from home, through pleasures and fears, to fulfilment. Her comments show how strongly she sees different forms of power as linked in her own self-empowerment. They also display her worries about her personal relationships, with her partner and children, which will be discussed in Chapter Seven.

> I see *a house*, look, this house, with me and my children. Well, to get as far being active in the community … look, I drew barriers, obstacles which came between me and being able to *join the group* in my own village. And I drew one barrier, there, bigger, very close to my house: that's my husband. Why? Because when you go to join in, even in our own village, well, it's *'Where are you going?* What are you going to do with all those women who are just going to talk scandal and worse? You're going to neglect the children; you won't have enough money even for clothes,' and so on.
>
> I drew this other barrier because there are many women who are always criticising us for *joining in*, even in our own village. They say, 'There go those women!' and what they say really gets to us. And here I put the men, too, the very people of my community, all of them in general, and the elected people, say the village land reform bosses who support us and so on, and how the same people take it on themselves to criticise the women who are trying to do something for our community. I'm telling you, these are the barriers I've had to get past to be able to *join the group*.

In the end, when I had the idea clear that I wanted to *join*, although they wouldn't let me and, look, there was such a carry-on – it was a real achievement because *I joined the village group*. My other achievement was when the other women elected me to represent them, for me that's an enormous achievement, for the women were saying, 'We trust you, Carmen, to represent our group.' Then I was *taking part* in something bigger, because in the group I was working in now, as representative of my group, I had the chance to share everything with 28 women, 28 representatives of groups. This is where I really developed, seeing how they worked in other communities; I hadn't had any idea at all how other women were working. Now, although the same obstacles as I'd had before were still there, I understood the idea of being an activist more clearly.

Taking part is a double burden. For me, it's meant a double working day, because I have to rush to leave *tortillas* (maize pancakes) to eat in the house, to take the smallest boy, leave the others, take them to leave them in a friend's charge, and then in the afternoon come back tired from a *meeting* and so on, and even so, another scolding, another banging and crashing. And it's a long way from San Bernardo to Alamo, two and a half hours, so it's five hours *travelling,* as well as whatever *I took part in*, and when I used to get back tired from the journeys and the meeting and still, another scolding – well, I could see more clearly from the women I'd met, how they kept on *taking part*, and they were tough, they had the courage for all this. Well, I said, 'Right, well, why can't I? I can do it too. If I want, I can do it, and I've got to do it.' Then I was scared, scared to speak, to give an opinion on all this.

But even so, when, later, the *organisation* put me in charge of training, that for me was another big achievement, now I was *taking part* at a regional level, now I began to destroy the fears, what I call the chains, the chains of fright which you always feel, when you feel the panic about 'Shall I go out or not?' And finally I feel in myself, where the other group members are, it is as if we are holding hands, all there together making an effort to struggle for something and then, well, I don't know how to say something well in a drawing, because I can hardly draw. Now with the training we've had, the sharing of experiences with other organisations ... I've had more need to learn and, after the journeys, the departures, the training workshops, like this one for instance – well, I have more motivation *to go out* and to struggle more. And now, at last, where I drew myself at the end, how I feel now, I place myself as being something more, with more spirit now, I feel more valued as a woman. I say, I have to go on fighting, and not for myself any more, but for all the other women, so that as some start on the road where we are a little ahead while others are just beginning.

There, I drew my husband, how the children see him now. Before, he didn't want to support me ... and now he's at home looking after the children, so how do the children see him, how do they see me? I feel strongly about this; I was telling a friend that once my daughter used to admire her teacher very much and, when she was in the kindergarden, always used to talk about her teacher. And one day I really felt it, there was something very odd, my daughter said, 'I want to be like my mother, be an elected adviser for *Sonora*.' So, that's how my daughter sees me, and I'm full of pride, of happiness. She sees me and how I'm taking part, how I'm working in whatever campaign we're in. I think this is a space, an achievement, it is an achievement when you win over your children in how they treat you. The boy, well, when his father comes in drunk, the older boy notices and says, 'Dad, look at this,' and begins to tell him things. And the older boy is eleven now and always backs me up, he asks me for money to buy things ... and I, one of the achievements I've had recently is ... I've won him over.

And one of the things I want most is to learn more, to be able to help other women too so that they can go out, further forward – or to be able to exchange what I've learned with other women, to see how they work in other parts of the country, what can help us and how we can help other women.

Summary of Chapter 4

'Power from within' was described at Tapalehui in terms of struggle and conquest, both of fear and of hidden, unconscious acceptance of 'power over'. 'Power from within' was the strength, valour and courage to throw off fear which enabled rural women to perceive themselves as 'able to occupy that decision-making space'. Men were very much an object and a cause of fear and the 'power from within' was defined in opposition to obstacles to be surmounted, barriers to be overcome.

In these cultures, 'power from within' was defined in terms of movement. The formula for liberation, for building the 'power from within' was 'to get out of the house and join the organisation'. All the rural women shared this narrative and had built a shared identity through it. 'Getting out' and 'joining' were key moments in all their lives, vividly celebrated. The bad old days before getting out were clichés of being shut in, of stagnating, of loneliness. Only later does the house also become a place of power. Going to the next village, even to Mexico City, are further symbols of liberation, freedom, self-acceptance, self-respect. The language of international feminism has been adapted here to a strong culture of male dominance in the home.

Notes

1. Few researchers take our children even into discomfort. Caroline Moser, an anthropologist we cite, did live for a year in a hut on the mudflats of Guayaquil, with the tide coming in beneath the hut and plank walkways, with her young children. Few others have been similarly courageous for their children.

2. Margarita is a graduate who works with peasant women, paid by a university project.

3. Mercedes González de la Rocha (1994) makes a similar point for urban women.

4. The Alan Guttmacher Institute, *Aborto clandestino*, cited with no further source details in Rayas 1998.

5. The newspaper *El Heraldo*, Mexico City, 11 February 1994, commenting on a book for adolescents and for training high school teachers approved by the Secretariat of Public Education, which is in charge of providing rudimentary sexual education in the public schools, cited in Lamas 1998.

6. On the metro in Mexico City, posters tell travellers to protect their families against AIDS, but make no suggestions as to how. The Director of the Mexican Red Cross advised in 1998 against the use of condoms 'because they have holes in'.

7. The sentence continues 'that would permit participants to organize and create their own workshops on the spur of the moment'.

8. INEGI, XI Census of Population and Housing, 1990.

9. In nearly every project in Latin America which Marcy Fink had known, at least one woman had been prevented from attending the project by her husband.

10. Tessa Cubitt and Helen Greenslade have a valuable discussion of 'public and private spheres' in Latin America and Mexico. The feminist emphasis is on understanding the public and private as a continuum where there is strong interaction, not on rendering all the private, public: 'This is not to argue that we are happy to see government inspectors in every bedroom and bathroom regulating sexual conduct' (Elizabeth Frazer, 1998: 64).

11. See also Cubitt and Greenslade (1997: 60).

5

'Power with': Getting Organised

Emma Zapata

One Story

Ana, who is Spanish-speaking, is paid by *Chiapas*, a membership organisation of Tzotzil- and Tzeltal-speaking women, as an adviser.[1] (Indian women[2] have been held back so severely until so recently that few in the whole country have yet become advisers.) She tells a painfully familiar tale in the name of the group:

This is the story we all tell, the story of all our stories, the reality of our lives, of our organisation. When there were just a few of us, we had the idea of selling the clothes[3] and table linens we make, so we sat down to talk. We spoke of the sadnesses that filled our hearts, but the spirit of our grandmothers spoke through us and we dreamed of a better world. So we said, 'Yes, we all agree, we've got agreement. Let's look for someone true to their word, for someone able to keep their word, to speak to us and put us on the right track.'

At first, it wasn't easy. We spoke different languages, we lived far apart, but we could see that if we all pitched in together, we could build an organisation. Then, along came educated women from the INI [Indigenous National Institute] who said they could help. They took care of the bureaucratic procedures for us and lent us some advisers to do the talking, and we went ahead.

But in their hearts they weren't sincere. Even some women from our own communities cheated us. They stole our money and took away our courage. So we all said we didn't want advisers like that any more. They were furious, and threatened us, they accused us and called us 'dirty Indian slaveys',[4] and that hurt, it clutched at our hearts. We saw that darkness was going to come back into our lives, that our embroidery wouldn't be sold, that we'd have nothing to eat and that once again our children would die. When we found that there were still good people whom we could trust, who told us to have faith, to manage our shop and sell our things, to go to the bank and see how much money we had, we felt wonderful. We want to establish our autonomy and that of our organisation, to manage our resources and elect our committee, according to our own customs and traditions.

Why is this story worth telling? For Ana and for me, it voices many of the problems faced by our women's groups: the lack of experience in working together, the limited social and technical know-how, the need to make money to survive, the unfamiliarity with competition, the vulnerability to officials. On top of these problems, the groups can only fight their way up to subsistence level by finding an economic niche in a highly competitive world. Then the officials advise on hierarchical forms of organisation and the women are excluded from the decision-making, alongside many other gender, family, social and community issues which also trammel the building of 'power with'.

Who is Writing?

So, where did I come from, to this research, to Tapalehui, to writing this chapter? I teach sociology at the Mexican College of Postgraduates in Agricultural and Forestry Sciences, which is a university committed to knowledge through practice, to learning through doing. For fourteen years, I have been learning here about the *power with*, from rural women. But I grew up in Colombia, on a farm, experiencing rural life at its best. Later, as a housewife with three children and not much English I moved to Texas and, in this new world, took a degree and went on to a doctorate. During my studies, two of my children were at the same university, so that we shared a fascinating experience. It was all personally and financially very tough, so that I have some understanding of what it is to be a mother who is facing a new world and transforming her life, as many women are now doing in rural Mexico.

When I came to this agricultural university, it must have been zest for challenge which led me to work for a gender-aware programme with peasant women, because agriculture and forestry are a sector of academia notorious worldwide for resistance to this kind of change. (The Colegio had worked with women since 1967, but only giving them technical advice while ignoring the specific additional problems they experienced as women in this society.)[5] The programme gave me the chance to learn about 'power with' from women's groups at several levels: grass-roots women in rural communities, groups of advisers, both rural and urban, and women colleagues and postgraduates in the university world. At Tapalehui, we were academics as well as peasant women and advisers, and this chapter will emphasise both shared and contrasting insights. My experience tells me that the struggle for self-empowerment will be a long one.

I have known some of the groups in this book for fourteen years; others I met for the first time at the workshop. More and more often I have seen women become social leaders through their awareness of the 'power with'. They talk to me about their everyday problems, and I have witnessed their determination to keep up the struggle in the face of all kinds of difficulties. All these experiences have taken me far from mere research projects, enriching and changing my whole life and leaving me deeply involved in the 'power with', in theory and practice.

The Organisations

As described in Chapter One, we explored women's self-empowerment with eight organisations. This chapter has been built around the experience and voices of all eight. First, I shall describe in more detail the four organisations represented at the workshop. These illustrate different forms of 'power with' and diverse ways of building and experiencing this power.

Sonora *Sonora* goes back to 1977, when the Foundation for Community Development withdrew its support from a range of groups in northern Mexico but the groups decided to carry on. When we visited *Sonora*, Evelina (change-agent) told us that those groups 'held community meetings every three months, attended only by men'. The women then realised that the men were getting financial help for the farm while the women were working in the fields and not seeing a penny of it. As Evelina said, 'When we realised that, we decided we had better go to meetings too.' By 1986, 60 per cent of committee members were women. Yet, when the organ- isation was registered and an executive committee elected, women could not vote, because their roles were not official; the formal positions were all held by men. At the same time, a loan from outside that had already been approved for the women did not reach them; they were merely assigned a hectare of land to work. The women also found a document proving that the Foundation had allocated funds for a women's bank. As these funds had been used for other purposes, the women used the document to place a woman on the organisation's audit committee. Later, the women set up an organisation of their own, which eventually became a Society of Social Solidarity (SSS).

Sonora want more say in politics and have worked to get it, beginning by getting to know each other. Their first meeting, of 220 women, lasted three days. Teresa, now an elected adviser, told us how 'the idea had come up of an organisation for women, like that for the men, because they never let us become leaders. We wanted to be leaders, to get funds, and to learn: these were the three objectives.' The technical advisory team of the old mixed organisation saw things differently. They said, 'No, that was only a moment of happiness, we weren't mature enough to have a regional organisation' (Teresa).

Here, the 'power with' was developed among women working in the same organisation as men. The women developed empowered leadership through experience, and their tremendous energy and creativity has allowed *Sonora* to build up 600 members in the north-west of Mexico and to create a national association. Groups of women made great advances in working together for a range of goals, from housing to income-generation to legal education. They did this from within, using funds from 'donors' to contract advisers for specific advice and training, not to hire long-term staff from outside like Ana or Isabel. Their long-term advisers, like Teresa and Carmen, are elected from and by the members and sent on training courses. For many years, *Sonora* was a women's organisation that took no interest in gender and even now not all members are equally aware of gender, nor do all want to improve gender relations. The members who became interested in gender did so through practice, not theory. As *Sonora* became larger and more successful, the leaders and many members increasingly felt that the obstacles they were meeting were created by women's position in society (see Carmen's tale at the end of Chapter Four). They began to want to talk to us and to other feminists to find out whether we had useful ideas.

Puebla North   *Puebla North* has some 200 members, all Nahuatl-speaking artisan women, in six groups set up in 1985 to co-operate in marketing. Again, the original organisation was of women and men, but here the men's disapproval of the women's economic and social gains led to conflict. When the women asked to manage the money they had obtained as loans or grants themselves, the break was inevitable. It even affected marriages. 'In the end the husbands said to the women who left, "Right, you decide. If you want to leave, I'm not going to try to influence your decision." [In the end], everyone took their own decision' (Maria, adviser and academic, *Puebla North*). On each side, the leaders wanted to sever relations completely, but the members were more tolerant, saying, 'You do your work and I'll do mine.' *Puebla North* is advised not by its own members but by a team of feminist but non-Nahua advisers (including María, Margarita and Guadalupe) from an NGO and a university, which began by getting the groups to evaluate their own work, then helped the groups use the evaluations to strengthen themselves. *Puebla North* is the organisation at Tapalehui which had been fired from the beginning (from the outside) with both a feminist vision and a commitment to the emergence of women leaders; *Sonora*, from a much more educated base, generated its own elected advisers from the inside but came to ask feminist questions much later.

Chiapas *Chiapas* was set up in 1984. The members were, in 1995, 873 Tzotzil and Tzeltal women from 23 communities spread across nine munici- palities in the Altos, the long-settled Indian highlands. They do embroidery, and weave on backstrap looms. As we saw from Ana's story, the women's will to get together came from the need to sell their work and to fight their way through the bureaucratic labyrinth that encumbers 'indigenous affairs'. Each municipality is represented on the executive, and each community sends three women to the general assembly. *Chiapas* is a membership organisation that, like *Oaxaca* (below) employs paid staff who are not members; in Chiapas these are an interpreter, two women working in sales and four advisers, including Ana. The advisers are paid little and have to make a living elsewhere, which limits their role. In both *Chiapas* and *Oaxaca* the paid advisers (like the NGO workers and academics advising *Puebla North*, or Teresa and Carmen, the elected advisers in *Sonora*) are feminists. In 1995 the organisation, already immersed in bitter civil strife, was still trying to keep its independence of the government. Now it has split into two, and the more independent group has been subjected to repeated threats, harassment and violence by the army and paramilitaries.

Oaxaca Unlike these three groups, *Oaxaca* is still a joint men's and women's organisation. All members speak Mixe. Here, it was the rising costs and declining quality of public services such as water, electricity and health care which gave people the idea of working together and approaching an international agency, although they had to wait two years for even a little help. In *Oaxaca*, the council is elected from all the member commun- ities, and oversees seven committees, which work in agriculture (including livestock), legal matters, women, planning, housing, public health and forestry. The women's organisation has some 600 members in twenty groups in as many communities, and is very much driven by the vigorous work of the seven women on the core women's committee. These last still have difficulties in reaching the communities to work, for lack of vehicles and drivers, and all their activities are hampered by delays in payment for work done. *Oaxaca* built its cohesion from the struggle to secure public services such as piped water and a mill for maize, but the paid (non-Mixe- speaking) advisers, including Isabel, still need deep commitment and determination to keep working in the face of the divisions and rivalry between the communities. Here, 'power with' is being developed among Mixe women in a mixed organisation, in conditions of extreme poverty. 'What has happened is that the increasing costs of public services have made women much more politically aware, because they've started ques- tioning many, many things they didn't notice before' (Isabel, paid adviser, *Oaxaca*).

Ethnicity and difference Of the eight organisations with which we worked, three (*Chiapas*, *Oaxaca* and *Puebla North*) are of Indian women who see their handicrafts as important to their identities. The experience of *Puebla North* as described by Linaloe, a Nahua change-agent, has been that of all three. 'The organisation began just by making crafts and ... because making them is a real part of their lives ... looking for a market is also a part of our lives because, although it's hard, we have to keep working at it, and besides it is very important because of the traditions of our region.' In building a women's organisation, there are pros and cons in being Indian. They are poorer, have less formal education and suffer discrimination unknown to the Spanish-speaking women, but their traditions do favour organisation. On the one hand, they have grown up apart from mainstream society, may not speak Spanish, the national language, and may be even more oppressed by their men.[6] On the other hand, their concept of 'community' supports the idea of 'power with', of collaboration and even collective work. The women are even more conscious of their dignity, and exact even more respect from advisers with whom they work than Spanish-speaking women. These three 'indigenous' organisations all have advisers who seek, in working with them, to strengthen the 'power with' and to promote autonomy and independence but all are outsiders, Spanish-speakers.

Five of the organisations are wholly or predominantly Spanish-speaking. *Sonora* works in the north-west; *Hidalgo*, *Jalisco*, *Puebla South* and *Veracruz* lie across central Mexico almost from coast to coast. The members or clients of these four organisations live in villages that have a present or recent tradition of collective control of land[7] but, at the same time, suffer from poor land and traditionally very poor access to credit, training or agricultural inputs. Living conditions for these Spanish-speakers tend, as is usual across the country, to be a little better on average than for Indians but, by Mexican standards, they are still poor and their poverty is a driving force in the search for 'power with'. All four organisations work to get better access to public services, to market their communities' products, to secure basic supplies, to run small projects to generate income and, for their main productive activities, to get funding and improve their skills and tools. (*Puebla South* has the most Indians and these live in significantly greater poverty and in a much harsher physical environment.) For all four, the relationship with their advisers is different from those of *Chiapas*, *Oaxaca* or *Sonora*. As for *Puebla North*, their advisers work either in universities or in NGOs, so that the organisations are the clients of advisers like María or Margarita, not their employers. One NGO is linked to the PDR, a political party in opposition.

Sonora, in the far north-west near the United States, has very different world-views. *Sonora*'s members are much more mobile, and as we have seen its advisers and change-agents have come from its own ranks. Physical appearance and culture make a great difference. As Carmen says:

> We're light-skinned [*gueritas*] and tall, and we speak Spanish, so we've been able to make more contacts and things have been easier for us, because all these things matter [in Mexico]. For example, the fact that we women from the North [of Mexico] speak out has made us able to work more with mixed groups of men and women, which is much more difficult for women who don't speak Spanish.

Sonora has more room for manoeuvre and uses it to build alliances for national struggles with many types of organisation: of Indian women, of men and of other Spanish-speaking women.

What is the 'Power with'?

Celebrating the 'power with' At Tapalehui we met as old friends and new. It was a time to express joy and satisfaction, both at seeing each other and for the chance to share ideas and exchange experiences for several days. We all also enjoyed the chance to discuss our differences. What were we celebrating? Why did we enjoy being together? People said:

> working in spaces like this is just pleasure, because it makes you feel understood ... I can say what pleasure it gives me to have the pleasure of working with women and not feeling incomplete ... Why should there always be a man about? (Carmen, elected adviser, *Sonora*)[8]

> One thing I really like is that some groups have managed to add a playful note to the pleasure they find in sharing, to the pleasure they find in work. In participating, in exchanging what we've learned ... the fun is very important, because men never take it into account and women do. (Felipa, specialist and academic, Hidalgo)

Their group has many meanings for these women. It enables them to solve basic problems, but it is also a place where culture is made and remade from the old and the new, a place where difficulties shared by all can be worked out together, a place for rest and for fun.

'The thing I like best about the organisation it that it lets us get out. We're not stuck in the house the whole time any more, we can come and talk, get to know each other. Before, we didn't have this chance to get to know each other, to talk about other things ... '(Carmen, elected adviser, *Sonora*). 'Of course, because they can share with other women, say, everything they are going through in their family, then they build up joint strengths, which makes them, well, more confident' (Isabel, paid adviser,

Oaxaca). That is, the 'power with' supports the 'power from within'. For another woman, the organisation gives her a chance:

> ... to relax a little, forget myself a little. I think that then it's what we appreciate most about the women's organisations, that sometimes the most important thing isn't so much to go and look after some activity or see to sales or work on the project. I feel it's more the opportunity we get to get out and talk – not in the depth some of us would like, but at least it's something, and we have more friends than we had before in this same community of twenty families. (Teresa, elected adviser, *Sonora*)

Again, this is a severe indictment of the past. As María said, the sharing of experience has made domestic violence, formerly seen as natural, 'not seem normal to them any more' (María, adviser and academic, *Puebla North* and *South*). The Mixe women use the men of their organisation to combat violence:

> Last year, one of the male members had beaten his wife. She was pregnant, so the case went to the organisation. Then we had to step in and as a result the man has stopped beating her. Besides, everyone talked about what had happened, even in other communities, and they say, 'Look out!' Because women don't stand for beatings any more ... There are many disadvantages to being in an organisation with men, but that is one advantage. (Isabel, paid adviser, *Oaxaca*)

Although the lighthearted face of togetherness is always there, it is the economic crisis that has brought the women together. The experience of the 'power with' has then helped them learn from others, share their own knowledge, get out of the house, find new paths and draw strength from knowing that they are not alone. They enjoy the company of other women and enjoy joining together to face the crisis and overcome unwanted traditions.

> I feel, as a woman, more appreciated than before. I mean, I want to fight, and not just for myself, but for all women. Because it's as if there are some who are only just starting out on the road where we are a little ahead, but they are only just starting. (Carmen, elected adviser, *Sonora*)

> They see how much it's worth to belong to an organisation, and tell other women never, ever to leave, because we'll be more united and it's the only way we are going to solve our problems ... because right now it is very hard to live and take the road alone, because this is a time to get better organised and to wake up. (Citlali, Mixe change-agent, *Oaxaca*)

> 'It's so stimulating that I believe working together is like an alternative

life, a different vision. Like you have to get out' (Xochitl, Mixe change-agent, *Oaxaca*).

Defining the 'power with' In the face of Latin America's economic crisis since the early 1980s, it seems strange to find groups that fight to organise and to find creative responses to global changes (see Chapter Three). It would have seemed more likely that the daily struggle to survive would leave people without the strength to act in new ways, that it would be each for herself.[9] But, as Arturo Escobar and Sonia Álvarez put it (1992), collective action is not only creative and comprehensive but may even conceal itself to resist unwelcome changes more effectively. As they argue, the literature on new social movements has had to change both its interpretations of them and its theories.

> According to these theorists, an era that was characterised by the division of the political space into two clearly demarcated camps (the bourgeoisie and the proletariat) is being left behind. In the new situation, a multiplicity of social actors establish their presence and spheres of autonomy in a frag-mented social and political space. Society itself is largely shaped by the plurality of these struggles and the vision of those involved in the new social movements. (Escobar and Álvarez 1992: 3)

Women at Tapalehui made up a kaleidoscope of identities rich in collective expressions, expressing their experiences as social actors in a variety of actions, from the focus group to the swimming pool or the dance floor. As we have seen (pp. 81–3), they recognised the self-empowerment from their own histories. The 'power with', they had seen 'in our own organisation', 'in getting organised in our own way', in 'letting ourselves play active, leading roles in our organisations', in 'being together, setting our goals and putting plans into practice'.

The joy of sharing, meeting, working and being together develops 'power with' as something 'that gives us strength and courage ... to go out and prove ourselves', as 'the power we are building out of the group'. It is the opportunity to grow together, to lose fear together and to become aware together of the society in which they live. 'Power with' works in many ways, and can also be found, for instance, when women of different generations or classes work together, for instance, 'When mothers and daughters share a close relationship, they can build the "power with"' (Felipa, adviser and academic, *Hidalgo*). In the past, women's knowledge was rarely taken into account (Leonora Cebotarev 1994). But for María, adviser and academic (*Puebla North* and *South*), 'One of the things I've been working on has been sharing, the search for collective, joint solutions.' All this has led to a new recognition of women's strengths by academics and advisers. 'There is great creativity in rural areas ... there are many ways of creating, even of creating culture' (Margarita, adviser and academic, *Puebla South*).

'Power with' can be expressed in different ways, such as the search for a shared identity, the chance to negotiate as a group, to share power, to seek the support of other organisations, to look for outside backing, all building up power in a creative, positive way. As we have seen, the women explain that power has always been something negative, something no one wants to talk about. In the group context, they say, power looks different and can be constructive and positive. Collective forms of organisation are much more suitable for feminist groups than hierarchy (Rebecca Bordt 1997). For Carmen (elected adviser, *Sonora*):

The group is a place where we can find support when we want ... I know we're all happy to belong ... It's as if we feel we're useful to the community, to the other women in the group, to society itself, and we don't feel involved only in this group or that, but to women in other groups in different communities. Because in the last general assembly [of *Sonora*], I could see that all the women were very happy, very content about everything.

Over the last seven years, Carmen has transformed herself from a shy peasant woman into a self-confident leader, a leader who enables others. She has three children. Her daughter did want to be a teacher but now, having seen what her mother does, she wants to work in the community.

'Power with' can link groups through acting together. In this case its force can be limitless. As Naila Kabeer finds in South Asia (1997: 119), it is the ideas and actions taking shape in daily life that determine the dimensions of power. The idea and practice of empowerment are the basis of any popular movement.

Organisation and the Search for the 'Power with'

From the Revolution of 1917 to the end of land reform in 1991, Mexico proclaimed socialist, collective processes, especially for the betterment of the poor. From 1940 onwards, these were empty words, used primarily to control in a sophisticated electoral machine of patronage that has kept the same ruling party in power since 1932 and made rural people extraordinarily dependent. This is a men's world in which patronage used to be directed only to men, as 'heads of households'. After 1940, little training or credit reached the 'beneficiaries' of land reform, who were nearly all men. For the First United Nations International Women's Conference, in Mexico City in 1975, the government enabled poor peasant women to form groups to cultivate one family-sized plot of land in each community.

This experience served to expose the array of barriers surrounding women and had little success.[10]

Araceli and Linaloe are Nahuatl-speaking peasant women, now change-agents in *Puebla North*. Linaloe (Araceli's aunt) now runs a new project of *Puebla North*: an ecotourist hotel. As we have seen, Linaloe is single at thirty-two, resisting the requirement of her community that a woman must marry the man her family chooses when she turns fourteen, and Araceli is following suit.

> The truth is that, before, we didn't know anything. Only now, since we've been in the organisation, we've learned so much. We have woken up to so much. Because before, only men were organised; they ran the co-operative and everything and the women always stayed at home waiting for them. It's only now that women go to meetings too, and join in, and get organised. We already know what we want: to make our communities stronger. (Araceli)

Working together gives these women who formerly belonged to their family rather than to themselves a feeling of participation and an opportunity to grow, to build the 'power from within' and to express themselves. They know where their interests lie, and have learned to make them known. Citlali (Mixe-speaking), now a change-agent in *Oaxaca*, had never left her village before she joined, but later she had the courage to speak in the great central square in Mexico City (the biggest such square in the world) during the Congress of Indigenous Peoples. Since Tapalehui, she has represented her people at an international congress of minority peoples in Barcelona. As Naila Kabeer argues (1997), shared experiences of subordination give shape to a collective identity, which is where the first steps are taken towards change. At Tapalehui, the rural women agreed on the importance of building a shared identity.

Forms of organisation At Tapalehui, careful attention to the way the organisation was structured was felt to be very important to building the 'power with', although all present saw groups as potentially enabling for women. *Sonora*, from its very first meeting, has been committed to building an organisation in which 'power over' is shared as far as is humanly possible. That meeting chose four areas in which to work – education, public services, production and health – and within three months, with a great deal of involvement of group members, they had located the main problems by place and axis of action. Then they wrote their internal rules and a work plan, and designed a regional strategy. Two women would work in each area, one running things, the other as her deputy. The deputy would train by shadowing the woman in charge, until her time came to take over. These transitions have taken place smoothly. 'There was no president or treasurer.

We formed a collective management' (Evelina, change-agent, *Sonora*). To relate to the government and to get access to funds, they have to have a formal structure, but they have managed to combine this with a flexibility which 'keeps us free of bureaucracy' (Evelina).

In *Puebla North*, the twelve members of the Women's Council take responsibility for specific programmes. The ideal of the supporting NGO and university is that leaders should develop, but not occupy permanent positions. These Nahuatl-speaking women leaders are elected by the women of their communities, three for each, for long-term training, so that they can support the group in the whole process from designing projects to securing funds and selling the crafts produced. The idea was to train and prepare the women in such a way as to make them self-sufficient, so that they could become an independent organisation. Annual workshops are held on human rights, culture, health in pregnancy and childbirth and the environment, with gender weaving through all themes.

In *Chiapas*, the members of the organisation learn by shadowing the advisers. 'None of the advisers goes anywhere without one of the women from the organisation, and that way they learn too, to get out into the world and know other things' (Ana, paid adviser). *Oaxaca* works in the same way, but of course within a wider organisation dominated by men. 'Another form of organisation has been put forward by the women of *Hidalgo*, where their system is that the leaders (although they don't call them that) rotate. The idea is that everyone will occupy the decision-making positions at some time' (Felipa, adviser and academic, *Hidalgo*). These groups are creating and proposing 'new distributions of power' (María, adviser and academic, *Puebla North* and *South*). These are, as María Luisa Tarres says (1996: 12), practical ways of developing socio-cultural alternatives to traditional relationships between men and women. So, for an academic:

> I think they have moved forward ... as women. They have become aware of themselves as political beings and are making their own decisions ... They have learned to negotiate with different authorities. For instance, although they [*Puebla North*] did not support the election of the present mayor, they are using their regional strength to negotiate his support. (María, adviser and academic, *Puebla North* and *South*).

The women are active not only in the organisations but in politics at all levels. As Naila Kabeer finds (1994), it is not enough for women to join in projects when they are restricted by the state, by society, by economic, cultural and ethnic structures. The 'power with' which they develop in political struggle is determined by the extent to which women's power goes beyond the project. Back in their personal lives, the women's activities challenge the division of labour in the family,[11] as someone has to carry firewood and water. 'The women of the groups have passed on the need to participate to their children and their husbands and, well, this has improved family relations ... The women's children wash clothes and make meals because their mother has her tasks in the group' (Margarita, adviser and academic, *Puebla South*).

Training for autonomy? These are groups of poor women lacking in many necessary skills for building organisations, as Ana described at the beginning of this chapter. At Tapalehui, we discussed Srilatha Batliwala's analysis of women's empowerment in South Asia (1993) (which we had translated into Spanish and had circulated to all the organisations, and of which we gave a summary to everyone at the workshop). On the third day, Jo Rowlands described PAEM in Honduras.[12] Both Srilatha Batliwala and Jo think it best to start work with the group on issues of power, and for the group to go on to decide on issues such as projects, education and training. No adviser at Tapalehui had ever known such work, and for me and for the other advisers, the idea was unbelievable. How could anyone go to a community and start talking to the women about power? Power must be always at the back of our minds, but we cannot begin by shocking people. The idea must be planted and nurtured. Yes, it is vital to speak of power, of conflict, of violence, but we begin with practical work on projects, training and education. When these are truly open and supportive, women can build the 'power with' and other powers by thinking about and discussing the experience.

In practice, the women share participative workshops, meetings, visits and any activity in which they can learn together. 'The process of participating has in part transformed who they are' (Lynn Stephen 1997: 194). Srilatha Batliwala (1993) found advisers[13] from outside to be usually crucial; in all the groups at Tapalehui except *Sonora*, outside advisers support the women through this process. In *Sonora*, the members themselves are the facilitators:

> Generally, this has been the job of women able to commit more time and put more into the group ... but this isn't because the rest couldn't do it; they all know how. The thing is, they simply have more time, get more support from their husbands and so on, and they become the teachers for everyone else. (Carmen, elected adviser, *Sonora*)

Workshops are one way in which a group is strengthened. In *Oaxaca*, says Xochitl (Mixe change-agent), it is in workshops that 'we realise that we are women, and that we have problems just because we are women, in how we meet childhood, adolescence, in how we meet maternity – all these things which give us identity'. *Sonora* attempts through 'chain-reproduction' to pass experiences from workshops such as Tapalehui through to all members. They know that this is not a simple transmission of what they learn, but believe that it is a duty to hand on what they gain from every workshop to refresh and maintain the networks between all the women.

To 'train' is, usually, to impart a standard skill. For the women in these groups, 'training' is different; it means awareness, Paulo Freire's 'conscientisation' (1973) learned from NGOs and academics. It means learning about and understanding situations that may at times seem complex and difficult but which they know they have the ability to grasp. *Sonora*, for instance, asked outside advisers to run one workshop on globalisation and another on federalism. They know that they can analyse facts critically, discuss and take a stand on issues, and that this will help them obtain and impart a different kind of education, moving towards better relationships between men and women. They know this is not problem-free.

The women think seriously about learning from those with greater 'power over' in society (see Chapter Seven). For instance, both academics and advisers can bring different, outsider perspectives and perhaps experience to organisations or groups. This can help, not through being 'right' but in bringing new insights; their reactions can help the group see and tackle their problems differently. The groups, therefore, want communication to be both horizontal and vertical; they want to build networks which include academics alongside both Mexican and international groups. Conventional 'development' has shown us problems of 'training' to which peasant women have had little or no access. One novelty introduced by the Tapalehui groups is the importance they give to real training, starting with a very inclusive definition of what is needed and of the creativity to be developed in obtaining, imparting or promoting training.

Both rural women and academics at Tapalehui wanted to relate more with each other. The academics dug far into these issues:

For the women to analyse their everyday reality and act for change, they must be aware. By this we mean ... that women, including us [academics] must know our own potential in a society where everything is against us ... and to change that, we have to change ourselves and the society around us. I think this is the most important undertaking. The material side (the income-generating projects) is of course important, even essential, but we believe that it must be tackled with practices which allow us to work both on women's practical needs, to get them interested and involved, while at the same time the activities lead to analysis of their lives and of how society works, in relation to them, and to us as women. I think we are opening up questions of practice not yet fully explored but still being developed. (Catalina, adviser and academic, *Hidalgo*)

What is leadership? At first, the efforts of women's groups set up in Mexico by government or NGOs are directed at survival, at breaking the cycle of poverty in which restrictive government policies have them trapped. In this struggle, the women also begin to work for qualitative change and better lives. There is not, however, a natural transition to successful leadership of the kind that can enable, not oppress. Commonly a hierarchy is imposed and only 'president', 'secretary' and 'treasurer' are trained. Often, a powerful clique then comes to control the group and may either cause it to collapse or monopolise resources in its own interests. Building the 'power with' in the organisations with which we worked is something different. The groups are analysing different forms of wielding 'power with', such as the leadership assumed by a few in order to help others by stimulating the development of their potential or raising their morale (Joanna Rowlands 1997a: 48). Women leaders must simultaneously cope with their family problems, generate informed policies in their own organisation and get them put into effect. Leaders must understand subordination to share the knowledge with others and work for a more equal society.

A Road Full of Obstacles?

Learning on the way The groups must struggle not only with their lack of experience in working together but also with their limited external credibility. As Arturo Escobar argues (1995), analysis must explore and emphasise all the obstacles groups must overcome to make themselves heard. Here, malicious gossip, family or community disapproval and domestic violence are all examples of cultural obstacles. The main economic obstacles are shortage of resources (land, water, credit, technology) for production and lack of skills and networks in marketing. Ideological obstacles appear in contempt for and denigration of their work, and their frequent exclusion from vital decisions. We saw at the end of Chapter Four how Carmen drew herself as surrounded by barriers set up to control and restrain her. Citlali (Mixe change-agent) from *Oaxaca* showed on how many fronts they must work:

> We get recognised as women in the organisation and in society and in families, where we also get oppressed in ways we have to change. Being a woman, she [another change-agent] was not allotted her share of village land by her parents, who shared out the plots only among her brothers. Now she has to look after her elderly mother, at the same time as helping other women in the organisation ... In other words, if we don't make space to discuss these things ourselves, if we don't take the time to do that, the work we do with the groups becomes just another activity without deeper meaning.

For eighty years, governments in Mexico have bound peasants to them with programmes, projects and subsidies which have created great dependency but little economic gain. Now, the women need to act in many different ways against poverty. In the groups, the change-agents and the women who have become more aware want to break away from this dependency, but not all members agree.

The Nahua women from *Puebla North* and their advisers were particularly outspoken about practical obstacles that proved familiar to others. For instance, there can be a downside to the flexibility of organisation of which the women spoke so highly. These women are personally very close to their advisers, but one adviser has to liaise between them and a 'donor'. Since she is charged by the donor with supervising their activities and helping them work to a schedule, she is in a difficult position. Another adviser illustrated the problems of the transfer of responsibilities:

> Among the leaders of the group itself, problems also appear once the women have been representatives [on a very small but wholly unfamiliar salary] for two or three years, in which they learn and build up the ability to negotiate in the region, while the rest begin to depend on them. Problems come with change, when the positions have to be given up and others take over. Leaving the position is hard for them, because they don't wish to, and the new women are often afraid of responsibility ... In spite of these difficulties, they have respected the system. Once their time is up, new women take over. (María, adviser and academic, *Puebla North* and *South*)

How can the groups find a way to reward past office-holders and continue to profit from their experience, while encouraging others to take their turn with responsibilities? In *Puebla North*, no other paid work is available, and one past leader has withdrawn from the organisation to market her crafts independently. Here too, a 'donor' created difficulties by making a grant to a leader, Julia, in order to promote her organisation. In local terms the grant represents a high income, but Julia has not found a way to help the group. She more or less fulfils the conditions of the grant but is isolated from the group. In practice she does not attend meetings and hardly talks to the other members. She has been rejected by the group with considerable ill-feeling against her and the 'donor'. In *Hidalgo*, one group had planned to rotate its office-holders but almost broke down when an authoritarian leader took over; another lost its land because the men of the community were jealous of its success.

The women have to contend with so many controls: of their culture, their men, their community, the government, the 'donors'. Jealousy is also an attempt to impose control, especially when a wife occupies a leading position in the same organisation as her husband. Teresa (elected adviser, *Sonora*) finds that:

> When women begin to seem likely candidates for a regional position of leadership, their husbands feel abandoned, which may lead to divorce. They're jealous, because we now know more than they do, since they aren't organised, don't get together, haven't become well-informed and don't get training. Well, we just don't have anything to talk about any more and they get mad. Before, for instance, when night fell, many men from the group came to talk with him, but not any more; now they come to discuss things about the group with me.

Teresa came into the organisation with her husband, with whom she has two children. She was very successful and is today a member of the state parliament and president of the state Committee for Environmental Affairs. Now, the couple are separated since he could not handle her political success. Teresa knows too that her son has problems with his peers because of what she is teaching him about gender equality. This kind of upbringing is not common in Mexico, and children do not easily accept other children who behave more fairly; the boy feels confused. Other leaders of *Sonora* have preferred to give up rather than face their husbands' jealousy. The women are therefore asking an international donor to pay for them to have workshops on gender, so that the women can come to understand better what they are going through.

Ana, a paid adviser to *Chiapas*, speaks of the difficulties of trying to work with women without causing conflict with their men. 'Yes, because so often it is their husbands who are the ones who cause trouble.' It was suggested that women should think about converting the men even before aspiring to formal positions. The conflicts arising from women's success within the organisation are also very real in organisations where there are men. Teresa (elected adviser) from *Sonora* believes that in such organisations the success of some women should be 'almost automatic [because] if women participate in an organisation, its leadership should be of women, too. I mean, part of the power should be women's.' Teresa thinks the same of political parties, which she sees as really out of date:

> ... practically in the Dark Ages. There are parties which are supposed to be very democratic, but only in their speeches ... because when you elect them, when you get them into power, they simply don't make any headway, they just talk and talk, they don't put women in a position to make decisions. Perhaps the only thing they support is the right to work, but only on certain things.

Cultural obstacles take time to overcome, but the women have, little by little, found ingenious ways of doing it. Meetings and workshops are one place where discussion of the problems they face allows them to assert themselves, personally and in the group. As Sharada Jain writes (1997: 10) 'conscientisation, women's mobilisation and gender sensitisation are inter-linked concepts'.

The 'power with' and politics For Lola Luna (1994: 40), 'The relation-ship between women and state in Latin America has been based on paternalism, under which family and state have been normative institutions, guaranteeing the maintenance and modernisation of the patriarchal order and thus excluding women from the political order.'

Women are at once excluded and 'protected'. The organisations with which we worked seek to change this reality by building 'power with' at all levels. In *Puebla North*, says María, adviser and academic, 'The idea came up of forming a regional organisation for the work already underway. The women suggested it because we were working with isolated community groups. As for us, we saw the women's interest and felt that the work was so demanding for us that it should reach more widely.'

The organisations have different forms of participation, but all are far from those cited by Sharada Jain (1997), Naila Kabeer (1994) or Nira Yuval-Davis (1998), where the mere presence of a woman is seen as participation, or one woman's membership of a decision-making group is seen as women's involvement in the planning process, or one woman, simply as a woman, is seen as representing all women. At Tapalehui, the academics agreed that:

> Independence should be established, so that in the medium or long term they can build their autonomy or independence. So I believe that advisers should work, deliberately, in such a way that the groups can in time become independent. This will not happen overnight but is a long process. (María, adviser and academic, *Puebla North* and *South*)

Building 'power with' is the opposite of neoliberal ideology. That glorifies individualism and competition, while the women are seeking organisation, solidarity and co-operation. One example is the National Network of Women, drawing together twenty-six regional organisations (including *Sonora*) of 16,400 women in twelve states (Patricia Alonso and Roberto del Prado 1997). This new structure respects the autonomy of the organisations, which are free to define their lines of action. In the face of globalisation, as in the organisations Arturo Escobar describes (1992), the members make their presence felt in different spheres through different forms of autonomy, in a fragmented social and political space.

'Power with' in academic life 'Power over' as it faces academic women is very different from that met by peasant women, but no less real. At Tapalehui we shared very disparate experiences, and sought to learn from each other. Few women academics can organise and develop 'power with'. Few women get academic jobs, particularly in agriculture or rural development, and those who do face great difficulties in getting recognition for their research. Like peasant women, we face hierarchies that exclude us from decision-making in our community. Team work in social science in Mexico tends to be seen as either trivial or subversive, something that should be weakened and undermined. Women academics are presented as a group when convenient, but when their work expresses 'power with', it is ignored. Research proposals are lost in bureaucratic labyrinths. Promotion for a woman demands greater achievements than for a man. Most senior scientists who decide promotion are men, with the power to judge, to delay, to hinder, all unchallenged. They may admit to the hierarchy only women who are anti-feminist. Success for a woman, such as securing more outside funding or publishing more than her male colleagues, is unforgivable. Assessments are based on hierarchy, not quality. It is common practice to deny recognition to a woman's academic performance. At the same time, the men use 'power with' from their own networks and social support. The academics at Tapalehui are aware, like the peasant women, of the hostility of their world but, like them, showed their determination to build alternative processes of sharing, to demand democracy and participation. The invisible here too must come forward, be allowed to speak out and have a presence. 'A drastic redistribution of power is in order by means of horizontal communal organisation. Destructive gigantism must be replaced by creative smallness' (Max-Neef, 1998: 63).

Visions of the Future

What did Tapalehui teach us about 'power with'? The peasant women, advisers and academics all saw the 'power with' in the work done and decisions taken together in these organisations with more horizontal power structures where decision-making is more open to participation. 'Power with' appears in the journey from 'me' to 'us', in the pleasure of being together, sharing and exchanging experiences, in the joy of new knowledge and of building positive alternatives, in taking action at any level, from individual to national, without fear. In formal politics, all groups challenge the 'power over' in action or hierarchy, in government, NGOs or their own organisations. They reject paternalism. They want to be themselves.

The means to women's 'power with' are their desire to learn, their commitment to themselves and their community, their positive images of themselves as women, horizontal, democratic forms of organisation, leadership that supports rather than dominates, the development of leaders, networking, collective support and self-criticism. Three of the organisations make traditional handicrafts for sale, which plays an important role in 'power with'. As capitalism evolves, new combinations of forms of production and representation redefine identities. For Nestor García Canclini (1982), this process wrenches people out of context and reassigns meanings to the advantage of dominant cultures. People skilled in traditional crafts are displaced not only because their products must succeed in new realms but because they have lost the world in which they were embedded, the 'indigenous' life and the rural market, and must move into new spaces such as middle-class life, the urban superstore, the museum and the new boutique. *Puebla North* distinguishes between crafts that preserve the community's identity, such as ceremonial clothing and women's dresses, and those they produce for sale in order to survive. Those crafts that are valued in shared spaces help them preserve their culture and give true value to their work.

Kenneth A. Maton and Deborah A. Salem (1995: 631) set out to explore the organisational characteristics of settings in the United States that proved supportive of empowerment. Studying a religious fellowship, a mutual help organisation for people with severe mental illness and an educational programme for African American students, they found all to have:

- a belief system that inspires growth, is strengths-based and focused beyond the self;
- an opportunity role structure that is pervasive, highly accessible and multifunctional;
- a support system that is encompassing, peer-based and provides a sense of community;
- leadership that is inspiring, talented, shared and committed to both setting and members.

Very unusually in rural Mexico, all eight organisations with which we worked had all these features. All were celebrated by the women at Tapalehui. Tapalehui differs in greater ambition (see Appendix): the women at Tapalehui seek not to join the mainstream, or to be comfortable with the mainstream, but to become the mainstream. Their goal is to change the world, although they have no illusions about how far there is to go or how much both discourse and practice still need to change in their own families and communities.

All the women want to build a new political force through the 'power with', in order to develop women's capacities and find solutions to such community problems as have remained unresolved through the limitations or negligence of their male-dominated assemblies.[14] Women are coming forward as thinking beings in leading roles in their own lives. From personal relations to national politics, the women tell us that the men will never suddenly have a bright idea and say, 'OK, we recognise you. Come on over and take a strategic position in making important decisions.' Bob Connell agrees with them (1995). Women who have stepped forward to build the 'power with' others will have to make big changes in gender relations.

Each woman, they say, must retain her individuality; difference is a source of joy. As Marcela Lagarde writes (1997), it is a contradiction of feminism that in spite of the struggle to bring women, half the human race, forward as a group, women do not accept anonymous roles. Each has her personality and as much right to decide and direct her fate as any man. To me, the leading obstacles to the building of 'power with' are the invisibility of women under Mexico's prevailing forms of patriarchy, jealousy, poverty, overwork, lack of skills, isolation, little or no representation in decision-making, aggression and loss of resources.

These women are building alternatives to 'development', collaborating with NGOs and academics. 'Development' itself is in doubt (Chapter Two), and interest is growing in the potential of hybrid cultures (Escobar 1995). The Nahua women at Tapalehui are skilled with computers. Citlali has taken part in a world congress. Many have presented projects that their groups have designed to international agencies or NGOs. Hybridity offers multiple pathways as alternatives to 'development', with cultural invention transgressing class, gender, ethnicity and nation. State policies have, at best, sought to satisfy basic needs. This attitude still prevails in state projects, in which basic needs are seen as opposed to human rights or equality of opportunity. The struggle for basic needs seems to be divorced from the pursuit of equality between men and women (Elizabeth Maier 1994) but in reality, these demands are interwoven. Basic needs can become strategies and political practice (Gita Sen and Caren Grown 1987). As Lynn Stephen concluded from examination of an array of women's groups in Latin America, in successful change, 'Basic needs are not tied solely to survival, but rather to constructions of identity and relations of power' (1997: 277).

'Power with' offers women the pleasure of learning with other women, some of them from other places and/or very different experiences, as at Tapalehui. They can meet other groups, travel, learn, create possibilities and construct utopias. They organise workshops, meetings and discussions, join in, make proposals. The 'power with' has helped them decide about their bodies (delaying motherhood or choosing to stay single) and to seek to renew, not discard, their cultures. 'Power with' has amplified their capacity to choose and propose actions, projects and forms of organisation, and to take more part in community decisions.[15] At Tapalehui:

We spoke of the need for all of us to become more aware, including peasants, advisers and academics, so that we can come to realise our own potential in a society where everything is against us. About the possibility of changing ourselves and our surroundings. While the material side remains unquestionably important, it must become a means to more fundamental change. We talked of ways of working at the same time to satisfy basic needs and to support women building the 'power with'. (Isabel, paid adviser, *Oaxaca*)

I always wanted to be an elected adviser ... I thought I'd never make it, and what I'm proudest of is to be with a group of women, to get them aware of the need to unite and to be able to do so much without becoming a tyrant, or vain, to still belong to the grassroots, without wanting to be more than a useful tool, at the service of the other women in the group, of my community, my municipality and Mexico. To be able to set an example for my children, to serve others even if there is no money involved. (Teresa, elected adviser, *Sonora*)

Summary of Chapter 5

Here we describe the organisations with which we worked, and their stories of 'the power with'. Again there is celebration, and rural women speak of the pleasure of the group that they may have joined expecting merely hard work for a little more income. The 'power with' supports the 'power from within' and vice versa; the 'power with' 'gives us the strength and courage to go out and prove ourselves'. Sharing, learning and innovation are described as pleasures, although in the context of a fight, a struggle ahead.

Forms of organisation were seen as very important. The sharing of 'power over', the role of all members in decisions and a variety of mechanisms to avoid hierarchy were discussed at length, not only for decision-making but for training. 'Training' is seen in terms of Paulo Freire's 'conscientisation' or development of awareness: it is not only about skills but about critical thinking. 'Leaders' are needed to encourage the work of the group: how can they be trained without the creation of hierarchy? What happens when they complete their period of office? The different groups came up with a range of solutions. Their group efforts imply a different and stronger democracy in everyday life.

The rural women also had much to say about formal politics, from their villages to the government. A national network exists and some groups are seeking greater collaboration at the regional level.

> The academics recounted the difficulties of building the 'power with' in a very hierarchical, male-dominated academic life. Both groups challenge the 'power over' in hierarchy and paternalism and want to build a new political force through the 'power with'.
>
> All at Tapalehui saw 'power with' in the work done and decisions taken together in organisations with more horizontal power structures and greater real participation. They are seeking to build alternatives to 'development'.

Notes

1. For definitions of change-agents, advisers etc. please see Chapter One, pp. 13–14.

2. Please see Chapter One Note 1 (p. 17) for the use of the word 'Indian'.

3. Heavily embroidered garments for women.

4. In the last century, 'slavey' was an offensive, derogatory term for a maid who did the most menial work. No word in current use in English is as pejorative as the Spanish term *pinche*.

5. They worked, that is, in a Women in Development style, not Gender and Development. See Razavi 1995.

6. The myth that there is no domestic violence in indigenous culture can bar them from help (Ana María Garza, personal communication). See Martínez Corona and Mejía Flores 1997a.

7. The land reform laws were changed in 1991 to promote the privatisation of collective land.

8. She does indeed use the word 'pleasure' three times.

9. Lynn Stephen (1997) argues that this is what happens to the majority of women in Mexico.

10. De Barbieri *et al.* 1993, Arizpe and Botey 1986, Aranda 1993, Zapata and Mercado 1996.

11. As in Nayarit, Mexico, and elsewhere in Latin America (Stephen 1997).

12. See also J. Rowlands 1995a, 1997a and b, 1998.

13. She uses 'change-agents' where we use 'advisers'.

14. As for the women in Nayarit described by Lynn Stephen 1997.

15. In many Mexican towns and villages, decisions taken by an elected assembly, over matters from the banning of alcohol to the building of a shopping centre, are the norm.

6

Power to Do: and to Make Money

Marta Mercado

Who is Writing?

Since I was at school, I have known that the keys to new ways of living are already in human hands, especially the hands of the poor and dispossessed; we can change the forces that hold us where we are, and the key is organisation. I came very young to work with peasants, fired by a Christian education about people living in bitter poverty. At university, I chose veterinary medicine because, although fascinated by chemistry and biology, I wanted to continue my rural work and hoped as a vet to combine both worlds. Later, when I knew myself better, it was the human problems that called to me. Luckily, my training emphasised social issues but, back with the peasants, I kept meeting problems I could not understand, let alone resolve. This took me to study rural development at the Colegio de Postgraduados, where I later joined Emma Zapata's project for action-research with rural women. Always, I have wanted to bring theory and practice together to see particular problems in their wider frame. I had already worked with Nahua women and wanted to continue, still combining veterinary medicine with working as an adviser with women.

I found Emma's project fascinating and deeply enriching. Not only did I work closely with the *Hidalgo* women who feature in this book, but I came to know women in organisations across Mexico. I had joined the thousands of people (mostly women) working with women in rural Mexico, as advisers, facilitators, trainers, social workers or some combination of these, whether paid by government or some independent organisation (see Chapter Three). As we have seen, much of their work is designed to control rather than liberate women, but among the more radical there is a national network, the Network of Advisers Working with Rural Women. Six years in the network were decisive in my becoming a feminist. I was privileged to be able to share all this with my partner Toño and, in time, my sons Ivan and Diego (now five and seven). Now, studying for my doctorate with a friend of Emma's at the University of Guelph in Canada,

I find the processes through which women organise, their self-empowerment and their new identities even more exciting. It was deeply satisfying to share in the project we are describing here, especially to visit the organisations and know them at first hand. At Tapalehui, I caught up with old friends and made new ones.

I chose to write about the 'power to', which I have seen so much in action. For Citlali, a Mixe change-agent and leader from *Oaxaca*, 'I understand that "power to" means that I'll say, "Yes, I can do it!" even if they tell me I can't. But when I feel I can do it, then what I am feeling is this "power to".'[1]

All at Tapalehui – rural women (whether Indian[2] or Spanish-speaking), academics and advisers – found a thousand ways of putting the 'power to' into words. The local women I met on the visits we made to the organisations did the same, as they described the goals of their work, their tasks or their problems with funding agencies, or told us how much training had helped them and how valuable it will be for the future. Above all, like Citlali, they spoke of the 'power to' when they told us that they now *can* act on their own. They are no longer, they say, meek, isolated women, afraid to mix with others; they know their own capacities to change their family lives and even those of their communities. As we shall see, they talk of the 'power to' particularly in connection with making money.[3] We originally felt that their financial gains were very small, as were other changes in their lives but, no matter how small these changes seem to us, they mean a great deal to these women and, at times, to those around them. Their understanding matters.

I shall explore first the meanings attached to the 'power to' by rural and academic women, and what the groups literally 'do', then the obstacles to their development of this power and, finally, the ways suggested by rural and academic women to seek or to support the 'power to'.

As an adviser, I worked in Feminist Popular Education. 'Popular education' (see Chapter Three) is education in both political awareness and useful skills; it can be truly enabling and liberating.[4] As an academic, my efforts are based on critical social science and, again, on feminist thinkers. For me, then, self-empowerment is a process of emancipation into which women's groups are brought through critical reflection on their specific condition and social position.[5] Self-empowerment takes shape 'when social change takes place in feminist terms' (Saskia Wieringa 1997: 8), around gender-specific awareness and organisation (Magdalena Léon 1997: 12). To me, it is of fundamental importance that a balance be struck between group awareness, organisation and personal growth. The process is not driven from outside: it may be encouraged, but the women themselves must develop and give shape to their self-empowerment. As we strive to encourage a feminist self-empowerment, as advisers or change-agents, we must never forget either the shared nature of the process or the rights of the individual. Because this is a difficult balance, processes of self-empowerment and ways of supporting them necessarily differ greatly between cultures.

In this chapter, the women's undertakings will become vantage points for describing their processes of self-empowerment. The simple act of doing has real significance, although 'power to' as a strong emancipatory force is created by their deliberate exploration of what 'doing' means to them. 'Power to' thus embraces capacities, skills, creativity and, at times, resistance. Processes of self-empowerment include new relationships which feature enriching, not oppressive, forms of power. This is a practical matter, and organisations must commit themselves to a long stretch of hard, daily work to make any advances. The processes face many obstacles, of which the greatest is the socio-economic environment. Manifold aspects of culture conspire to prevent individual women or their organisations from pursuing new goals.

We, the authors, take a stance as women and academics on changes already achieved. We delight in women's new-found struggles for inclusive ways of living, not based on social class or ethnicity but consciously and critically rejecting and transcending their everyday oppressions. In the sense that the group efforts on which we report imply a different and stronger democracy in everyday life, they are a part of a social movement of women not only in Mexico but in all Latin America (Chapters Three and Eight). Women are gaining control over their own actions. 'As women go forward, they want to exercise new forms of power. That is to say, their progress involves getting organised, becoming aware, realising where they stand' (Isabel, paid adviser, *Oaxaca*).

Microcredit As we have noted in Chapters Two and Three (pp. 49–50 and pp. 24–5), there is much debate among activists and academics about the benefits and drawbacks of microcredit. We see microcredit as problematic, but ask whether the peasant women at Tapalehui are turning it to their advantage and particularly whether they are using it for self-empowerment. We argued in Chapter One (p. 17) that they have the right to their opinions, that their opinions matter. We should admit that the women still in the groups with which we worked are the successes: some women do withdraw under family pressure. Worse, some women break down under the demands and/or fail financially, although these are hidden problems which we did not reach at Tapalehui.

What is the 'Power to', for Rural and Academic Women?

Clearly, all at Tapalehui understood power as a force, a force of strength and ability to act, projecting women into the future.[6] The 'power to' enables them to build a future different from that mapped out by custom, and becomes a subversive, rebellious, provocative form of power. We all spoke of what we do, and how we do it. Every story emphasises the importance of belonging to an organisation, because this is what had helped each rural woman transform herself. As we see in other chapters, they claimed that before getting organised they 'could not', but now they can say, 'I can'. 'Now that we belong to the organisation, we are learning so much, we are waking up' (Linaloe, Nahua change-agent, *Puebla North*).

The women at Tapalehui described the changes in terms of awareness, willpower and action.[7] All of us, rural and academic, work to make spaces for ourselves, spaces that will give us a say in society and a right to our opinions.

Table 6.1 shows the different tasks undertaken by each of the eight organisations. When we explored together what each group at Tapalehui wanted to achieve, some women were constantly looking ahead, thinking through what they want and imagining ways of achieving it. For me, imagination and the ability to set objectives and create utopias seem essential to self-empowerment. For Citlali:

My goal, or what the women of our organisation want to achieve, is equality, you see, between husband and wife or in the community, and for us, as women, always to be taken into account. In meetings, for instance, or when leaders or officials are elected, we want to be considered too. Not only men should hold these offices, but women too. That's what we want.

Margarita, adviser and academic, *Puebla South*, wants:

To design work strategies with women's groups ... and to encourage the use of [appropriate] technologies designed either by our team or other institutions. These reduce the women's workload and give them an income ... We also want to work with the idea of gender, because what we are trying to achieve is equality between men and women – for the women's work to be valued and respected and for the woman, the peasant woman with whom we work, to take the place which is rightly hers.

Other academics strive for 'quality fieldwork' (Felipa, academic and adviser, *Hidalgo*) and seek to link their teaching, research and advice in support of self-empowerment:

We teach on the masters programme just because we want to tie our experience in the villages into teaching and research. For me, this is the ideal,

TABLE 6.1 Power to

Name	Gender	Principal activities	Guidance	Number of groups/ members, language	Funding
Chiapas	Women	Livelihood projects (training and organisation, production costs and quality control, management and accounting, management of bank accounts, use and maintenance of sewing machines, clothes design, treatment of clients), human rights of Indian women, domestic violence.	Outside and self	873 women, 23 communities, Tzotzil and Tzeltal speaking	World Food Program–INI (National Indigenous Institute)
Oaxaca	Mixed-gender	Livelihood projects (tortillas,[1] huipiles,[2] farming, poultry, family gardens), organisation and training, human rights, gender awareness.	Self and outside	20 groups, Mixe speaking	NOVIB, IDEX-Agency, Dutch and Australian Embassies, Government departments, Ministry for Social Development (SEDESOL), Federal Office for Protection of the Indian Population
Veracruz	Women	Livelihood projects, co-operative shops, food shops, mills for cooked maize, sericulture, coffee processing.	Self and outside	100 women, 7 groups, Spanish speaking	National Centre of Indigenous Missions, Miserios
Puebla North	Women, one male technical adviser	Social welfare, livelihood projects, (farms, tortilleria, mill,[3] handicrafts for sale), organisation and training, gender awareness, latrines, stoves, health care, nutrition, housing.	Outside	6 groups, Nahuatl speaking	CILCA. Additional support: SEDESOL, National Indigenous Institute (INI), National Institute for Adult Education, Comaletzin, C.P., PACMYC, MacArthur

Region		Activities	Market	Groups	Funders
Puebla South	Women	Livelihood projects, farming skills, organisation and training, gender awareness, leadership development, rotating credit, vegetable gardens and traditional medicine.	Outside	4 groups, Spanish and Nahuatl speaking	Bank of Holland through CILCA
Hidalgo	Women	Livelihood projects, organisation and training, gender awareness, rotating credit.	Outside	2 groups, 37 women, Spanish speaking	Ford Foundation, UNIFEM
Jalisco	Women	Livelihood projects (livestock, cacti, cochineal insects, cochineal for dyes, turkeys, mill, co-operative food shop), community and reproductive health care.	Outside and self	12 groups, 500 women, Spanish speaking	Miserios, French Caritas, DEMOS, Embassies of the Netherlands and Canada, SEDESOL
Sonora	Women	Livelihood projects, training, education, savings, credit, housing.	Self	29 groups, 630 women, Spanish speaking	IAF, Solidarity, state government, Ministry of Agrarian Reform

Notes: 1. *Tortillas* – flat cakes made with maize flour; 2. *Huipiles* – heavily embroidered blouses; 3. Mill – the mill is to grind maize into flour, the *tortillería* to make the flour into *tortillas* (both traditionally done in the home by hand, and occupying several hours of each woman's day).

although it obviously demands a tremendous joint effort. Then the experience has to be formalised and expressed in teaching as well as research. I
feel that an immense effort is necessary from all the women involved. (María,
adviser and academic, *Puebla North* and *South*)

All these women are speaking of a 'power to' expressed by getting
organised, designing projects, getting money, teaching or training, achieving
change and valuing our work. Let us take a look at each of these expressions.

'Power to' organise   All the groups first organised to make money to
support their families, but now work for social as well as financial ends
(Table 6.1). Almost all place great importance on awareness of their
position and condition as women (Chapter Four). Each organisation has
committees for specific areas, which sounds dull, but these mechanisms
have been developed through experience in working together, and their
voices give witness to the control they have achieved over their personal
development and over the tasks which strengthen their 'power to'.

Three committees are formed in each community. That is, there are six of
us, but each has her duties, her field of work, so there are three committees
to each group: committees in charge of making *tortillas*, of the cornmill, of
making *huipiles*,[8] of the weaving, of the vegetables. (Citlali, Mixe change-
agent, *Oaxaca*)

We hold meetings once a month, when we plan what to do. Everyone is
responsible for their own work and for social welfare. Six women handle
livelihood projects, *tortillas*, the cornmill and handicrafts. We divide everything among us to manage the whole programme. Because just one woman
on her own couldn't handle it all. (Linaloe, Nahua change-agent, *Puebla
North*)

Well, here we see how the regional committee works. It really has the same
functions as those of each community, that is, to plan the organisations'
activities, get funding for its activities, manage projects, make sure things
get done, advise the groups when asked, or provide training or services when
asked. (Teresa, elected adviser, *Sonora*)

All the organisations, except *Sonora*, set themselves up with the help of
women advisers from outside who expressed their own 'power to' in giving
this help. Each adviser has her own understanding of gender, whether she
is professional or academic.

Our team is more ready to say our work is in gender, because some of us
have been in touch with feminist thought by taking part in the feminist

movement from time to time. We've tried to use this experience in our everyday work with women who are basically 'indigenous', although this work is mostly about their immediate needs. This is where marketing their handicrafts comes in. We've tried to offer guidance and training in some things: one thing we did last year was help them understand how everything came down to costs of production, help them learn how much it costs to make this or that, how to set a price, how much the wool costs, get them involved in the whole process. (Ana, paid adviser, *Chiapas*)

If self-empowerment is to continue, learning to be leaders (see below) and change-agents is fundamental.

'Power to' design projects All the groups have livelihood projects (Table 6.1),[9] and what is unusual in Mexico is that none has been imposed from outside. The women themselves have decided on them, sometimes through a thorough examination of their needs.

We made an assessment, and filled it out in a workshop with the women, where the need for livelihood projects came up. The process didn't begin with the projects; they were a result (María, adviser and academic, *Puebla North* and *South*).

The women never forget their desperate need to produce either income or replacements for income (as by growing food or making clothes) and one objective is always to make their lives easier, less crushed by poverty. This is why we call them 'livelihood projects'. They see their projects as supplementing consumption, in addition to bolstering the family budget. But such activities are always among many others, such as welfare, health, appropriate technology or even workshops where gender identity is explored.

Intense debate still surrounds the idea of income-generation. On the one hand, people will simply not be able to stay in rural communities without more income. On the other hand, are the projects 'income-generating' if they have to run on tiny amounts of credit and, if the women's time is costed at more than a couple of dollars a day, they cannot make a profit? Basic foods cost little less in Mexico than in the United States or Europe. Unless they are part of a strong organisational process directed towards autonomy and gender awareness, the only thing 'income-generating' projects do is exploit the rural population. When it is women who are seen as cheap labour by government or NGOs, they are even more at risk than men, as their expectations are lower, and their existing workload for family and even community is ignored, being seen as 'natural' to their 'womanhood' (Ma. del Socorro Centeño Rodríguez 1996).[10]

The image of the projects as a means to an end beyond income is more familiar to the academics than to the women who do the work.

I believe the so-called income-generating projects are for basic needs. They don't produce profit so much as things to be consumed as well as sold. In this sense, they are a means for women to join in, to have their ideas heard ... They are the ones who decide which way they want to go, what kind of skills they'll need and ask for. (María, adviser and academic, *Puebla North* and *South*)

These women stayed at subsistence level, but they [the projects] gave spaces for reflection where women could talk about the problems of their daily lives. This process started branching out, and now the academics have made a theoretical proposal, so to speak, for these projects to be approached from a gender-based [feminist] perspective. (Elena, adviser and academic, *Hidalgo*)

Rural women attach much more value to the direct products of the projects. 'All the activities spring from basic needs, such as "I want credit to buy shoes for my children".' (Isabel, paid adviser, *Oaxaca*)

In the communities, the women join in these projects because they say, 'Yes, they're useful, they're a big help, a real help.' The communities ... have their projects. Let's say there's a group of women at the mill. So the fund is useful to them, whatever's over from the mill. If anyone gets sick, if their husbands get sick or the women themselves or their daughters, they can go and talk to the mill committee, where they get support or ask for a loan. It may not be interest-free, but it helps. So the whole thing works for them and they talk about everything. I think they get a lot out of their work. (Linaloe, Nahua change-agent, *Puebla North*)

For Linaloe, the earnings are profits, although the academics might argue that they are only a fraction of the local agricultural wage (which is low) and simply not worth the time. She says, 'We've found that the pig farm makes profits, because the women who run it kill the pigs themselves and sell them as prime cuts. Because if we sold them live, well, there wouldn't be any profit, because whoever bought the live pig would make the profit. So the women kill them, make a profit and use it to buy things.' Some apparently commercial activities may be profitable not in money but in working time saved (Ana Fernández *et al.* 1994).

And the *tortilla* shop too, because that saves time ... We have to make them by hand. So now they can go and buy *tortillas* and save time and come to the meeting. They also use the mill, because before we had to grind the corn by hand and now we go to the mill. There we can see that [the project] helps. (Araceli, Nahua woman, *Puebla North*)

The groups have developed very rich dynamics. Instead of merely running their projects, they examine their workloads and suggest ways to lighten their chores instead of simply adding work (see below). Clearly, the groups do not exist to make money. They analyse their activities and the needs of their communities, which opens up the possibility of cultural, social, educational and other activities. As their needs are strategic as well as practical,[11] the analysis of what it is to be a woman in each of their communities and regions, and in Mexico as a whole, pervades their activities. 'Then they got organised to set up livelihood projects, including a programme of workshops on gender, minority issues, politics etc.' (María, adviser and academic, *Puebla North* and *South*).

Power to get funding Each group has or has had funding from international agencies as well as national and perhaps local government, which they negotiated (usually with help from their advisers). Almost every group supports income-generation with rotating credit,[12] and made their own rules about loans, repayment and interest. The women make regular payments come what may, even if they have to take on extra work to do so. In *Puebla South*, one Nahua group has a rotating fund to buy gas stoves and gas:

> I asked them where the money came from for the rotating credit. 'Well,' they said, 'that's right, we have put a little more work into things that allow us to make money. It may not be much, but it is a lot better than having to walk for I don't know how many hours to fetch water and firewood [for cooking and hot water] and other things. This work we're doing, well, it lets us make money.' That's what they say, and proudly too. Although they have to work more to pay back the loan, it's work of a different kind. As they say themselves, 'It's a different kind of work, we do have to work but it's easier, less exhausting.' (María, adviser and academic).

The work that is 'less exhausting' is embroidery (of table napkins), which they can do at home at odd moments, although the returns per hour are very low. *Puebla South* has other livelihood projects, and wants to set up rotating credit for more conveniences for the home, such as gas stoves and collectors for rainwater. (The nearest water is an hour's walk in the dry season, and fuel for cooking is further.) It is the women who decide what they need. Unfortunately, no one from here came to Tapalehui, but I heard their ideas when Jo and I visited them.

Only *Sonora* have a savings-and-loan association. This is a new idea, as in the past the government allowed organisations only to receive savings, not to lend. They had to put any savings in banks, and only banks could lend, so that a whole area of independence was closed off; only small, informal groups could save together and lend to each other, usually in tiny amounts for consumption. 'Now that we have savings and loan, we're making long-term plans. It's as if there's a kind of independence guaranteed now. They won't just depend on credit any more, and won't have to go out to look for someone to give them credit; they'll manage their own resources' (Carmen, elected adviser, *Sonora*). (This, of course, would make them a 'sustainable' organisation on the model now promoted by the World Bank and other agencies, but *Sonora* are seeking independence, not to follow a fashion.) 'We have women who sell *tamales* [corn dumplings], food, cloth, clothes, everything' (Teresa, elected adviser, *Sonora*). In *Sonora*, funds go both to group projects such as livestock and to individuals; any member can apply who belongs to a group and lives in the area. The rules on eligibility, timing and payment are clear. Members have responded warmly and their businesses are growing.

> Some women decided to work with meat, to kill their cow, sell meat and make *machaca* [dried, shredded meat]. These were new members, six women who decided to ask the savings-and-loan association for a loan, and use it to start the business. They said they'd pay it back from their earnings. We made the loan, and they paid it back in two months. Now they look after their own sales. The same thing happened at the shop – the women paid off the loan from their profits. The first loan was of 4,000 pesos,[13] and it was a grand experience. (Teresa, elected adviser, *Sonora*)

There is even an effect on migration. 'Women leave the area, and the groups shrink. But with this kind of project we've found that the project, that participating in the organisation nearly makes them a living' (Teresa).

Power to learn Training, education and analysis are fundamental to self-empowerment as we understand it. A cognitive element is part of the process. 'New knowledge is essential to arrive at a new understanding of gender relations and to destroy long-held beliefs which contribute so much to constructions of gender' (Nelly Stromquist 1997: 8). *Oaxaca*, *Puebla South* and *North*, *Chiapas* and *Sonora* in particular have built up and been enriched by new knowledge and skills. Although, as I have said, all the groups plan their activities within areas they define, all have training. This usually includes technical issues and keeping basic accounts for the projects, as well as the women looking at their own lives as women. In *Oaxaca*, for instance, they have wanted to study their bodies and sexuality, from cervical smear tests for cancer to domestic violence. Isabel (paid adviser) described a case of violence reported to the main organisation by another member, in which the man was punished (see p. 92, Chapter Five).

I recognise from my own experience Naila Kabeer's account (1997: 125) of the development of awareness: 'Interests spring from different dimensions of social life, all rooted in experience. Some come up when practical experience leads to new observations and knowledge so that previous thoughts can be reconsidered.' *Sonora* exemplifies this process. For years, livelihoods have been at the centre, but now the women themselves want to learn of gender issues, inspired by their own experiences. 'We haven't introduced gender yet, or worked on it or anything like it ... We are really here [at Tapalehui] to learn so much ... We think you have to understand it very clearly to be able to get it across to other women' (Teresa, elected adviser). But practical experience is itself a form of education. 'It's like when a member joins a commission to deal with the bureaucrats, because then she can learn how things are done, how the other members of the commission speak, how the whole business has to be carried out ... But also, when we leave home to exchange experiences with others, to travel' (Teresa).

Other groups have programmes to develop leadership, sometimes in top-down ways that work with notions of the transmission rather than the development of knowledge. 'I think like a leader, too. So we get advice there ... we get special training. As leaders we can train others, prepare a workshop for other leaders and run a workshop. We can offer training or design a project for the community' (Linaloe, Nahua change-agent, *Puebla North*).

> We don't do it just to have more leaders or get workloads down, but because it means that the other women of the communities, of the groups, won't be as dependent on the advisers any more ... They know how to deal with the authorities, they can start work on their own without having to wait for the adviser to turn up, for the leader to go and tell them what to do – how to deal with red tape or whatever. So that means more women are informed, which is organisationally empowering. (Isabel, paid adviser, *Oaxaca*)

At the same time, it is worrying that such preparation is limited to very few women, leaving the development of the rest of the group problematic. Across Mexico and Central America, many NGO and government initiatives promote the setting up of women's groups and fund the training merely of a president, secretary and treasurer for each. Often, these posts have gone to women who already have considerable 'power over' the other women and are thus endowed with more 'power over' and 'power to', encouraging them to misuse both power and funds. All at Tapalehui are deeply committed to avoiding this pattern, but the women trained may still use their knowledge to personal ends rather than share it. Stephanie Riger (1997: 70), using a rather different definition of empowerment, asks 'since when does the empowerment of vulnerable groups and persons simultaneously generate a sense of community and strengthen the bonds that hold society together? Does it perhaps promote certain individuals or groups at the expense of others, intensifying competitiveness and lack of cohesion?' This problem explains our concern about how to encourage and strengthen the groups, a worry shared by the change-agents and rural women. As Citlali says (Mixe change-agent, *Oaxaca*), they want to be shown the way.

> I think it's one of our basic worries. Yes, how can we manage this? We may understand clearly what's needed, but maybe we sometimes need education, information, training in how to do it. Maybe we are great believers in changing the world and changing the conditions of women's lives (in this case peasant and Mixe women), but it's very difficult to get the tools. I mean, a way of doing it that's right or will work, in the sense that it is suited to the place, to the kinds of women, and also takes into account our own education, our own awareness; even that is important.[14]

But problems are not everything. Training also emerges as the space where 'power to' can grow and can be reproduced. The Indian women at the workshop showed much optimism and enthusiasm about the training they had received, taking great satisfaction in the things they *can* do. (See also Linaloe's words on p. 33). 'When I joined the organisation, I learned to take part. And I have the right too, as a woman, to come out [of my community] like this. And I also have the courage to learn to speak and to attend the workshops too, and the meetings' (Citlali, Mixe change-agent, *Oaxaca*). I think training has opened doors for these women, allowing them to express themselves as they would never have believed possible. Their talk reflects their personal growth, drive and self-empowerment, all of which 'imply conscientisation, or a break with the silence imposed both on their class and on their gender' (Kabeer 1997: 144).

> The other women told me that we are learning so many things that now, instead of going to talk with their husbands at night, they talk to Sonia [another member] about Article 27 [the article of the Constitution under which land reform was repealed in 1991] or the death of Colosio [the national presidential candidate of the ruling party who was assassinated in March 1994]. They don't go and ask the men any more, but Sonia, and that's what's caused the trouble. One woman said that maybe the men are realising that they're losing the place they've always had ... And the women, they're not all going back home, most feel better when they break with the usual way of doing things, the traditional way. They are breaking with all that. (Teresa, elected adviser, *Sonora*)

The academics at Tapalehui also see the training positively:

> They've been trained in things they'd never have believed possible ... in

management, right out of the reach of peasant women. I think, now they've
started, they've developed skills ... and I've seen group learning on so many
things, from skills for their projects to how to organise and relate to other
groups. This process of constant learning and training in the groups lets
them develop more independence. (Felipa, adviser and academic, *Hidalgo*)

On the other hand, Felipa says, the work is like sowing seeds, and needs
to be professionalised through their postgraduate programme.

The results so far speak to the viability of self-empowerment. As women
acquire greater access to and control over all kinds of knowledge and other
resources (Batliwala 1993), the process will become independent and will
grow of itself, supported by the links between self-empowerment and an
increased say in decisions. In the long term, everything will depend on
how far women are able to challenge and change present political priorities
(Kabeer 1997: 145).

Changing work   We have seen how much the women value participation.
María, adviser and academic, speaks for *Puebla South*:

   ... and on the other hand our relationships with our husbands. Now, we're
   respected, because we have improved our homes, like with the stoves. Before,
   we had to ask them for everything all the time, and now that they've seen we
   can handle a loan, that we succeed in what we are doing, they don't fight
   with us any more.

Teresa (elected adviser, *Sonora*), says the same of *Sonora*:

   It has given her, well, a certain status in her family. For instance, she tells
   me, 'Guess what? The boy doesn't want to work in the fields with my
   husband any more. Because when I have to go to a meeting he prefers to
   look after the house for me, take care of the children, buy groceries – he
   prefers that to helping his father. He doesn't ask his father for money any
   more. They ask me, because I'm the one who gives it.' She's surprised how,
   with her taking more money home, or almost making a living for the family,
   her husband has been pushed into the background ... Her husband stopped
   saying that she wasn't looking after the children well, that she hadn't kept
   up with the washing. Now he says, 'You're leaving me because you have
   someone else.'

Gonzalez (1991) thinks that changes in peasant households in Mexico
have undermined patriarchal control, as agriculture brings in less income
and the women and young people bring in more. For the rural women at
Tapalehui, money can change relations in the family in their favour, but
this can also bring problems. For Teresa, elected adviser of *Sonora*:

We've had so many members who start going ahead but then turn back, leave and end up frustrated. They get to a crisis with their husbands, and for two or three months they can't give all that we can because they're all mixed up, or separated, or looking for a new mate, because we [women] still refuse to accept that we can cope on our own ... We have to talk about gender, because we have to understand what's going on in order to find a way forward.

Sonora and *Puebla North* want to bring the men into this process, but there is no experience in rural Mexico in working with groups of men on such matters. There has been urban work, but little has been published.

Self-empowerment, then, requires constant reflection and adjustment. 'And we say how we've had to adjust to the changes we've gone through as women. Not as mothers, not as wives, but as women. How are we adapting?' (Carmen, elected adviser, *Sonora*).

Obstacles to the 'Power to'

Around the world, the current fashion for empowerment in poor countries came just when the IMF and World Bank imposed neoliberal policies which have brought suffering and loss to the poor (Stromquist in León 1997). (See Chapters One and Three.) Indeed, the World Bank has adopted a language of empowerment which shifts the burden of responsibility for change on to the poor. By credit and training, the poor are to be 'empowered' to better themselves. For us and for the women at Tapalehui, this is a contradiction in terms. The women are desperate to maintain their families' standards of living against falling incomes, and welcome credit and, when appropriate, training, for any small gain they can make. Yet they know that they have still to challenge the 'power over' that keeps them poor. At this point, we need to recall the grim picture of rural Mexico sketched in Chapter One. 'In Mexico, the income of 45,560,000 people (half the population) is insufficient to meet their minimum daily calorie requirements' (*La Jornada* 1996: 46).[15] In Mexico, 80 per cent of rural families are poor, and 70 per cent of the extremely poor are rural; the average rural wage in the early 1990s was only 63 per cent of the legal minimum wage in Chiapas, 57 per cent in Oaxaca and 44 per cent in Guerrero. For Julio Boltvinik (1995), in Mexico 'poverty kills and rural poverty kills even more ... More than two thirds of deaths of rural children would not happen if their mortality rate was that of the urban upper class.'

María (academic and adviser) studied nutrition in *Puebla North* and found the Nahuatl-speaking families to be eating too little food and too little protein. Hunger came up again and again at Tapalehui, where Linaloe

(Nahua change-agent from *Puebla North*) said, 'It hurts us to have to say
we don't eat meat once a week, sometimes not even once a month.' In
1999, things are even worse in, for instance, the states of Chiapas, Oaxaca
and Guerrero where the army has been sent into rural areas to bring back
order, so they say, and control armed groups such as the Zapatistas and the
Popular Liberation Army (pp. 7–8, 38–9, 50). Overwhelming poverty is
made more crushing when the government sends the army in; in Chiapas,
where there are now 50,000 soldiers, some 30,000 rural people have been
driven out of their homes and are living in camps while the coffee beans
rot on the bushes.[16]

The groups have come together to struggle, encouraged by support from
international agencies, NGOs and government. But, as Isabel says, 'Things
are now so bad that it is almost impossible even to keep working.' Everyone
gave their own examples. Teresa uses the idea of 'strategic' needs, adopted
from international feminism. 'It's all down to the resources we can't get,
to the national economic crisis. That's why women concentrate on basic
needs and pay a little less attention to strategic needs.' From the academic
perspective, Felipa (also an adviser to *Hildago*) thinks that neoliberal policies
have simultaneously encouraged women's groups to think up projects that
bring them income or services, and made it increasingly difficult for them
to succeed. Isabel described the struggle to meet 'donor' conditions: 'You
have to be on top of the numbers, on top of making money, and there's no
time for anything else.' Getting money has become the Achilles' heel of the
organisations. For Linaloe (Nahua change-agent in *Puebla North*), 'Well,
the donors tell us what to do. They make themselves felt, make the
conditions and the decisions.' The academics detest the conditions under
which they must work with the groups. As Felipa says:

> When women get money from the donors, the very first requirement is for
> the groups to become self-sufficient, independent. They [the donors] allow
> the least money they can and expect that to get the groups not just going
> but independent. I think this is impossible, unfair, because many men's
> groups get money for much longer without ever getting off the ground. But
> women's groups are expected to become independent and self-sufficient in
> two years, with minimal support.

Stromquist (1997: 81) calls this the 'economic component of empowerment', which 'requires women to commit themselves to work which will
give them a little financial independence, no matter how small at first or
how difficult to achieve. Income-generating projects are hard to achieve,
because they are risky, time-consuming and, at first, inefficient.'

The 'power to' do more and more work is not an unmixed blessing and
both rural women and academics had a great deal to say about it. All the

rural women agree that the organisations mean even more work, and leave them rushing from task to task 'with no time to think or take a wider view' (Isabel, paid adviser, *Oaxaca*). They agree also with Xochitl (Mixe change-agent, *Oaxaca*):

> Women's work. Well, yes, it goes up. When we go to a meeting or to the organisation, well, we have to leave the housework not done. You just have to forget something that needs doing here to cope with something else there, and then you still have to do the first thing when you get home. I mean, that's why we have more to do. We leave our jobs at home to go and help the other women.

The academics were even more outspoken, more articulate and angrier about their workloads. They too need to work in several places at once. In their universities they not only have the same teaching, administration and research as the men, but women are a tiny minority in this field and under intense pressure to do much more. At the same time, says María, academic adviser to *Puebla South*, the rural women need the very best the academics can do, but this work is hardly recognised in the university. The academics also have housework and childcare. They feel they have no personal space and, like the rural women, no time to think (Catalina, María and Felipa), which harms the work done. A real downside to the 'power to' came through from almost everyone.

Building Up the 'Power to'

As I have tried to show, possible ways forward are strongly inter-connected in our idea of groups working for empowerment. Everyone at Tapalehui has analysed what they have done and what has come of it, which has led us to challenge our society's ideas of women. Awareness has enriched each woman and each group to which we belong, rural woman or academic.

One possibility is a different kind of project, where reducing women's work comes first. This means finding specific solutions. As we saw, *Puebla South* got money to set up revolving loans, and the women decided to go for gas stoves and rainwater tanks, to save themselves the work of fetching wood and water from further and further away as the environment deteriorates.

> So I think a different kind of project seems to have developed, let's say in the medium term. It's agreed that the women will be able to think up ways to make money, once they have a little less to do. Things like shops making *tortillas* for sale are steps towards reducing women's work. I think this has really paid off. (María, academic and adviser to *Puebla South*)

In *Sonora*:

> We said, 'we can't go on like this, we have to change so as not to put in more
> and more time and work. Our families should help with the projects too,
> because they get something out of them, too, not just us, the women. The
> truth is, we didn't get anything out of our projects, because all the gains
> went to our families.'
>
> That was when we started to discuss collective projects at an individual
> level. They are collective because we had to belong to the group, we had to
> be organised … And individual because each was responsible for her bit.
> The project would be the same for everyone, a 500-hen poultry farm, but
> each woman looked after so many hens at home with the help of her son or
> husband. Or of the cow. Because the cow belonged to a cattle-raising project,
> and we thought this would get our work down a bit. We even got better
> results this way, got the original money back and kept going longer. (Teresa,
> elected adviser)

Carmen, another elected adviser from *Sonora*, wanted to change our
basic thinking:

> We should use this [meeting] not just to comfort each other, personally or
> as a group, but to find a way of thinking positively about our work. For us,
> as women, more work … means more satisfaction and the chance to learn,
> as leaders or just by joining in the projects. The idea we should work at is
> how to share the new work as much as possible, how to get the rest of the
> family on board, because if we continue working and encouraging other
> women to think, OK, it's true that we've got more work, but we have to
> hang in there, we have to go on because we have no choice, because it's the
> only way to get anywhere, but, I mean, we can't be heroines either.

Everyone agreed that this is an urgent problem, but not everyone thinks
the work can be reduced. I doubt that the academics can do it, much as
we need to, yet I think it is absolutely necessary to create spaces for
reflection, to improve the quality of our work. The demand for new spaces
speaks of the need for the groups to link themselves with policy-making
at higher levels, to get involved with municipal and regional as well as
national policy. As Kate Young argues (1997: 113):

> If policy makers are to do more than simply listen to women's demands, the
> demands must be attached to some political imperative. In politics, the will
> to act only arises in the face of some political force. To gain enough political
> power, women's organisations must try to work more with other groups
> seeking social transformation.

The workshop I was much struck, in writing this chapter, by the importance given to simply belonging to an organisation, particularly among the
rural women. The way we all feel about belonging to a group is essential
to group empowerment (Chapters Two, Three and Five). This speaks of
an organisational power fundamental if 'the activities performed are to
broach the wider context of women's lives' (Naila Kabeer 1997: 144). This
is genuine 'power to', for the activities are not sterile, they do not only
entertain women nor are they pure work. On the contrary, it is clear from
their meaning in women's lives that they are practices that enable transformation and self-empowerment.

Women's 'power to' is produced and reproduced through these activities.
Everything the rural women said about it expressed drive and motivation;
they may be worried at times, but never defeated. On the other hand,
uncertainty and even, at times, despair at the immensity of the task can be
heard in some of the talk of outside advisers and academics.

As we said in Chapter One, women change-agents are truly amazed at
what they can now do: 'Yes, I can!' is liberation for them. Their talk of
workshops and training is of spaces that have real meaning for them.
Advisers, on the other hand, demand more training and chances to learn,
and are simply not as elated as the rural women. Imagination has played
a central role in the work. We have probably all at some time imagined
new private and social selves: imagining utopias and struggling to create
them are vital to social change, and dimensions are multiplied when a
group brainstorms together. Workshops and training sessions, as spaces
available to learn and talk, have played a strategic role in this group search
for utopias. They have allowed women to exercise 'power to', by getting
organised, earning money, raising money, and above all by making changes
in their own lives. The change-agents demonstrate their capacity for reflection. Their opinions come from thoroughly planned and analysed activities.
They are alert to the ways they must go and to the needs that must be
fulfilled for self-empowerment.

Where Next?

I have explored the understanding which rural women, advisers and
academics have of 'power to', how they exercise it, the obstacles faced and
the alternatives available. I must move to the wider context. In the first
place, the organisations must enter wider fields of action. As Srilatha
Batliwala writes (1997: 203), 'If women's empowerment is to transform
society, it must become a political force, an organised mass movement
capable of challenging and transforming existing structures of power.
Empowerment must ultimately include poor women in regional, national

and international mass organisations.' The organisations with which we worked do have important links with wider spheres, but I believe more are needed for them to build real political force or to influence regional and national events and penetrate international networks, to 'begin to demand that resources be assigned through the policies themselves' (Naila Kabeer 1997: 144). Women's control of their own sexuality must also be assessed more clearly, as it is a cardinal factor in self-empowerment. We must call attention to, study, analyse and document the construction of gender identity in every context, to enable change-agents, advisers and academics to design more effective strategies in support of self-empowerment.

Lastly, I want to call attention again to the need that advisers and academics express for space to think. They talk of being overwhelmed by their workloads and, although they delight in the achievements of organised rural women, they do not feel they have made comparable gains. This delight is still palpable and underlies the alliances at Tapalehui. 'This work has also given me great pleasure, that's certain, and though I also get support from other advisers, what I've got most out of, day by day, has been listening to the women. This listening to the women has been truly wonderful' (Isabel, paid adviser to *Oaxaca*).

Summary of Chapter Six

Rural women at Tapalehui revel in the 'power to', which they express in terms of action, of their power to build a different future. They revel in new skills, in getting organised, designing projects, training others, achieving change and learning to value their own work, new or old. They express this power very much in terms of everyday practicalities such as committee work, making money or getting funding, which they see very differently from us. What sounds tedious to the authors is liberation to the speakers as they develop a feeling of increasing command over their own lives. Not all is mundane: the 'power to' includes awareness and critical reflection. Often the material gains are small and the costs of effort great, but what we might see as exploitation is expressed as a joy.

To develop the 'power to' is to face many new problems, from coping with new skills to conflict with husbands. Organisation and training are seen as central and critical. Yet the 'power to' do has its downside for both rural women and academics, they have to be learn not to undertake too much. All are under pressure to overwork: the rural women by declining family incomes, the academics by their institutions.

Notes

1. We opened the book with a similar expression from Citlali.

2. See note 1, Chapter One, for the use of 'Indian'.

3. Magdalena León (1997) translates the English-language 'power to' as *'el poder para'* (the 'power for'), and uses it very much in Stephen Lukes' (1974) meaning of the 'power to have a say in decisions'. We translated it as *'el poder de hacer'* or the 'power to do', and the rural women at Tapalehui attached this rather to making money, and to specific skills and physical actions. Differences in translation may therefore account for the differences in discourse between León and ourselves. There was no intentional difference in principle.

4. Gender was at first ignored, which limited women's gains, but now feminists have made Popular Education invaluable to women too by including gender awareness.

5. Very comparable with Batliwala 1993, Kabeer 1994, 1997 and Rowlands 1995a, 1997a, b, c; we all owe a debt to Freire 1973.

6. Nearly all: see Chapter Seven for Pilar Alberti's understanding.

7. Compare Lagarde 1992.

8. Traditional embroidered dress.

9. *Proyectos productivos*, or productive projects, in Mexico.

10. The frameworks within which women's groups or local organisations can get funding are extremely complicated (one reason for the existence of advisers).

11. The concepts of strategic and practical gender needs were introduced to international feminism by Caroline Moser (1989), now at the World Bank. Many women have a practical need for water, not because only they need water but because it is their work, their role to provide the water for the family. Clean, accessible water would help them in their existing roles. But women have strategic needs, to stop their men beating them or to have a say in decisions. We have three comments. First, donors tend to twist the concept to give preference to 'practical' needs as seen from outside, not as defined by the women concerned, and to avoid strategic needs. Second, once women become aware, they may define any need as strategic. And third, the terminology can help people think (whether peasant women or students), although it is also abused.

12. Under which the women borrow and repay in turn, often initially from a fund supplied by government, NGO or international donor.

13. Some £800 or US$1,300 at the time.

14. This is very characteristic. A notion remains that there is a 'right' way of doing things, a neutral 'tool' which can be brought in from outside.

15. As quoted by Zapata and Mercado 1996.

16. David Stansfield, personal communication.

7

Power over: Domination, Oppression and Resistance

Pilar Alberti

Who is Writing?

First, like my fellow authors, I must introduce myself. Imagination has driven the course of my life, bringing me from Spain to work with Indian women[1] in Mexico. Studying far away in Madrid, I was gripped by the Indians of the Americas, their archaeology, ethnohistory and anthropology. I left my country, my family and my job to travel first to Peru, then Mexico. I joined an archaeological dig in Peru, near Cuzco, and first explored my fascination with Indian women with my undergraduate dissertation on the priestesses of *acllacuna* who worshipped Inti, the Inca sun god. I then studied gender and ethnic identity in Mexico, among three generations of Nahua women (who belonged to an organisation of craftswomen) and also met Mayo, Mixe, Otomi, Tarahumara, Tzotzil, Yaqui and Zapotec women. For my doctorate, I examined the Mexica religion and Mexica goddesses as models for Mexica women today. I was privileged to work with many parts of the women's movement in Mexico (see Chapter Three). I came to live in Mexico in 1992 and to work at the Colegio de Postgraduados in 1994, teaching about theories of gender, problems of rural women, research methods, ethnicity and domestic violence while working with rural women. The link between practice and academia in our team of gender researchers seems to me to be of the utmost importance, enriching our work with peasant women and our teaching, research and writings. I have learned so much from peasant women. Dignity is not lost even on the edge of extreme poverty, and dignity and imagination are central to women's self-empowerment.

What is 'Power over'?

This is a sensitive subject, and in this chapter when I quote from individuals, I shall use categories (peasant leader,[2] adviser, academic) rather

than even fictitious names. All had the courage to express critical understandings of the power exercised over them through institutions or
organisations, at work and at home, by women and men. We also explored
'power over' among and between academics, advisers, change-agents and
group members. We learned so much from each other, and I must protect
that freedom of speech. We had to be very brave to criticise and accept
criticism as we did at Tapalehui.

My role at the meeting was to run the 'more academic' focus group. I
found it important to listen to women who seek to support self-empowerment in organisations of peasant women. How do they further their own
self-empowerment, and what personal and professional difficulties do they
meet? One academic said, 'I relate power to oppression, to imposing on
others and to control over others.'

As we saw in Chapter Two, there is a substantial literature on 'power
over'. In Mexico, the leading feminist Marcela Lagarde defines power
itself as 'power over' (1990: 31) in its most negative forms.

> Power consists primarily in being able to take a decision which will affect
> someone else or in acting to force, confine, forbid or prevent. Whoever
> exercises such power subordinates and degrades, forces actions, exercises
> control and assumes the right to punish, seize material property, infringe
> symbolic rights and dominate in every respect.

Such understandings of power are natural in Latin America with its history
of colonialism, dictatorships and military governments. Citizenship and
democracy are starting to emerge now, but amid corruption, extreme
poverty and the power of local bosses, especially in rural areas and among
Indian groups.

Michel Foucault has a different understanding of power as it connects
individuals and groups (1989: 238).

> [P]ower is a set of actions that act on other possible actions. It functions in
> the field of the possible, or inscribes itself in the behaviour of actors by
> inciting, inducing, seducing, facilitating or hindering, expanding or limiting.

Even 'power over' relates free individuals to one another. If power is
exercised in a state of complete alienation between individuals, it ceases to
exist. From this, a basic feature of power relations between individuals and
groups can be inferred: resistance.

> Relations of power and the rebellious nature of freedom therefore cannot be
> separated from one other. The obstinacy of the will and the intractability of
> freedom lie at the very heart of a power relation, which they constantly
> question. (Michel Foucault, 1989: 240)

Precisely this rebellious nature of freedom made itself insistently felt in women's discourses at Tapalehui, which is why I must remind you that power itself does not exist, only power relations.

Forms of 'power over' Women at Tapalehui identified three basic forms of 'power over':

- that exercised by institutions over individuals;
- that exercised by individuals over others, in this case over women; and
- the 'power over' to be found inside a single person (pp. 26–7, 147). This is the tyranny we exercise over ourselves, which comes from the tension between duty and wish. Often, the judges and police inside us are much stricter in their dealings with us than are other people. This situation is more common in women.

Academic Women and Advisers on 'Power over'

We were surprised to find from our tape-recordings from Tapalehui that the 'more academic' group had much more to say about power over than the 'more rural' group, and the 'peasant leaders' least of all. Although the latter suffer more from 'power over' and suffer more forms of it, they showed much less tendency to talk about it or unpack it. For them, it is a very large feature of life, but not intellectually problematic. When the comments are put together, those of the peasant leaders sound weaker and are fewer. After wrestling with this problem, I have decided to separate the two, although this will leave the more academic women dominating the chapter. I shall also organise the chapter around specific relationships through institutions and between individuals. The institutions I have selected are government and politics, 'donors', the family, universities and religion (the last two only for the 'more academic' group, as only they really discussed them). These were the formal institutions discussed in detail at Tapalehui.

For the women with more formal education at Tapalehui, 'power over' proved an uncomfortable topic.

> I believe that women could exercise all forms of power, even 'power over', the power of domination, because we are talking about the power women could have, not what they want. Some women use the 'power over', like older women, mothers-in-law, power within the family. Perhaps their power is not oppressive in the manner of the oppressive power wielded by men. When we talk about the exercise of power, we ought to emphasise that women wouldn't necessarily want this power of oppression, because then we would be copying this male-centred model which isn't, of course, at all good for society, you know? (Academic)

Institutions If we begin with institutional 'power over', we find ourselves asking, why do people put up with it? How is it legitimated? What is the state? We need to analyse the justification of power, and how 'power over' can go beyond all limits to historic excess, as with fascism and Stalinism. Such 'power over' generates resistance, by individuals and groups. In Mexico, institutions including the state have been decisive in tending to restrict women to the role of mother and wife, while limiting their reproductive and other rights (for example, to abortion or to making decisions over their property) and denying them certain privileges. The 1971 Law of Agrarian Reform made land pass after the death of the husband first to the wife, then to the son, but the amendment to Article 27 of the Mexican Constitution by the 1992 Law of Agrarian Reform prevents peasant women from inheriting land; the consequences for widows and elderly women can be terrible. At Tapalehui, the academic women explored a great range of institutions implicated in the 'power over'.

Government and politics Women who seek to become policy-makers face both concrete and cultural obstacles. The system resists women, especially at levels with greater power. The first step to women at the top must be in open commitment. So far, however, this has not been enough in Mexico. Election promises to women are not necessarily kept, and even women who become policy-makers can face severe limitations.

> I believe that women's influence has to be felt everywhere, even in politics, even beyond politics. That's why I've always said that women and men should share power, because there is so much left to be done in politics. So, a new turn – I mean, politics has always disqualified women in practice – a new turn has to be given to political practice, because men aren't going to do it on their own. If they wanted to, they'd have done it by now. So, we have to get to the political positions where things get decided. They must be occupied by women with the vision and awareness to give things a new turn. (Academic)

Women are still determined to take part in politics, at national and international levels.

'Donors' Under neoliberal policies (p. 48), the state has been forced to cut back on its old activities and leave the people to meet their own basic needs, including much education and health. National and international funding agencies have become more and more important to the provision of basic and wider needs. Popular and peasant organisations have taken on new roles. Some are now self-sufficient, but were dependent on the support of funding agencies; many continue dependent. Agencies differ in their

ways of working, objectives, conditions imposed, origin of funds and degree of support to women's groups. Many may force women's groups to work in particular ways, imposing 'solutions' alien to their culture or wishes. Others have a mechanistic approach to 'including women' in projects – the 'tick the box' approach, which can be useless or counterproductive. Normally, the agencies think only in terms of using their 'power over' the grassroots women to 'help' them, not to liberate them or to promote their self-empowerment. Occasionally (p. 8) such coercion has positive outcomes, but normally the culture of the agencies, constantly expressed through the 'power over' bestowed by their wealth, is didactic, controlling, male-biased and ethnocentric.

Women's organisations have a better record than men's in Mexico for repayment of loans on time;[3] women are more efficient administrators of limited resources. Yet the amounts granted for women's projects are very small, when compared to the salaries of senior agency staff (especially in international agencies) or to other projects they fund. Tensions between 'donors' and women's organisations are common. The amount may be too small, or may be excessive, when women have not yet developed the capacity to make good use of funds; this can destabilise the whole organisation.

Some of us at Tapalehui think that 'help' for poor people to meet their basic needs (clean water, good nutrition, education, health care, housing and community services, for instance) through getting organised can itself be intended to control rather than assist. Financial 'help', however limited, which uses women's cheap or free work to help people survive may, they think, distract attention and energy from the need to confront the state. The 'help' may have successfully stopped them getting organised to more purpose, and have forestalled armed resistance which could have brought political pressure to bear for change in the misery and want of the peasants. 'We must analyse this, because we so often ask ourselves what we should really be doing. Perhaps we are holding back, stifling changes which would have exploded long ago' (Academic). Violence and repression are everyday affairs in Mexico, and among Mexican social scientists at the turn of the millennium, the idea of social change coming through violent revolution is more current than in, say, the USA or the UK.

In many very poor rural areas, especially where people are Indian, there is open revolt, as by the Zapatistas (EZLN) in Chiapas or the Popular Revolutionary Army (EPR) in Guerrero. In others, however, I think that many of the most pressing problems are being relieved by the peasant and Indian women, which suppresses potential revolt against the economic and political model that the government is imposing. In the words of the Nobel Peace Prize laureate Rigoberta Menchú, 'We, the women, are not the problem. On the contrary: we have often proved that we are the solution' (Reyes, 1994: 14).

Universities 'Power over' is very noticeable in universities. We heard at Tapalehui how women who have taught from a feminist perspective or sought to move to more flexible, more participative, less hierarchical structures, or worked for greater gender equality in treatment, salaries and promotions, or for a greater visibility in academic work have suffered for it.

> As academics in the institution, we are subject to its forms of evaluation. We must produce this and that, which is part of the pressures they impose and isn't empowering at all. On the contrary, it becomes a source of constant anguish, as they want you to do something here and something else there and to participate in this or that. Bureaucracy wears you out dreadfully, and is tremendously disempowering ... The methods of evaluation are designed by men, which worries me greatly, because the methods are hierarchical and the men always get their own way. They manage to make things look as if they were doing more than a woman who is really doing more and with better quality, but they end up looking better qualified. All this really gets you down, alienates you, frustrates you horribly. (Academic)

Our British colleagues tell me that this problem is worse here than in the UK, where at least if a woman does what is asked and publishes respected books and articles, this will be recognised. Here, it may not be. Envy and jealousy are found in universities, as everywhere; here, women who have worked hard and well for outstanding achievements frequently meet these emotions, from both men and women.

Although the link between theory and practice is so important, especially in programmes to improve conditions for the poor, women's projects may just be left out of consideration even in institutions that otherwise make this link. There may be respect for the design of projects, consultancy, training, evaluation and the bringing of theory and practice into the classroom – so long as the participants are not women.

Both feminism and simple awareness of gender have become increasingly important in the social sciences. In theory, work in rural development, income-generation and public policy must include women as possible agents of change and action. In practice, to get funding, applicants for funding for research or for development projects must incorporate gender, and they do.

> At the university, they seem to recognise the need [for gender studies], but I think they are keen to get the money, I don't think they are really changing ... Some professors say that gender isn't an important field, and still use the

word when they want money. I think most of the male professors have the same attitude, and talk about us as 'those crazy women over there', but we crazy women are productive, get money and do things they don't. (Academic)

Any work calls for intellectual and physical effort, especially when daily pressures of work are increased by the 'power over' wielded by the institution against academic women who want change. What price must be paid? Is it worth it?

I wonder why we work so hard, why we believe it's up to us to change the world, why we must give our lives to this cause. We get so wrapped up in this fantastic amount of work that we feel that if we don't do it, the world will come to an end. (Academic)

(Our British colleagues tell me they agree.)

At the centre is a very important issue: the ethical commitment that women take on when we work for change side by side with other women. This is work for change, not just for pay. Such a commitment is truly enslaving, and exercises a moral 'power over' that stops excesses being questioned because they benefit the cause. Women academics and advisers working with women's groups rarely limit the time and effort we put in. Our work and the pressures build up and can even cause health problems, physical and mental. Franca Basaglia writes (1983) that we women build our identities around 'being for others' rather than 'being within oneself', to the point that we must be for others to justify our own existence. This 'apostolic' sense of mission can lead us to devote our lives to a cause. Of course, not all those working with women share the commitment; some use the gender fashion simply to get funding.

The family In Mexico, the institution of the family is valued very highly. Government propaganda promotes the idea of the family as the basic cell of society on which rest the pillars that support the nation. Yet the contradictions between the ideal family and daily practice cannot be ignored. The number of families headed by a woman is increasing; in big cities, many street children are completely uprooted from their families. Declining wages, unemployment and alcoholism have taken from many men the role of sole provider and violence is common in many homes. Family and values are changing in this crisis, and the 'power over' wielded by the male head of household is questioned.

We can't generalise, but traditional values are definitely being questioned inside the family. There's change, you know. It used to be normal for a wife to be beaten, for children to be beaten. Now that's being questioned inside the family, so I believe that family values are changing. (Adviser)

Women as well as men wield 'power over' in the family (see p. 72), especially older women. In rural Mexico you may still find the extended family, with several generations of relatives and in-laws living together. Here, the mother is fundamental, because she is the central axis around which the family revolves. She has considerable 'power over' which grows over time. One academic wants to see the powers of older women questioned:

> It's the power of knowledge. I mean, I'd say it comes from experience, this power to dominate the children, especially when young. The power of older women over other women and other family members ...

Traditionally, men have the main power to control the rest of the family and make decisions. This has become rooted in our ideology, politics, religion, philosophy and culture. Yet we can still see points of resistance that lead to questioning and change.

Religion We also talked at Tapalehui about the power of religion over thought and action, and the way it affects community life through its influence on women's behaviour.

> I think that when we criticise Catholicism, we forget that the rest are just as sexist. Anglicans are the same, and Baptists, Jehovah's Witnesses or the Church of the Light of the World. Women are subject to awful control. I remember one woman with a hernia who decided she didn't want any more children because she suffered so much when she got pregnant. But she couldn't get an operation [sterilisation] or take anything [contraceptives] because her [Protestant] pastor wouldn't allow it. This is a real step backwards, and any step backwards alarms me, because the religions are taking advantage of people's poverty to get into the villages. They turn up with piles of money, get into rural communities and impose all these reactionary ideas. (Academic)

Men and women can be subjected to 'power over' by any religion. Yet some groups resist, and struggle for equality within all the religions, including women who claim their rights to share in religious leadership.

Although Mexican law protects different religions, religious intolerance is used by local leaders to promote conflict in rural areas, especially in the state of Chiapas. Here, followers of a minority faith are often driven out of their villages. The organisation, *Chiapas*, with which we worked, struggles against such intolerance.

'Power over' between individuals The first kind of 'power over' is exercised through institutions, the second is that wielded by individuals, as by men over women (although gender is itself an institution). Michel Foucault (1989) defines protest movements as responding to such expressions of power. Women's struggles conform to his model of protest movements: they are not limited to one country, although they differ between countries according to politics and culture; their goal is to change the nature of power, so that men are criticised not for being men but for the way some use their power over women's lives and deaths; their response to power is direct, since women aim their criticism at the nearest form of 'power over'; they revolve around questions of identity, rejecting abstractions about 'women' as a group, and all the ideological, political and economic talk that ignores the differences between groups of women and between other social groups; they question the way women's existence as separate, distinct individuals is ignored and reject the description of women as all the same. When women are subjected to control over and dependence on another individual, 'power over' is present in both the domination and the resistance. Academics and advisers at Tapalehui had a great deal to say about this.

The rural women in mixed organisations of men and women have had some difficult experiences (see Chapter Five). An adviser at Tapalehui said:

> What happens in mixed organisations? What happens to women? They say, 'They don't recognise our worth at home, nor our work with other women, let's hope that the mixed organisation will pay some attention to us.' It doesn't. What do the women do in this organisation set up by men? Well, they cook for the big meetings because they have no practice in public speaking. The saddest part is that nothing is done for them. They are simply being used.

The power exercised in such an organisation extends past feminine roles from home to organisation. Women's support must be feminine, in traditional women's chores such as cooking – but again, this 'power over' is being questioned and resistance is appearing. Mixed organisations need to rethink the place of their women members and find ways of working that guarantee participation and representation to all members, women and men. By clinging to authority, they increase the risk of losing the women, who prefer, when not full members of mixed organisations, to go and form their own.

'Power over' in marriage For Joan Scott (1986: 44), 'gender is a primary form of power relations. Between couples, when women become even a little aware of their rights, "power over" sparks greater conflict because the resistance to it grows.'

And so, says an adviser:

Couples are always engaged in struggle. In my case, I feel we're always arguing about nothing. We sit down, start arguing again and get mad again, until at last he gets the point. It's a long process, and a month later we have the same argument over again. You have to talk through the same thing, over and over, to remind him that we're only asking for what's fair, so it's a bit tiring. But when we manage to convince them, when we manage to make ourselves heard, we get ahead and you can get on with things. The problem is when your partner gets set in what he thinks, and things don't work any more.

Working women must handle pressures at work as well as the chores at home, which can lead to separation and divorce. But changes in women's lifestyles are not easily accepted. Much public opinion is hostile to women's new attitudes, and women's families also set limits on new behaviour. Even at work, conflicts erupt when men feel threatened in the spaces of power that they have controlled for so long with no competition from women.

When a woman starts to change, she faces real problems with her partner just to get him to accept this process. I've seen this in the university among many women colleagues whose partners just wouldn't accept it. I think many feminists had the same thing in the sixties and seventies, that men wouldn't accept the changes. (Academic)

For single women, it is also hard to find greater equality.

It's hard to find a man who's different. I really think they're few and far between. When I was at college, there were thousands of men, and I re-member once a man telling me in a very aggressive tone, 'Men don't like women like you,' because of my feminist thinking. I took it as a compliment, because I wanted to be different, but he meant to be nasty. Women students really suffered systematic hostility among all those men. I don't think this is just the circles we move in, it's really widespread. Over the last few years, women have changed a lot and men haven't been able to. They hold on to authority. All they want is submission! (Academic)

Even for advisers and academics, a 'good' wife is submissive, makes no difficulties for her husband, never contradicts him, and suffers his rudeness or adultery in silence. Again, this notion is under strong challenge in societies and a world claiming the right to a change in thinking at the turn of the millennium.

'Power over' between academics and advisers Power is also exercised over women by women. Problems between women have often been denied or concealed in case they weaken the women's struggle. Women try to

keep a united front, but outside the political arena it becomes vital to
investigate the power plays between women, to find problems and solutions
in the interests of self-empowerment. To one adviser:

> Contact between academic feminists and NGOs seems to me to be essential.
> The main problem I see is jealousy, mistrust. I feel that the academics could
> help us not by organising the information but by giving us the tools to do
> it ourselves, as advisers who might want to do research.

In 1987, the National Network of Advisers Working with Rural Women
was set up to give advisers and academics the chance to meet and talk. It
has been kept going by hundreds of women working in gender in rural
areas. In this Network, 'power over' and the resistance it produces create
a dynamic process of constant transformation.

> This has been extremely important in enabling links and contacts, but it's
> been my experience and observation that there's a barrier between advisers
> and academics at these meetings, as if they see a separation between academic
> and field work. (Academic)

Advisers and academics have still been able to work successfully together,
as shown in the materials published by the Network.

'Power over' inside us The third kind of 'power over' is that which we
internalise, according to the norms and social values that determine what
'should be' (see Weber 1990). There is great variety here, but once a rule
is internalised, it may be individuals themselves who enforce it most
severely. For women, this may be expressed as the 'glass ceiling',[4] or the
'Cinderella complex' (Colette Dowling 1982), or simply a lack of the
necessary self-esteem (Nathaniel Branden 1997). Here too, 'power over'
subjugates and oppresses.

The academics are gloomy on the subject.

> We give ourselves to listening, to supporting change, to reviewing the experi-
> ences of other women, but what happens to our own growth as human
> beings? And when we talk about empowerment, we should ask ourselves
> where our own empowerment has got to. I feel that my job gives me great
> satisfaction and has helped me a lot – and that's just why I have trouble with
> my partner, because of my own process of empowerment. (Academic)

> I enjoy what I do, but I really don't have a personal life. At times, I feel
> completely alienated, because my work follows me everywhere, even home,
> where I get phone calls, or a student may bring me a paper to read at eight
> in the morning so that we can discuss it at ten. I love to read, I love to go
> to the movies, I love to have fun, but I can't. It's as simple as that. (Academic)

Almost all the academics agreed. Our work has taken over our lives and closed off many other opportunities for fulfilment. Once a certain degree of gender-awareness is reached, everything has a new meaning, from the smallest action to life itself, and we become more sensitive to and critical of all discrimination.

> Once you know that gender [feminism] is an essential part of your life and of everything you do, you become very much aware of everything relevant. I mean, no matter where you go, you immediately notice the discrimination, and think, 'Well, am I just a rebel, or what?' It's also exhausting, and sometimes, even if you want to shut your eyes to what you see wherever you go – it gets like a sieve that you put every personal experience through. You have to work with this constructively, not destructively, or there comes a moment when you feel completely exhausted and frustrated. (Academic)

'Exhausted' and 'frustrated' are two adjectives that describe the academics' (and I dare say the advisers') feelings once they find out that a more equal society graced by gender relations less grounded in 'power over' is still very far off. One adviser commented that the more 'anguished' discussions were to be heard among the women with more formal education, more exposure to urban life and international feminism, not among the more rural women who confront so much more daily suffering.

Rural Women on 'Power over'

For rural as well as more urban women, power was 'power over', something that can never be positive, must always be contained.

Institutions

Government and politics

> So, you have the power which comes with the municipal post to which you've been elected, but how much power have you really got? In the first place, you belong to a minority, to the opposition party, and second you're a woman. I don't know how much you can influence decisions. For the first reason, nobody ever pays any attention to you, and still less when you are a woman. They just listen. We sort of took stock of what we had done, once our three-year term was over, and we found the only thing it had been good for was to open a few more doors. You know, to get the mayor to see us later [after our term of office], or to try to be there when the municipal structure plan is being made, to get our own ideas in, you know? (Peasant leader)

Peasant women attributed some of the problems they met in positions of more power to their lack of experience, perhaps internalising oppression. Certainly, these political institutions are reluctant to let women in, and are dominated by men.

'Donors' The rural women experience 'power over' in two ways in their relationships with funding agencies: as an imposition, and as a necessary promoter of change. One leader spoke of imposition:

> Perhaps some members of the funding agencies are interested in helping us women do what we want, and in how we are going to do it. But basically, the funding agencies' policies don't work, they don't think women should empower themselves, they only think of their own interests. To me, it's in their own interest to have a hand in the organisations, to know what we are doing, so that they can watch out and not lose their power at a given moment. I think that's it, that they're afraid of our getting ahead, of being pushed aside by us some day. (Peasant leader)

Even new forms of imperialism may be welcome and may be seen as subverted to women's own ends (see Citlali's words, p. 1). These two visions of the same power relationship display the duality of power and resistance, the constraints and opportunities experienced by rural women working with Mexican and foreign 'donors'. The second is particularly controversial, seeming to legitimate in this case what we often see as an unacceptable use of 'power over' by donors, to impose behaviour on poor women that donor agencies often cannot achieve by other means.

The family The Indian women at Tapalehui had most to say about the family, although there were clearly echoes for others. In Indian communities, marriages used to be arranged by the parents.

> Almost everything is changing now. The girl and her boyfriend take the decision, and she doesn't tell her father anything. Before, her father decided, and the girl's hand was asked in marriage two or three years before the wedding. Once a week, or once a fortnight, her future father-in-law would bring messages for the bride and give them to her father. The girl didn't even know her husband to be, she had no idea whom she was going to marry! They met on the way to the registry office to register the marriage. But nowadays the girls decide themselves. So I think that the girl has been empowered. (Peasant leader)

For all the talk of change, it does not reach everyone. Indian women, as I know from my own work, are very vulnerable over health care. In villages far from the towns, especially where women speak no Spanish, they have almost no access to health services because they are afraid to go to the clinic or the doctor's on their own. They depend on their husband's permission or on his willingness to take them. Sometimes it is even the husband who goes to the doctor and explains his wife's illness without her being there, so that she has no chance to explain things to the doctor herself. Women's fear of doctors (who are usually men) is one reason for their refusal to go to hospital. Their feelings come from distrust, ignorance and embarrassment at having to bare their bodies before a man not their husband.

> She went to the doctor, not feeling well, and the doctor said, 'Come in and take your clothes off.' So she asked herself, 'What is this man going to do to me?' and the doctor said, 'Right, now lie down here,' and the woman went and grabbed her clothes and said, 'I'm out of here, I know what this man wants to do to me.' This woman was very frightened because no one had ever told her about this, you know? And when she got back to her village, she told the other women, 'You'd better not go and see that doctor.' And they said 'Really?' 'Yes.' 'Oh dear, that's why I never go to the doctor.' (Peasant leader)

The insensitivity of some doctors working in places where most people are Indian peasants to women's reluctance to let a man other than their husband see them undressed, and the ignorance among peasants about what doctors do, explain why only a small number of women consult rural doctors.

Women's diets are known to be another source of inequality. 'Well, what I've seen in my family, my brothers – we made the meals, my brothers ate more than me. Yes, they eat more. That's why women are weaker' (Peasant leader).

Childbearing is very important among Indians. Women who do not get pregnant are insulted, threatened and beaten by their husbands, because if a couple is childless the woman is seen as guilty. There is no recognition that men can be infertile.

> Yes, he beats her, he tells her, 'You're no good, you're useless as a woman.' Or he sees other women. 'See, I had children with the other woman, get out of here,' and when he starts kicking her around, well, it really is a problem, it is. (Peasant leader)

Laws of inheritance used to be different, although changes in the national law (p. 132) have made them more similar.

> My father owned over eight hectares of land, apart from his share in the village land. So, we are three sisters and only one brother, and my brother promised to leave everything to my mother while she was alive. He said he'd take care of her, not us, because we inherited nothing. Even my nephew got the house I helped my parents build ... Now my brother has the land ... but

he can't stand my mother and even took away the tiny part of the plot that was still hers to plant. So I ask my mother, 'Now what?' But my mother only says, 'But he's a man, he's my son.' (Peasant leader)

'He's a man' and 'He's my son' are two good reasons for a mother to give up what is rightfully hers. In this case, 'power over' has been internalised so deeply that the victim herself is convinced that this is the way things should be done, and sees no reason to rebel.

Change has come in Indian and Spanish-speaking villages as women begin to bring their children up differently, but the Spanish-speaking women had more to say about this.

Like, starting to tell our daughters they can do the same things. That if their boyfriends are demanding something they [our daughters] have the power to make a decision. I have a fifteen-year-old daughter and already I tell her, 'If you think your boyfriend is demanding and wants to order you about, you don't have to accept that. You're the one who has to decide.' (Adviser)

At the same time, women looking for a new kind of family can often not help feeling guilty, because they are breaking with and questioning a scheme of things accepted by society.

The family as it used to be is changing, but we haven't yet understood that it's changing. So we, the women, feel bad when we say, 'My husband is treating me so badly, he's holding me back so much, that I'd better leave. I like the organisation more, it's giving me more.' So that makes us feel bad, because we're breaking away from our family, you know? (Adviser)

'Power over' between individuals

Women and men In community action, 'power over', resistance and the desire for 'power over' are very clear.

In my community, in the mountains, women never participated and no one bothered about us. The men always argued when women went to a meeting about community land, or the school, or to any kind of meeting. But now we too have the courage to speak out. Because several women go to meetings, we now talk back. Because before, the first thing they used to say to us was, 'I'll bet you women aren't going to use your *machete*' [an agricultural tool]; they mean, you aren't going to do any work, 'All you come here to do is talk.' They shouted at us, you see. But we talked back. (Peasant leader)

I'd say that we should speak out at meetings and tell them we want that power. Because we, the women, would like the same thing they have, to feel the power of giving orders. [You have to] talk to them first and then establish equality in power. (Peasant leader)

Wife and husband In the group of more rural women at Tapalehui, much was said about the pressure a husband may bring to bear on his wife when she wants to go out of the house to the organisation, or when he, on his own, decides to have another child, or when she needs his permission to do what she wants with her own belongings or her own life. 'In the village where I used to work, girls of thirteen or fifteen had children, but their husbands had already decided they would only have two. The decision was his' (Adviser). The academics supported this: 'You always need your husband's consent, you know? Even the institutions require it: they demand the signature of "a responsible party" and that party is your husband' (Academic).

The peasant women spoke of the husband's 'power over' his wife:

Before, Indian and peasant women never joined in and were never allowed to get together with the other women members. I mean, because their husbands, their partners, wouldn't let them, not even when there were meetings in each community, in their own village, would they let them come. (Peasant leader)

When a man does let his wife join in, he usually requires her to carry out all her duties as wife and mother first:

He didn't approve. I mean, I wanted to be with the other women and do things with them. I loved joining in, and teaching them a little of what I knew about the mill [for corn for *tortillas*]. At last, he agreed, so he said, 'OK, so long as you don't let me down.' I mean, his mind then wasn't what it is now, his mind was full of things, of bad ideas. He said yes, but that I should respect him, because when women started to go out like that, often they forgot all about their husband and children. (Peasant leader)

Some women had to give up important roles in the organisation because of their husbands' bullying, when they began to fear their wives would achieve more than they. 'So then, the woman who kept the books and was in charge of the organisation's finances started to get into trouble with her husband … Her husband made life so difficult for her that in the end she had to give up the organisation' (Peasant leader). Positions of power are risky for women, because they get criticised by husband, family and community: they have to pay a high price for their empowerment.

Academics and organisations 'Power over' is likely to be present when women academics study peasant women's groups or their projects, as all parties at Tapalehui were well aware.

> Some researchers only come and do their research and then never come back, which I feel is bad. There should be an agreement with these researchers, that they can do their research and then send us a copy when they write it up, their results, because it's worth it. This matters to us because it would help us improve our organisation which is often worth more to us than money. I feel that would only be fair. (Peasant leader)

But getting academics to comply depends very much on 'how far the organisation has got, its maturity and the capacity it has to build relationships with outsiders' (Adviser). When the groups are weak, these relations can be a problem, as when the groups:

> ... don't like what they want to study ... because they don't give any information back ... that's where the mistrust comes from ... [For example, in *Oaxaca*] an academic wanted to write up all the information about all the groups, and we felt that she wanted to make use of our work, and we were only going to do the donkey work. [This made us] blow up. We've got far enough to learn from failures and frauds. Donkeys aren't temperamental unless you teach them to be. Relationships between academics and NGOs must be laid down very clearly in future. (Adviser)

Advisers and grassroots women   It is hard to draw lines in this relationship, because the advisers' work is so closely related to the grassroots. Here, personal and emotional factors co-exist with commitment, but also with dependence and manipulation.

> All this sets up friendly relations between advisers and women, and a certain dependence develops. But I feel there are different kinds [of dependence] involving everything from emotion to resources. At the beginning, the advisers devote themselves to getting money, until, little by little, a gap appears between adviser and organisation. At the beginning, they see you as a superwoman, because you have to be all kinds of things, lawyer, secretary, psychologist. It's too much work for us. (Adviser)

> In many cases, we risk getting in the way of women's building the capacity to help themselves. Mutual dependence just has to be got rid of, because women come to depend on advisers. (Adviser)

To weaken this power of advisers over members of the organisations, one strategy suggested was to define the role of the adviser very clearly:

> When the identity [place or role] of the adviser is not clear, dependence

follows and they end up making excuses all the time. 'OK, the women already know that, but now they have to learn this.' Then their affection and friendship for the women get muddled in, they don't know how to cope and wrong things get done. (Adviser)

When advisers limit their personal involvement, there are new risks, related to the power of knowledge:

Their desire is for women to become more independent and to handle their own resources. The advisers made the women responsible for all sorts of things, like being in charge of their income-generating projects, of the management, of the accounts. In the end it was a real mess, because the women didn't have the experience or the skills to manage the projects, so the advisers had to come back in. (Adviser)

The peasant women are keen to promote autonomy:

We don't want them to depend on the adviser, to see her as a god, on the contrary. We want the women to handle their own affairs, not depend on the advisers. That's what the leadership programme is for, to make them more independent. But we also don't want to limit this to just one area, but for it to spread and for other women to get this kind of training. (Peasant leader)

When we'd only just got organised, advisers helped us, but now we don't have advisers any more, we do practically everything. And we can. We decided long ago, because when we had them [advisers] they used to get in the way, because we'd suggest something and they'd say it was impossible. They always wanted a say in what we were going to do. Later, we've had problems even when we only want advice on one thing. Even if they are only here for a month, they want to stick their noses into everything. They try to take the decisions for us. (Peasant leader)

At Tapalehui, dependence on advisers was explained as a continuation of other dependence by women, on their husbands, their children and on other authorities like the government's welfare programme. Although the peasant women do admit that they need some advice, they say that ground rules such as mutual respect, and an agreement on the tasks to be done and over what period, must be laid down in advance.

Peasant leaders and grassroots women The peasant leaders stand out in their organisations, and have access to resources and information that other women do not, which gives them 'power over'. The organisations need the right strategies to train people in working together and handling disputes.

If the knowledge isn't shared by everyone, what happens is that the president gets control of the budget and keeps it for herself. But what we did was to balance the cash among us all, so everyone knew about it, and we got into fights, really bad fights. It isn't that easy, there's lots of trouble with these things, because the women don't realise how much receipts matter. They often lose them, or they agree something with other people with the community and then lose the documents, or a woman gets into a fight and then takes all the group's papers and never gives them back. (Peasant leader)

The fact that a woman is a leader doesn't automatically mean that she'll try to help other women ... Some men are awake [to our needs], while some women use power to oppress. The simple fact that someone is a woman doesn't necessarily make the system democratic. (Adviser)

When the men realised that the women's suggestion was getting a lot of attention, they got really scared and banded together. When this woman from our group got on an executive committee, when that executive committee took power, the woman said she knew many didn't like her being there and she was going to begin blazing the trail and other women would follow her. And, well, she's in a very difficult position, she's been boycotted, but she's very clear that she represents women and she's held to that vision of solidarity with women. (Peasant leader)

'Power over' inside peasant women Women leaders are in a difficult position. Their personal fears, lack of self-esteem and of support from their family, their insecurity and powerlessness to change things make it hard for them to be active, or to empower themselves. Peasant women spoke of these fears and the efforts they have made to overcome them:

I'd ask myself what I'd have to change in us, because if we are not sure of what we want – see, things can change, because they actually have changed, you know – but if I don't take responsibility for what I want, there won't be any power, we won't get any power, even if things do change. (Peasant leader)

On the inside – at least, this is how I feel – on the inside I'm still scared. Oh, I don't know how to say it, but sometimes you say, how am I going to break this barrier, this chain? And sometimes it is very hard for us to break ... We advance very slowly, but not enough to break it yet. (Peasant leader)

What are we going to do, personally, to enable us to get these powers we want? But we have to change too, and there are costs and losses we often don't want to accept and that hurt us badly. (Peasant leader)

This last quote has three key phrases in self-empowerment: *we want power*, *we have to change* and *there are costs and losses*.

Responses to 'Power over'

Peasant and academic women between 'power over' and empowerment Everyone at Tapalehui talked about experiences of 'power over', but academics and advisers had different approaches from the peasant leaders. Here, I want to give my personal opinion, because I think that the greater anguish expressed by the more academic, more formally educated group was related to their greater awareness of inequalities in relations between women and men. Some of my co-authors might say that the difference is rather in expectations, that the academics expect more and are more frustrated when they fail to achieve it, but to me their greater awareness leads to more consciousness of the obstacles and greater anguish, because a better world seems more difficult to achieve. We are all agreed that discussions in the 'more academic' group at Tapalehui were often more anguished than those in the 'more rural' group.

We all agree that the peasant women did not express anguish and dissatisfaction as much as the academics and advisers at Tapalehui. It is my opinion that peasant women do not experience them as much, that they identify 'power over' but do not perceive it or feel it as intensely. The ways in which peasant women evade this power are more immediate and concrete, and confined to daily events. They set more limited goals and have the satisfaction of reaching them. Perhaps this is why they feel less frustrated.

The academics and advisers, on the other hand, devote themselves to gender and have read widely, talked to many people and written about their experiences, through all of which they develop a very critical vision of society and of relations between men and women. In my view, they see the profiles of the 'new woman' and 'new man' more clearly, and the models they propose are further removed from tradition. For peasant women, the reality they live as women is closer to the traditional model. They have not, in my view, developed the same critical awareness of tradition. For them, the distance between the traditional woman and their 'new woman' is less than for the academics. (Not all my co-authors would agree.) I think that their less critical perception of reality protects them to a degree from the anguish and frustration to be heard from the academics and some advisers.

'Power over', power as resistance, and change 'Power over' and revolt cannot be separated. At Tapalehui, for peasant women, advisers and academics, 'power over' was a form of domination and repression. Their words still tell of a closely related power, that of resistance (Joan Scott 1986), which can sometimes change and in time transform 'power over'. When power structures really inhibit change, there are high costs at the personal, family, community and organisation levels if the change is forced.

The balance between 'power over' and the power of resistance is difficult to strike, but the will exists for change and to find ways to achieve the 'power to', 'power with' and 'power from within'. We are on the way to find the keys that will open the way to our utopia, to the advances in self-empowerment we seek for peasant women, for ourselves and for the women of the world.

Summary of Chapter Seven

Three forms of 'power over' were discussed at Tapalehui, existing always in power relations:

- the power of institutions over individuals;
- the power of individuals over others; and
- the tyranny we each exercise over ourselves.

The academic women have by far the most to say about 'power over' and express the most distress about it. They are deeply conscious of the obstacles faced by the rural women in the face of donor power, by women in politics who seek change and by themselves in universities, seeking the truth. All are seeking to change the world in ways unacceptable to powerful institutions. As women, all also face the 'power over' in their daily lives, public and private, with other individuals, colleagues, partners, families. For most, the home is the most difficult place in which to change the 'power over', which again annoys the academics even more. Even in work with women's groups, problems can arise between academics and advisers, advisers and change-agents, change-agents and peasant women: lines of command are difficult to escape. The academics are particularly conscious of their failure to overcome the tyranny we exercise over ourselves; we can create our own 'glass ceiling' or 'Cinderella complex'. For all, however, the will to change is there and hope for the future is real.

Notes

1. See Chapter One, Note 1 for our use of the word 'Indian'.

2. *Peasant leader* will include all the peasant women, including change-agents and advisers elected from among the members.

3. This tendency is worldwide. See Hulme and Mosley 1996.

4. Burín 1996. The glass ceiling may also, of course, be created purely by others.

8

Levels of Power: from the Person to the World

Emma Zapata

Dimensions of Power

The word *empowerment* is used to mean so many things (Chapter Two). For the World Bank, to be empowered is to get things done, from financial operations to tiny micro-enterprises which could be just one woman who cannot even afford to set up a street stall but walks along the street selling titbits she has cooked that day. The World Bank does not question the economic or personal relations involved or how power is exercised. For George Bush and Margaret Thatcher, the word refers to privatisation and lower taxes, claimed to 'empower' the poor to choose and pay for their own health and education. For women in India there is a strong link between empowerment and 'self-employment'. For Naila Kabeer (1997) the concept comes from the grassroots, in poor countries and rich. While some NGOs support empowerment, some restrict it. DAWN (see pp. 20–21) sees NGOs as possible supporters for groups in search of change. For Srilatha Batliwala (1993) empowerment is a slow process, hard to measure or to establish evidence of. She suggests that work to support empowerment with a new group should begin with concrete action such as specific projects chosen by the group, at the same time as more abstract work, say in self-esteem and leadership. Public policy, as a support to the empowerment process, must develop new approaches from 'development'; it must enable women themselves to control the process. Empowerment can only be self-empowerment, but only a part of empowerment is personal. Other conditions must be met, in other spaces and at other levels, so that together they support the process. Srilatha Batliwala also identifies the search for empowerment with grassroots feminism, struggling to go further than Women in Development (Chapter Two).

It was Jo Rowlands's ideas that led us to read others on empowerment, and so to Tapalehui, where we talked of self-empowerment. There, all agreed with Naila Kabeer and with Jo that empowerment comes from no external agent, but is rather a process that begins within the person and enables her to value herself, change herself, grow and reach more autonomy. We give most emphasis to the power from within. Outsiders such as advisers and NGOs can support the process but not empower the person.

At Tapalehui, we all came from specific regional contexts with contrasting gender relations under which women build different personal identities. Here, we have listened to the voices of the peasant and Indian women, for it is they who live and feel the power. We have tried to be as open, as transparent as possible, to use their words not to prove our own points but to show the changes through which they have lived.[1] Our concern is to be as inclusive as possible, to reconstruct our understanding from the bottom up and express a new vision.

> If women's personal narratives both present and interpret the impact of gender roles on women's lives, they are especially suitable documents for illuminating several aspects of gender relations: the construction of a gendered self-identity, the relationship between the individual and society in the creation and the perpetuation of gender norms, and the dynamics of power relations between women and men. (Personal Narratives Group 1989: 5)

I want to celebrate not our project but the women's achievements. The peasant women at Tapalehui had tremendous experience and had already achieved so much; they have made themselves dynamic, free to travel, creative, proactive. As they said, when they 'get out of the house', they learn, grow, advance, rarely stop on the way or, if they do, only in order to continue the journey. They are no longer willing to be ignored, they want to be in the front line, not suffering and not passive. They want to enjoy life, have fun, break with tradition. They want not only 'to act but also to get access to resources. At the personal level, to control not only their bodies and their lives but resources ... To build together a strategy to defeat oppression' (Lucía, adviser on credit). These groups build and establish new identities in a world shattered by economic crises and political conflicts. They offer a mosaic, rich in cultural diversity which comes through in action, in planning and carrying things through, organising, learning, expressing themselves while they note their differences and seek to resolve conflicts among themselves. Later in the chapter I want to explore the spaces in which different kinds of women have power, as individuals, and may be able to influence relationships.

Power cannot be studied as an abstraction or an isolated event. Self-empowerment, the capacity for power, is a complex process, as the woman can change, go back, halt on the way, reflect, look behind, think and go on. In this chapter, I shall explore different environments in which women live power, in levels to which they have access and where they have the opportunity to empower themselves. I do not think that there is a moment of being 'empowered enough'; on the contrary, people must always go forward, grow, develop. Not all the women and organisations we visited or who came to Tapalehui are the same, or engaged in the same empowerment process. They have different perspectives on the same issue, and the results of their decisions will be different.

Power as such does not exist (pp. 129–30), only relations of power, sometimes apparent in subversion, acceptance or resistance. As the last chapter showed, women at Tapalehui showed the rebellious face of freedom. Above all, they exposed the tensions created by the 'power over' that holds them back. But tension turns into delight at the 'power to', the 'power with' where they build up their strength and capacities with others, and the 'power from within' that enables them to go out, go beyond 'power over'. This chapter will explore how these different aspects of power come together in different dimensions (Rowlands 1997a):

- personal power, as women develop a sense of confidence and ability and overcome internalised oppression;
- relational power, or power in relationships, as women improve their abilities to negotiate and influence the nature of a relationship;
- group power, where women work together for goals they could not achieve alone.

Personal Power

At Tapalehui, women's talk of their personal development tended to confirm that of the PAEM women (p. 32) (see Rowlands 1997a: 112), reflecting some similarities between Mexican and Honduran society. In all cases, 'The process of empowerment is both experienced as a feeling of personal change and development, and also manifested, or demonstrated, in changed behaviour' (Jo Rowlands 1997a: 114). In Honduras, women's understanding of empowerment was explored systematically, while at Tapalehui we were learning from extensive discussion, so that we can only make loose comparisons, but the language at Tapalehui shows strong similarities to the PAEM experience. For the PAEM women, personal empowerment was about increased abilities: to formulate and express ideas and opinions, to participate in and influence new spaces, to learn, analyse and act, to organise their own time and to obtain/control resources, along with an increased sense that things are possible. I feel that all these are recognisable in earlier chapters of this book.

Peasant women at Tapalehui say that they are not the same as they were 'before getting out of the house'. They talk of movement and growth against being shut in and stagnating. They are no longer willing to accept suffering as natural. Their vision of women is dynamic, as 'a flood of events, a peak of wisdom' (Teresa, elected adviser, *Sonora*). They can defy fear, pull away from it, leap barriers, break chains, seek other spaces. They can dream and fly far away. They reject the traditional model of the submissive woman, who suffers her husband's adultery in silence; they demand new ways of thinking. Each is aware of her own reality. They can express what they want, what they dream of and what they hope for themselves and their children. This is how they put it:

> A teenage peasant girl can want to be a dancer too, can't she? Or a composer, or a musician, or painter, or an astronaut. What do I know about it? My daughter, for instance, really made me laugh, because we were on the bus and she suddenly said, 'When I grow up, I want to be a dancer.' Later, she told me, 'I want to work with cows,' and 'I want to be an astronaut.' But I say that any woman in the world can have these desires. So, why shut ourselves in, and say, 'No, peasant women just want to raise better crops' or 'have a better stove to cook on'. It's impossible. I think a peasant woman can want to do things and can want to have unlimited powers. (Carmen, elected adviser, *Sonora*)

The peasant women are critical of their cultures, because they want to construct their own identities, to reject what they find oppressive and sustain what they value, destroy what undermines them, support what strengthens them. They do not use the word 'oppression', but they express it; in the house they feel trapped, not only because they are physically enclosed inside the house, but because they are in the house in order to be at the beck and call of the family. Yet they fear breaking with the family, although they begin to recognise that this is not their fault alone when it happens. Some live these changes as achievements while for others the changes mean suffering, although, paradoxically, these women reject this suffering.

The peasant women see themselves as being supported in personal empowerment by their longing to learn more and more, their acceptance of responsibility to themselves and to their community, their new value as women, their democratic, egalitarian groups, their joint decision-making, their training as change-agents, the opportunity to learn by shadowing the work of others and the capacity for self-evaluation. The PAEM women gave a list of conditions 'encouraging' personal empowerment which is different, yet again very familiar from Tapalehui: activity outside the home, being part of a group and joining in its activities, ending isolation, travelling, wider friendships, time for themselves, support, sharing problems and literacy (which gives access to even wider groups). This is how women at Tapalehui talked of building 'the power from within' in Chapter Two, 'getting out of the house and joining the organisation', a joint process by which women take the power to move out of convention, and build it by working with others and developing new powers to do. When I think about the conditions that make self-empowerment, especially as regards 'the power with', more difficult, I believe that they are the *macho*, male-dominated culture which keeps them invisible, envy, overwork, poverty, lack of training, poor access to community decision-making, conflict and the loss of resources.

The academic women, on the other hand, claim the powers to learn, understand and analyse, and the power over their own sexuality (this last is also a claim of several advisers and of the *Sonora* peasant women). Generally, academic women have the power to do and to speak, but within themselves some recognise little empowerment since they have accepted the chance to be responsible for others and to make mistakes. To change themselves and be free is to choose their own paths. Like the peasant women, they have an ideal of marriage that cannot be fulfilled. And not only can they not find their ideal partner, but some men who appeal to them reject them because their academic achievements are seen as threatening.

Power in Relationships

Peasant women Relational power, or the power to change relationships in a direction they want, is a vital area for women. The peasant women talk about the changes they have made in the home, in relationships between generations, between change-agents and grassroots women, among the women in the organisations and with other organisations. They share ideas with other women and with groups far away. They convince themselves that they are able to do, to meet, to talk, enjoy, feel pleasure or, as Sonia Álvarez *et al.* write, 'They construct or configure new interpersonal, interorganizational and political-cultural linkages with other movements as well as with a multiplicity of cultural and institutional actors and spaces' (1998: 15). And they set limits:

> And they decided they didn't want to join a mixed [gender] organisation, they weren't interested, because they wanted to grow, to decide about their own lives, about their organisation, able to build a group for themselves. (Ana, adviser, *Chiapas*)

We have said that women in Mexico and Honduras find that the relationship they find it most difficult to change is that with their partner. They get the children to help more in the house and change how they are bringing them up, but the husband remains a problem. They transform themselves, break with daily routine, get out of the house, go to the organisation, manage their own time, make time to learn in workshops where they discuss the economy, politics and cultural icons that perpetuate negative attitudes towards women, but may get no change at home.

Some have made real advances with their partners:

> My relationship with my husband has enriched me greatly. There are moments of disagreement, but commitment carries you forward. I remember once, about a year go, getting back from a two- or three-day workshop, and a man I worked with, but who didn't get on with my husband, offered me a ride home. I got in tired out, and my partner made a real drama out of it which just flattened me. In the end I said, 'Look, if you're expecting me to say I'm sorry, I'm not going to, because I've nothing to be sorry for.' And then he thought, and changed his attitude. (Xochitl, Mixe change-agent, *Oaxaca*)

But more often the relationship proves the most intractable of all, as we have seen in Chapter Seven.

Change-agents and advisers   Change-agents and advisers lack an international association but, as we have seen, have created the National Network of Advisers Working with Rural Women. Personally, they have been able to develop their work into a profession, to build up their own skills and to do research (in which many have learned not to regard people as objects, but as subjects). They use meetings to network and to extend and strengthen themselves. One area in which they have particularly developed their creativity is in designing and running workshops, courses and role-plays, all linked to the central understanding of how traditional values may be barriers or, with critical awareness, may dynamise change. Their practice with grassroots women makes them more able to subvert, transform, raise consciousness, discuss, criticise. This group understands that their work must be on many fronts and at many levels, from social structures to daily life and interpersonal relations.

> Hence the strategies aimed at *concientizacion*[2] – cultural-political interventions such as promoting workshops and courses on gender power relations, addressing sexual discrimination in the workplace, teaching reproductive health, and helping participants in popular women's organisations who faced domestic violence – were also deemed crucial to the struggle against women's oppression. (Sonia Álvarez 1998: 228)

They make their personal changes very much in relation to the group:

> I feel anything which means a change of thinking or of tradition is always a challenge. The communities where we work are traditional, *macho* [male-dominated] ... It is a challenge to begin working on things like that with the

women. Changes in thinking are very slow, they happen slowly, over the years ... For the advisers too it is a challenge, to work on new issues. (Elena, adviser and academic, *Hidalgo*)

I don't agree that we, the advisers, should now start punishing ourselves. I agree that the work of adviser and organisation should be separate. I feel that you yourself begin to withdraw, because there comes a time when your life isn't your own, it belongs to everyone but you do have to protect yourself. I believe this separation has to be slow. (Ana, paid adviser, *Chiapas*)

Relationships between organisations and advisers (women or men) are not always transparent or easy. The peasant and Indian women want to meet advisers on equal terms, with mutual respect. Anyone trying to support self-empowerment has to work on and accept the process in themselves as well as in the organisation. The process of empowerment needs to be respected and understood by both parties.

Academics In this diverse group at Tapalehui, in a very friendly atmosphere, the academics argued that their problems, though different, were not less serious. As we saw in Chapter Six, the peasant women are more pragmatic and delight in their achievements while the academics hardly recognise their own successes and always want more. The academics are supercritical of the obstacles which confront them and the utopia they want to reach. They say that they want power, not a male, hierarchical model of power, but a shared power that will let them fulfil themselves, the power to decide, the power to do.

It is postmodern theory that has emphasised relations and concepts of power. Academics are involved in institutions that are real arenas of unequal power in daily life that comes out in conflict, envy, competition and resentment. We may understand such

micropolitics as 'an organizational underworld in which we all participate'. Micropolitics is about influence, networks, coalitions, political and personal strategies to effect or resist change. It involves rumor, gossip, sarcasm, humor, denial, 'throwaway remarks', alliance-building. (David Morley and Kevin Robins 1995: 175)

The outcome for academics may be seen in anxiety, stress and fear. They do not feel that, as feminists, they are succeeding in academia in what they want to achieve. Although they speak highly of the place of feminism in relationships that they have been able to build, they return always to how much further they want to go.

As for their work with women, the academics speak of it with delight and satisfaction yet feel that the ethical commitment can work against them, as overwork becomes unavoidable and they become enslaved to their commitments, unquestioning because the cause is good. Like the peasant women, they have built their identities through living for others, not for themselves. They want to be missionaries, to work for other women and men. Ana (paid adviser, *Chiapas*) said, 'Yes, it's good, but we also exist as separate individuals ... and what happens is that we can solve the problems of others and forget our own ... ' As Marcela Lagarde says, 'We live by supporting others' (1997: 11). The work of the academics at Tapalehui is like sowing seeds. They must also develop themselves and their own awareness, design ways of working and constantly improve their service to peasant women. In a sense, they feel that society sees women only as labourers whereas some, including those at Tapalehui, believe that women can also transform and create.

In academics' close relationships, progress has also been limited and again the expectations of the academics are high. Some have been able to get their partners to help about the house, and although two suffered violence from their partners, they did manage to end it. The academic women unpack the problems of 'power over' far more than other groups (Chapter Seven) and Felipa (academic and adviser, *Hidalgo*) told how 'My daughters and I are caught up in this [reproduction of oppressive structures]. And men are too, in their role as unconscious oppressors and sometimes as very aware and self-interested oppressors.'

Individual women and national and international power   Some women at Tapalehui had been able to join in international events. Peasant women and advisers from *Sonora*, *Oaxaca* and *Puebla North* had been abroad to international congresses on themes of direct concern to them such as food and sustainability. National events are easier to get to, and several are active in the National Indigenous (Indian) Congress. Teresa has been elected to the state parliament, others from *Sonora* to state and municipal posts, Citlali and others to community posts; a *Veracruz* change-agent is an elected member of the governing party in the state of Veracruz. New attitudes have arisen from these changes:

> [In] the women who have emerged as leaders, who have joined with other women, who come to the workshops and all that, you can feel the change in the way the awareness is passed on, not just the knowledge they have acquired ... but the drive to get out. Citlali's case is very obvious. She got out of her community, and now she's on the top committee there. Since then, she has had many problems and restrictions, but she has got across to the women of her village a new way of being active, even in the community itself. So other women also want to get out, also want to know and are

behaving differently. They want to be a part of the world. (Xochitl, Mixe change-agent, *Oaxaca*)

These women raise the question of how to enter modernity and still be Indians.

From their homes, all these women can build regional networks. They speak of politics and want to learn more about things that affect or simply interest them. They get local change going. In the community, they have a presence, an image, and join in decisions over communal land, which is new. They are present and active in village meetings over the management of public services.

Academics, of course, have much better access to national and international events, but the events tend to be academic conferences with all their hierarchies and conventions. Perhaps they give access to greater power in academia, but they open little opportunity to change relationships within or outside universities.

Group Power

Group power in the local community In their communities, women's groups co-operate to solve some of the problems they share, get involved in all sorts of activities and think up creative projects. One group has a mobile washing machine which is passed on from one home to the next. Another owns and manages a hotel in a tourist area on the basis of a project put forward by the group. Sales of ice and retailing of meat are among the activities of another group. Domestic violence is no longer considered normal and some communities have got it under control. These women know their rights, 'which worries the men a lot, because then they have to admit that the women have rights' (Carmen, elected adviser, *Sonora*).

> If projects are to take gender into account, then obviously they're meant to change power structures ... not to use power against others, in a repressive way, but to use the power to control your own life and resources. The simple fact of having power over resources gives the women a power they didn't have before. (Ana, paid adviser, *Chiapas*)

In their university communities, the academics are only just beginning to learn to understand their own micropolitics, in which their relationships are again

> about power and how people use it to influence others and to protect themselves. It is about conflict and how people compete with each other to get what they want. It is about co-operation and how people build support among themselves to achieve their ends. (David Morley and Kevin Roberts 1995: 174)

Although they have worked hard to co-operate and build support, they are only now becoming aware of the obstacles and beginning to seek a better understanding of the theory. To the British authors, these groups of academic women are both impressive and a delight to visit; to the Mexicans, the groups fall short of what is desired. It may be that the academics expressed more distress than the peasant women at Tapalehui because the peasant women use their groups as an outlet while the academic women do not allow themselves the time or the trust to use their groups in this way. The peasant women may use the 'power with' for mutual support in a way the academic women do not, and set more achievable goals.

Group power at the regional level The peasant women's organisations all seek involvement at the regional level, although some naturally have more influence. This is very welcome. 'I valued being there [because] it gave [me] the chance to understand the problems I've met in an elected, political post' (Carmen, elected adviser, *Sonora*). All the groups have thought up novel forms of organisation to create new ways of working: joint leadership, rotating leadership, division of responsibilities, individual projects under group management, horizontal accountability, power sharing and others. They have also asked the academics how to organise their records and memories of their years of experience for future use.

Puebla North, *Sonora* and *Veracruz* are strong, dynamic organisations with a regional presence. *Puebla North* and *Sonora* (Chapter Five) originally belonged to larger 'mixed' organisations, but decided to form women's groups because they felt that the men's power was holding them back; they also wanted not only to manage their own resources but to extend their regional influence. All have high regional profiles.

The government's neoliberal policies imply a big reduction in the numbers of peasants through the loss of land and jobs, but these women are determined to resist and have the capacity to do it. In the face of economic crisis and rapid change, they run projects which above all are not imposed from outside but designed by peasant women through their own participative assessment and critical evaluation of their needs. Initiative is being taken by the grassroots women who also evaluate their activities and work. They have transformed concepts of productivity and profitability, using social profitability (Alemán 1997) and gender profitability.[3] They not only manage their projects well but can present their needs to secure funding. Their projects are extremely diverse: public and social services, savings-and-loans associations, food supply, subsistence farming, production and sale of handicrafts, nutrition, housing, cattle, poultry and sheep, piggeries, photocopying and courier services (Chapter Six). They have claimed and cultivated land. Women realise that they and the young now contribute more than half the family income: the world has changed and they value the opportunities despite the new problems. Although the projects increase their workload, peasant women value them for the skills they have acquired, in areas they would never have dreamed of: management, computers, group learning, negotiation, sharing experiences, achieving independence.

For them, 'income-generating projects' become opportunities to learn about gender and social and technical matters. They run the projects so that each and every aspect involves growth and learning. 'For me, it's crucial that it's the women themselves who take the process forward and shake off dependence on outside bodies' (Jo, British academic). On our visits as part of this project, we saw enormously interesting, truly excellent results in groups that rely on themselves and elect their own leaders.

At Tapalehui, the rural women put forward solutions such as organisation, co-operation and mutual support rather than the individualism promoted by neoliberalism. Rather than accept the homogenisation encouraged by globalisation, they promote and respect a diversity of ways of organising in fragmented spaces. For them, participation should be an active, unrestricted process which should take more women into community, municipal and regional action. Because peasant women have been able to learn new things, make new contacts and take new action, their organisations hold many meanings for them. The opportunities are not only to meet basic needs, but for cultural growth and discussion of shared problems. Linaloe (Nahuatl-speaking change-agent, *Puebla North*) acts as a training specialist at the regional level.

These are the strategies observed by Álvarez (1998: 297) in the new Latin American feminist movement translating María Luiza Heilbron and Angelica Arruda:

> ... imbued by such values, manifest, for example, in the decentralization of the movement and its autonomy *vis-à-vis* other actors. Such decentralization expressed itself in the debates about representation, direct and equitable participation, non-monopoly of the spoken word or of information, in the rotation of occasional tasks and responsibilities, the non-specialization of functions, the non-delegation of power. In sum, organizational horizontalism was extolled as the perfect incarnation of the organizational principles of radical democracy.

Group power at national and international levels At the national level, organisations such as those represented at Tapalehui achieve individual or joint representation through processes in which they engage as groups. Their search for resources for training and income-generation gets them involved with national and international funding agencies. The power of these is felt by the grassroots women in two ways, as an imposition and as a welcome force for change. Peasant women have the critical capacity to analyse 'donors', deciding which best suit their ends in ways of working, in the amounts they lend or give, in their objectives, their requirements and the resources available to women's groups. Peasant women know which donors seek to strengthen the place of women in organisations, and they turn to these. They have succeeded in writing proposals, negotiating, setting conditions; they carry through the projects they want. *Sonora* suggested and designed a training programme on gender relations and another to discuss themes constantly heard but little understood, such as globalisation, the North American Free Trade Area, devolution, sustainability. They also suggested a workshop for their partners: unless their partners change, they will continue to be a cause of worry and distress.

In the international arena, the relationship with donors lies within what Sonia Álvarez (1998) has called the transnationalisation of feminism (Chapter Three). NGOs have moved into niches left empty by the withdrawal of the state. The relationship between peasant and Indian women and the NGOs is double-edged, for 'NGOs can indeed be an effective fragmented, decentered, political subject in a postmodern world, but the cost of flexibility, pragmatism and fragmentation may well be reformism: their capability to promote radical change may weaken' (Gustavo Lins Ribeiro 1998: 17).

In Mexico, these women's groups have a place that gives them some power in the Network of Rural Change-Agents and Advisers, in the proposal to create a Platform of Action for Rural and Peasant Women (*Puebla North* and *South*), in *Sonora*'s National Plan for Women and in *Sonora*'s creation of the National Network for Practical Co-operation among Institutions supporting Rural Women. Some change-agents and elected advisers contributed to the design of the Ministry of Agriculture's[4] Programme for Rural Women. *Jalisco* and *Sonora* have been active and creative in conceiving, forming and contributing to organisations of national scope.

All the groups lack power at the national level to transform society or convince it of the need for change. But the power they know they have is the power to understand, and to know what they can achieve on the basis of what they have done so far. They have managed to get out of the house, join other women and together demand a place in decisions by the community, the country and international organisations.

Mexico's plans for 'development' have been almost tangential to women, and especially to peasant and indigenous women, failing to give them any real power. Although included along with men in plans for education and health, women have been regarded as reproducers, marginal to economic and political development. In rural areas, opportunities for training and credit have traditionally gone to men. For instance, for the 1975 United Nations Women's Conference in Mexico, the government created a scheme to make land available specifically to women, under the Land Reform Programme. In each Land Reform community, land is held by farmers from the community (see p. 132 for the changes of 1991, particularly in inheritance). Under the 1970s scheme, each such community has a plot of land 'for the women', equal in size to the other plots, each of which was to support a family. To get this one-family plot, fifteen or more landless women had to form a group and apply to use it. Around 2,500 such UAIMs[5] were set up across the country and generated change through conflict rather than success. In terms of production and employment they were marginal, and in this they exemplified the nature of all Mexico's schemes for women. Government handouts have tended to keep women busy as passive objects of programmes and projects (and throughout this century bureaucratic paternalism has kept rural groups in a permanent state of dependence). Paternalism has sought to bring women into the market through social microprojects or as paid labour. More recently, the economic crisis has been key in making women's participation visible and making their presence felt (Chapter Three) and there is a demand for real recognition of rural women.

The difficulties that women meet in building organisations at the national level illustrate how unsuitable and unattractive the political structures are to women. Social policies include women only vaguely, sometimes attached to other groups, such as children, while they remain invisible. At the same time, the budgets are tiny and red tape encumbers all activities outside limits set by the state.

The groups involved in Tapalehui do not want to be a political clientele, but nor do they want to give up the meagre resources they can get from the state. Therefore, they diversify, mobilise and look for alternatives. 'They go to the institutions to demand … the things they want to do. They don't just wait for them to appear but go and ask for them to improve their lives' (María, academic and adviser, *Puebla South*).

Notes

1. Sue Frenk has a valuable chapter on the difficulties, in J. Townsend *et al.* 1995.
2. Paulo Freire's 'conscientisation' (Chapter Two).
3. Dueñas *et al.* 1997, Zapata and Mercado 1996.
4. The Secretariat of Agriculture, Ranching and Rural Development.
5. *Unidades Agrícolas e Industriales de la Mujer*: Agricultural and Industrial Units for the Woman.

Summary of Chapter 8

This chapter explores how the different forms of power come together in different dimensions of power at different levels.

The dimensions of power are:

- *personal power*, the growth of self-esteem and defeat of the 'power over' internalised by the individual;
- *relational power*, or the power to change relationships in the direction the individual wishes;
- *group power*, where individuals work together for goals they could not achieve alone. Group power is active at many levels, in joint projects, in the village, in the region, in the country and in the world.

The chapter first presents something of the personal power of peasant women and academics, and then examines the levels, from the individual to the international, at which different categories of women represented at Tapalehui have individual or group power in relationships with others. The change-agents and advisers have developed particular personal strengths through their work as, in rather different ways, have the academics; all feel tensions between their commitments and their own needs. Some individual peasant and Indian women at Tapalehui have been able to participate in national and international events. Turning to the groups, all the peasant groups have some power in their local community and some have a regional and national presence. Their international contacts are primarily with 'donors' and the 'transnationalisation of feminism'. The academics have put support for rural women's groups before the building of their own, and claim very limited group power.

9

Where Next?

Emma Zapata, Pilar Alberti, Janet Gabriel Townsend and Joanna Rowlands

Where Next? Emma Zapata

At Tapalehui we were all both researchers and researched, all took our places at the centre of discussion and on the edge, which helped us to a better understanding of our own work as well as that of others. As authors, we allowed our own individuality full play both there and in writing this book. In the face of a subject such as empowerment, everyone is afraid, but, because we could share our thoughts, discussing and examining power together was a joy. Our very open discussion of relationships between NGOs, MOs, grassroots members, advisers, change-agents and academics depended, as we said in Chapter One (pp. 14–15), on long-established trust. The academics put their doubts to the women in the organisations and were open to their criticisms, challenges and fears. The academics are more critical of their projects than they, because the peasant and Indian women's first concern is with survival: if the project contributes, they are too busy to ask if it is the most profitable use of their time. Yet they joined our project to explore and discuss power, because they wanted to learn, to think about it, to know and to deconstruct. All the voices can be heard throughout this book. Their intonation differs. Some are more emphatic, others debate or criticise, most are optimistic and assertive. We all know that we must understand the 'power over' that holds us down, and consciously defend ourselves against it.

We talked of the unhappiness created in us all by the oppressive faces of 'power over', of that intangible power which oppresses us and turns us into oppressors, sometimes unawares, sometimes with our consent. This happens because we are all actors in an authoritarian culture in which we cannot but affect others and be affected by their actions. We explored the distress of powerlessness and the fears of responsibility. Yet our study included everyone's happiness in sharing their thoughts, peasant and Indian women, change-agents, advisers, academics; everyone talked of their pleasure at witnessing the achievements of other women, getting involved in discussions of self-empowerment and putting it at the centre of analysis.

One right the rural women claimed was that of pleasure, of enjoyment, the right to include happiness in plans for change. Such happiness might not mean living without men, but would demand a different kind of man capable of understanding the changes women are living through.

The revolution at Tapalehui was to talk of power in positive terms, as self-empowerment, as building ourselves and building with other women. All of us who were there believe that for the peasant and Indian women this depends on mobility, on new powers of movement (Chapter Four). They take action, get out of their homes and join in; they fight their fears. Group ways of working will give more opportunity for this than hierarchy, not only among grassroots women but in links between groups and at different levels. The ways of working they suggested respect both individual rights and the differences between groups, and will help to move towards the utopia they imagine. The changes to which they aspire are not only inner and personal but reach all levels, involving all women in all spaces, transforming everyday life. We must see power as expressed in changing relationships, with change taking place not only within the individual but in all kinds of relationships. Power should be at the centre of discussion. The women at Tapalehui think that men reject the subject as soon as it comes up, because equal terms cannot be achieved without a sharing of responsibilities. At present, there is a bias in responsibilities and a new, more balanced and harmonious relationship has to be found on emotional and economic levels, in the 'power to do' in public and in private. This objective is one of the most difficult to achieve.

The women at Tapalehui came from different economic, political, cultural, ethnic and geographical worlds, bringing the diversity of identities and activities we have seen. All the rural women, each in her own reality, are acquiring modern know-how. They have taken on management, planning, the use of computers, the fight for gender equality, resistance to domestic violence, demands for reproductive health and rights – all modern, international themes. Their concern is to turn these things to their own ends. The rural women and their ethnic groups are very diverse and their world views equally dissimilar; they each have a multiplicity of roles in daily life which they have taken care to think through. What brings them together is a belief that only through 'power with' can they make the changes they desire. The Indian women use positive elements from their cultures for their own self-empowerment, while being very critical of other elements they see as belittling them, holding them back. For all at Tapalehui, critical awareness is of great importance in self-empowerment.

This is a revolution. By defining empowerment as self-empowerment, hierarchy and oppression can be toppled. Men will have to empower themselves, to take new powers and depend less on the 'power over', to recognise the rights of women and strive to reach a more harmonious world.

> To the extent that social movements shake the boundaries of cultural and political representation and social practice, calling into question what may and may not be seen as political; to the extent ... that the cultural politics of social movements enact cultural contestations or presuppose cultural differences – then we must accept that what is at stake in social movements in a profound way is a transformation of the dominant political culture in which they have to move and constitute themselves as social actors with political pretensions. (Álvarez *et al.* 1998: 8)

Where Next? Pilar Alberti

At the beginning of the twenty-first century, change seems to be the key word in all our lives and countries and for the very planet we live on. Our work shows the self-empowerment of peasant women to be attainable and desirable. We have witnessed both success and setbacks in the struggle to make it come true. Most important, it is linked to the worldwide women's movement. The United Nations' Fourth World Conference on Women in Beijing was preceded by great activity among feminist organisations, NGOs and ministries as they prepared evaluations of the situation of women and designed solutions. General awareness rose dramatically. There are suggestions that the theme is again disappearing from view, and many funding agencies merely pay lip-service to gender in areas such as human rights, sustainable development, health or education. Even so, awareness of gender has grown.

In Mexico, women have made headway in the state (through the National Programme for Women), in universities (courses and postgraduate degrees on women, gender and masculinity), in organisations (as through feminist meetings) and in culture (new mentalities growing from changes in language and in the habits and customs of both Indians and Spanish-speakers). It has taken the struggle of generations of women to get so far. Now we continue the struggle in the face of obstacles both within us and outside us. I believe that the inner limitations present the greatest danger and obstacle to processes of self-empowerment. The glass ceiling of empowerment rests on internalised oppression, on the Cinderella, Scheherezade or chameleon syndromes.

When peasant or academic women, or women in general, think that they 'cannot' do, think, achieve, get, have, feel or live, this is the Cinderella complex (Dowling 1982). These feelings of impotence, and the desire for other people to take care of us limits women's capabilities and personal development.[1] At Tapalehui, the syndrome appeared as something overcome (Chapter Four). The chameleon gives its name to a syndrome through its capacity to mimic (Fabra 1996), to adapt its appearance to its surroundings and protect itself against danger. Women mimic in social contexts, adapting their personalities to be accepted, by parent, relative, woman friend or husband for instance, and to escape rejection. Women may deny their own identities by denying their wishes, preferences, thoughts and differences. The Scheherezade syndrome takes the chameleon response further, but only with the opposite sex (Abelin 1996). Women may become insecure about their own values and desires and begin to identify with those of their husbands until they give up their own point of view entirely. Their wish to please leads them to silence their disagreement to avoid conflict. They are silent on 'men's business' (politics, football, work, money and so forth) or express their husbands' views. Many women have their capacity for analysis and criticism impaired by preferring silence to contradicting their 'better half'. Many fear to lose their husband, lover or boyfriend if they disagree with him, so give up their individuality as women and as human beings. In rural and urban Mexico, for instance, it is not uncommon for women to vote for their husbands' choices of political candidate. The pretence of having no opinion or separate identity, in order to manipulate and control a more powerful husband, is even more common. Although these syndromes were recognisable to some degree at Tapalehui, an even greater number of strategies are available to fight them. Group discussions help create awareness and work to overcome the obstacles, and the feminist movement has contributed in analysis, criticism and solutions.

For me, the degree to which women's practical and strategic needs (as defined by them) are being met is an indicator of women's self-empowerment. In Mexico, there has been progress on two fronts. First, government and international agencies are funding many projects to meet the practical needs of the people, making use of women's skills and experience. Health care, nutrition, education and housing are only a few examples. Such projects are politically attractive, as they can be summed up in numbers that enhance the image of the politicians who promote them, even if the gains are short-term and basic problems are not in fact solved.

Second, Indian women developed a stronger gender and ethnic awareness in the 1990s. In Mexico, the Revolutionary Law for Women drawn up by Zapatista grassroots women in 1993 (pp. 38–9) is a response to practical needs. From basic needs to the right to choose a husband and decide how many children to bear, the Law closes the primary circle of existence. The Law expresses the thoughts not only of Indian women, but of peasant and urban women, workers, teachers and housewives across Mexico. We can all identify with these demands to some degree. Women's self-empowerment has allowed them to lay claim to the first level of human existence.

In March 1996, at a meeting preparing for International Women's Day, grassroots women suggested broadening the scope of the Revolutionary Law. The new rights claimed, very strikingly, fall in the area of strategic gender needs, of women's needs to change their relative position in society. I think that some of these rights are very important, not for being novel (they were all alive in women's hearts and women felt they had to be achieved somehow) but because they were expressed for the first time. The right to express their feelings, to defend themselves verbally against insults or criticisms by relatives or others, to demand change in traditions that exclude or offend them, to rest, to have fun, to visit other places, to be different: all these may seem to be rights so basic that no demands need be made, because they should be a part of daily life already. But this is not the case, and the act of demanding them makes their absence all the more noticeable.

Where next? I would like to be optimistic, to trust that the new century will be better for women and men, to believe in utopias, to struggle for them to come true, and to look towards the future as the end of a film in which the remote, dark horizon can be vaguely discerned as the sun comes up behind the mountains, bearing with it the promise of a new day, filled with light and hope.

Where Next? Janet Gabriel Townsend

In crude terms, 'getting out of that house!' has been promoted in rural Mexico by offers of credit to women working in groups. In Bangladesh, academics measure women's 'empowerment' in terms of their increased mobility: women in groups are 'empowered' not if they feel they have taken new powers to themselves and celebrate them in the terms we have seen, but simply if they get out of the house more. Many in reality feel disempowered, forced for the sake of their families to go against their religious beliefs by going out to earn a little more income (Kabeer 1998). I told a (male) Marxist colleague about this, and his reaction was, 'That's what we used to call proletarianisation!' This is important. These women are being bribed to enter the labour force, to become self-employed.[2] Marta has said that this can be exploitative (pp. 115–16). As for the Western women who celebrate their entry into the labour force (Chapter One, pp. 36–7), the Mexican women know that 'getting out of that house!' is a part of their self-empowerment, even when it subjects them to new forms of 'power over'.

The practice of bringing millions of women into groups to engage in livelihood projects in the context of other forms of personal development (literacy, education, health) is almost worldwide. International agencies, governments and international NGOs all engage in it, although rarely in truly enabling ways. Often microcredit now dominates. This is, however, a two-way process: women have been willing to get out of that house, and some women delight in having done it. It may be that in Mexico and Latin America the small economic gains alone would not have kept women coming out, and that the novelty and the rewards of talking and sharing are the gains that really draw them. One reward appears to be a new feeling of power and control, but the increased control is in their daily lives and their immediate surroundings. It takes them into a whole new world of external controls and to a much increased engagement with national and international capitalism.

As we have said, talk at Tapalehui in the 'more rural' focus group turned repeatedly to 'What shall we do with the men?', and special discussions were held on this theme. The peasant women in particular see improved relationships with men as the next step in self-empowerment.

- 'It isn't enough to work with women, and for women to know their rights.'
- 'It's vital to give men a chance and a space to think.'
- 'The question is, how are networks going to develop among men so that they can give each other support in changing themselves?'

These same questions have been arising in academia and in the 'development industry', but we heard them first at Tapalehui, from peasant women. The Oxfam journal, *Gender and Development*, published a special issue in 1997 on 'Men and Masculinity'. In January 1999, the Swedish Ministry for Foreign Affairs[3] ran a seminar in Lusaka, Zambia, on *Men's Voices, Men's Choices: How Can Men Gain from Improved Gender Equality?*, which came up with some interesting answers. At the peasant women's request, after the workshop we circulated contact addresses of men's groups working in masculinity to all the NGOs with which we worked, and later to the National Network of Advisers to Rural Women. A seminar like the one in Lusaka would get great support from the peasant women at Tapalehui. Many academic feminists fear that more attention to men will simply return power and funding to men, but perhaps we should also listen to the thoughts of peasant women. For them, these questions are at the cutting edge of women's self-empowerment. They feel empowered, and have the right to know how they feel. They want to see work done with men, and they are experts in their own problems.

Where Next? Joanna Rowlands

Where has Tapalehui brought us? What came across most clearly at Tapalehui was enthusiasm. In the workshop itself, there was no shortage of passion or of a clear sense of optimism, particularly from the 'more rural' women. All the talk about processes of empowerment seemed to help bring their dreams closer, even if slowly and step by step. For the 'more academic' women, the passion was there, but the optimism was muted, perhaps through a fuller awareness of the scale of the challenges ahead. This illustrates the dilemma which arises if we use 'empowerment' as part of a 'development' discourse: how far, given the size and complexity of the changes needed, can the individual or small organisation hope to go towards its dreams before coming up against immovable obstacles? Are we really, if we are honest, talking about 'empowerment-within-certain-limited-parameters'? The powers the women describe and get so excited by are real. But so too is the 'power over' wielded over the lives of others by the 'big boys', the wealthy magnates, the mega-corporations and the people with their fingers hovering near the nuclear or biological trigger. Yet, should we be defeated by their 'power over'? Given the failures so far of many attempts to challenge manifestations of 'power over', who can say that myriad local solutions, local initiatives, will not produce the changes necessary on a broader scale over time? In that sense, the optimism of so many voices at Tapalehui is to be encouraged.

Outside Tapalehui But what of the women who were not at Tapalehui? This book has sought to learn from those who were. What about the organisations we visited before the workshop, which did not send representatives? We were not surprised this happened, but it would have been good to follow them up, and we regretted that our funding did not allow this. Perhaps they were too busy surviving to take time out to come. Perhaps the gender problems the women who did not come would have had to face (such as childcare or family obligations) were too pressing. Or then again, perhaps they were not convinced that the workshop would be a useful way to spend their time, perhaps because they feared an outside agenda. We can only speculate, and the answer is probably a mix of these reasons. Certainly when we visited, great interest was expressed, even enthusiasm, but as any researcher knows, this tells us little.

And what of the other women in the organisations that sent someone to Tapalehui? The peasant women there were nearly all leaders in some capacity; they were women who had reached a certain point in their own empowerment path, whatever route that had taken, which made it possible for them to be there. Perhaps there were many more who might have come, had the workshop capacity been greater. But maybe the workshop consisted of women 'by-definition-already-empowered' who would therefore be unrepresentative of empowerment processes in Mexico? Perhaps they began with some sort of advantage that would make them different from others? Maybe, for some. But some women in the 'more rural' group had very clearly started from nowhere and fought their own way, sometimes reluctantly, into leadership in their organisations. This gives their accounts a credibility and a possibility of at least coming near to the experiences of some women who were absent.

Also absent were 'non-organised' women. Like the 'poorest of the poor', these women are very difficult for outsiders to reach. What about their empowerment? Did the discussion at Tapalehui tell us anything about their needs, their processes? Are there some bottom line conditions that have to be in place for processes of empowerment even to start? That would require us to see empowerment as somehow separate and different from everyday life. But if empowerment is seen as one aspect of human development then that perspective does not work. Watch the small child developing new confidence as it tries, fails, tries again and finally succeeds: new powers are exercised, growing out of self-confidence and self-esteem. Some 'non-organised' women, of course, will be following an empowerment path that does not happen to include being part of an organisation or group (see p. 35). Not reaching for 'power with', or not outside a family setting, is completely possible and does not have to impede the development of other forms of power.

Two voices Throughout the book, the various authors have drawn on the words of the 'more rural' women and the 'more academic' women, setting up a counterpoint between the two voices. To the Western reader – to me, at least – there is a bit of a jolt every time I move from the one to the other. Hold on a minute, I ask myself, what are these 'academic' women doing here?[4] But perhaps the label was wrong: perhaps instead of 'academic' we might have chosen 'intellectually trained' or some other phrase. We did not, because that would have been patronising, implying somehow that the 'more rural' group was not intellectually capable or did not have valuable, valid ideas and things to say. We wanted to acknowledge that exposure to particular ways of thinking, often Western in influence if not origin, might condition the way that each group of people approached the tasks and topics of the workshop. We also wanted to acknowledge a certain familiarity with language and abstract ideas that was certainly evident in the transcripts and which acted to a degree as an impediment to exploring topics in a more personal way. We wanted to recognise that these things introduce a form of power, particularly given the nature of

Mexican society and culture, which could easily lead to self-silencing of the 'more rural' women, had the groups not met separately: the culture of patronage, deference to the powerful, respect for the 'educated' would come into play.

Despite this jolt, however, we have seen a great similarity of problems, struggles, challenges between the two groups, although expressed at times in very different language. We did not identify a different range of experience between the two groups, in terms of the forms that power takes. Perhaps the jolt, then, is artificially induced by the labels we chose to use. We seem to be looking at more of a continuum along which women can move. Indeed, a couple of women at the workshop did move between the two groups. The crucial thing is that concepts identified in Honduras (Rowlands 1995b, 1997a, b, c), which the Tapalehui workshop was to a degree testing, apply not only to poor, peasant Mexican women who had organised around small livelihood projects, but also to women in very different social and cultural situations. While making no claims to universality – and the model of empowerment we are using does not allow that, based as it is on unique individual life trajectories and circumstances – it is still intriguing that the talk at Tapalehui revealed a broadly shared experience of 'power from within', 'power with', 'power to' and indeed 'power over', despite the very varied life circumstances of the participants.

The 'more academic' group was not alone in using a language influenced by Western thinking: the 'more rural' women can be seen, at least in places, to have taken on some of these discourses as well. They talk of 'practical and strategic gender needs' (Moser 1989, 1993), of 'equality with men', of 'democracy' and 'the gender perspective'. 'Gender' itself (*género*) is a new use of a Spanish word, as it was in English. Have they been influenced (knowingly? unknowingly?) by external, foreign agendas? Well, yes of course, as has any group that has had things required of it, directly or indirectly, by foreign funding agencies. But their use of international discourses of 'development' and 'feminism' is very selective; it is not an uncritical adoption of ideas. This is what they select.

The psychological dimension From the Tapalehui workshop it is clear that in talking of empowerment, we talk of psychological processes as well as political (in the usual sense), economic, social or cultural processes. These are distinctions made in Western culture. But in examining power in their own lives, these women are not making such distinctions, not putting their lives into those boxes. Their lives are a whole, where different aspects overlap and interact, exposing such distinctions for what they are: intellectual constructions that have served particular purposes in the evolution and maintenance of particular systems of organisation and functioning of human endeavour. Most of the literature on empowerment produced to date has been produced in academic disciplines constructed within this framework (Chapter Two). Yet when you look at what is involved for empowerment of women, you have to look at the totality of their experience; ignoring some aspects because they do not fit the analytical box you work with is not helpful in the long term. So, for example, Marc Zimmerman (1995) is able to look at personal empowerment from a psychological perspective, without any mention of the development of 'power from within', or of the particular challenge of empowerment within close relationships (Chapter Seven). Why would a community psychology approach (see Appendix) lead to those particular absences?

In analysis of 'development' there has been much writing on economic and on personal empowerment with no thought for the real psychological aspects of the process. This enables a thoroughly instrumentalist approach to emerge, which often fails (Kabeer 1998). There have been many words written about new social movements, but within them there is a curious absence of the psychological aspects of 'participation' or 'organisation'. A central missing process in much of the literature on change is that of undoing the effects of internalised oppression. Of course, this can happen as part of an instrumentalist approach,[5] but is in that context good luck rather than good management. If empowerment is a goal, then encouraging the process where self-confidence and self-esteem are built and nurtured is a critical component. We have seen, in the preceding chapters, how central that process is to the Tapalehui women. Why, then, has there been such an absence of attention to this?

The challenge I would like to throw out to the 'development' community is to take on the reality of the very complex psycho–social processes within which individuals exist and with which they engage in any process of change. It looks like a different universe from development theory and discourse, but of course, as soon as you stop to think, all development processes take place in the context of complex psycho–social processes. This is really stating the obvious, since the agents of 'development' are human beings. Within the development literature, there are places where we have been feeling our way towards understanding the social and even the cultural. A major step has been taken with the more recent critiques coming from post-colonial, post-structuralist perspectives, and attempts to bring concepts of identity and difference into thinking on 'development' and on who sets the agendas. Apart from some writing on identity and some theory of popular education, we have stopped short, so far, of grappling with the psychological dimension and with the interactions between the psychological and other dimensions.

I am a little hesitant to encourage this focus, since the field of psychology is as ethnocentric, male-biased and rife with inaccuracy and limited perspectives as any other field of study, and power is a big debate in that field too. But nevertheless, psychology must be recognised. The processes we are trying to encourage (particularly those who approach 'development' wanting to transform human relations into something more just and less destructive), all take place in a framework where the individual's ability to handle change and to recognise and take opportunities as they arise is what determines the end result.

Recent events in world markets have illustrated this. Markets mostly function well if people believe they will. This belief is sometimes based on calculation, but is often influenced by other factors, many to do with confidence, willingness to take risks and so on. As soon as something happens that makes people lose confidence, then everybody sells up and a crash happens. It is salutary to recognise the centrality of psychology to the well-being of nations and to the abilities of individuals to meet their daily needs. Of course, markets are more complex than this, but the point holds: psychology is a significant factor. What do people fear is going to happen, and how does that make them behave? But then, also, what could be done to tackle the fears that are misplaced? In the mid-1980s, there was much concern about women's projects that did not work out according to plan. Individual human beings make decisions in their lives for a whole range of reasons, and one of those clusters of reasons is how we feel, where we feel threatened, where we feel safe and what our assumptions are (grounded or not) about what will happen if … Our actions are governed at least as much by this as by calculated decisions.

There is also, of course, a psychology of groups, with another literature attached. I suspect that, if we go into the detail, we will find that fear enters into the frame in many guises, in both individual and group decision-making and action. Here we make a link to the question of who has 'power over': people act as if they are going to be facing scarcity at any moment even when they have plenty of resources behind them. The individual's fear of losing their job may be far greater than the actual likelihood of that happening (except, of course, during times of significant market upheaval and in very precarious sectors of the labour market). And fear makes people accept circumstances that they would not otherwise tolerate. I include the fear of conflict. Many women I have met will keep their mouths shut rather than risk what might happen if they expressed their opinions, whereas, when they venture to speak, often they receive a positive response.

Tapalehui has reinforced for us the idea that empowerment must encompass the entirety of the human being and their interactions with other human beings and collectivities of human beings, i.e. the psychological, the political, the economic, the social, the cultural … In so doing, empowerment has to encompass whatever aspects of 'sameness' and 'otherness' as apply in the particular case, and to acknowledge and face up to whatever apparent contradictions are thrown up in the process.

A discourse of rights We came away from Tapalehui with a very clear sense that 'power with', 'power from within' and 'power to' are dynamics, potentials which can be fostered and can grow, to great effect. But where do we put this against the real challenge of the abuse of 'power over' that dominates so many aspects of the lives of most women and poor people – particularly as it relates to the distribution and use of scarce resources? (Some 'scarce' resources, of course, are not really so very scarce: but access to them is very skewed and unequal in the current distribution.) Some resources are scarce because unequal distribution of other resources has enabled changes which would not otherwise have been possible, such as dense human occupation of areas that are naturally desert. The exercise of 'power over' is a complex, pervasive reality to be explored.

It is time, therefore, to link the discourse of empowerment with the discourse of rights. Not the kind of rights that in Mexico (as in other places) mean expectations from the state, where the individual gives up power to the state in exchange for (often illusory) services. But the rights, human rights, where each individual has dignity and can expect to be treated as what they are, a unique individual member of the human race. In terms of empowerment, this creates two challenges. 'Power over' is a zero–sum game. That is, 'power over' is limited: if women have more rights, then men have less power over them. One challenge is the max-imisation of capacities to develop and magnify aspects of power that are not zero–sum: capacities to create, involve, generate, collaborate or co-operate, for instance, can grow without loss to anyone. My work both in Honduras and with the Tapalehui workshop illustrates that there is great scope for this to happen, and to be encouraged and supported. There is great potential for real change and transformation.

But the second challenge is harder. In order not to put empowerment into a small confined sphere, we must apply ourselves also to 'power over' and question matters of distribution. So, for example, in Honduras as well as Mexico, the women found that although they were achieving many changes and becoming more confident, with higher expectations both of themselves and others, they had difficulty and made less progress in the sphere of their own close relationships, particularly with male partners (Chapters Seven and Eight). There were some success stories, but often women would say 'I know I should, but … ' or, 'I know I want to, but … ' There is often a caring relationship, perhaps with support and encourage-ment for the woman, but there is also a power relationship that limits and confines. The ambivalence between the two faces of the relationship can be challenging and many women do not manage change in close relationships that parallels other changes they achieve. 'Power over' is about control, and about scarcity; it is also about perceptions, real or unreal, of control and scarcity. The controlling behaviours can become stronger when challenged because of perceptions that may or may not be well founded, that negative change will follow. So, again to use the example of close relationships, some women find their tentative steps towards initiating change in the relationship can provoke violent responses. Again, we need understanding of the psychological issues: in this case, the man who finds it hard to accept the possibility of his wife having more freedoms and more participation in decisions could usefully look at why that is. But what support does he get in this? Yet without this parallel change in men, the options for women like the ones at Tapalehui who do not wish to compromise what they believe are limited.

Avoiding the issues Much of the language of 'development', in particular about disadvantaged groups or poverty, is couched in terms that avoid confronting 'power over'. It is really quite extraordinary, but look at the language of 'partnership' (the recent fashion for collaboration between Northern and Southern NGOs, or between 'donors' and organisations, as 'partners'). The major funding bodies in particular have leapt on to this notion of partnership. And the talk about globalisation and the economic language commonly used in that context make the problems all look structural, avoiding any recognition of power or power imbalance. Many international NGOs talk about 'working with our southern partners' with no hint of the unequal nature of the partnership, often despite the best of intentions. The language makes it all impersonal, as if human beings had nothing to do with it. We have heard much about how work with women is essential in development, how women play a clear role in supporting economic activity, and how, to solve particular problems, women must become empowered. There is little evidence of any understanding that this might mean women exercising more 'power over'. One useful thing about using the language of empowerment is that it puts the notion of power back into the discourse. But this will not help if the kind of power that needs attention is neatly side-stepped.

There is a real dilemma here, when powerful organisations talk about empowering women. Unless they are only thinking in terms of power that can be given and therefore also taken away again (which is tokenism rather than empowerment), if women or some other group become newly empowered, then they have to let go of control over the consequences. Or rather, they have to be aware that they may no longer have any say in what happens. Otherwise it is not empowerment. This is a real difficulty for organisations that themselves have to be accountable for public funds, and that have a particular vision of what 'development' might mean. It cannot be assumed that the funders and those receiving funds will have the same priorities. This is nicely illustrated in an account of a workshop with rural women in Bihar, one of the poorest parts of India, in 1988:

> We asked them what their dreams were. What would they ask for if some god or goddess offered to make all their desires come true? Their answers baffled us, their wisdom challenged our narrow notions of development. Their list of desires was the following: my own identity, leisure and time to dream, recognition and respect, love, affirmation, freedom. Satisfaction of basic needs like food, shelter, came somewhere towards the end of the long list. (Kamla Bhasin 1995: 12–13)

Current systems of project planning and evaluation, on which upward accountability rests, will therefore have to come under scrutiny, and take more account of processes, such as the development of agency, rather than of specific, tangible end results. And those processes will need to encompass the possibility of a loss of control on the part of the funder. How many agencies are willing to give unconditional financial support to organisations moving in a direction that is not that desired by the funding body?

This is an area that most people and organisations shy away from. Most uses of the term empowerment that I have come across in the literature talk about it as if it was this cosy little thing that you can do somewhere, as if it were unrelated to power and politics, whereas, of course, politics is central to empowerment. The politics of 'power over' and the distribution of powers are crucial. It is one of the difficulties I have with Foucault's discussions of power as process, power as knowledge (Chapter Two p. 23 and Chapter Seven p. 130). He fails to tackle the distribution of these processes of power, who controls the flows, and why; which kinds of flows pass through which kinds of people; he does not allow for the people through whom it flows.

Challenging power relations One of the clear messages coming out of Tapalehui, which was repeatedly expressed, was this: 'This is what we've got to do, we've got to get to grips with our levels of confidence and our ability to act in the world and so on, but what are we going to do about the men?' The 'more rural' group kept coming back to this: what are we going to do about the men? The peasant women were clear that you can go so far working with women on their problems, but that at some point you have to begin to take on 'power over', particularly if you are working on control over resources and the way things are done. 'Thank you for letting us use a plot of land in the community for the women to raise crops, but actually, a quarter of a hectare, of the worst land, is not enough.' You reach a point where someone with 'power over' will have to give it up, or some of it at least, if change is to come about.

Women empowering themselves challenge power relations. When you start to challenge power relations, things begin to happen. People get defensive; people get scared; much controlling behaviour appears; you notice very quickly that you are up against something. In my research on empowerment in Honduras (1995b, 1997a, b, c), PAEM had done excellent work, analysing their situation, working out that what they most needed to change was access to basic grains, devising a plan, gaining the support of the government food-marketing organisation and securing funds to set up a grain warehousing project. At the point when the project was ready to go, PAEM came up against local politics in a big way. A local organisation felt threatened by their project and, not wanting to permit it to happen, pulled all the political strings they could to sink the project. When 'power over' in the hands of one person/group is challenged, conflict arises.

Handling conflict in ways that deal with 'power over' and work towards non-zero-sum solutions where no one loses out is arguably the biggest challenge for 'development'. Very few people have been willing to face up to this challenge. Those who do call attention to it risk being labelled as old-hat socialists, bleeding-heart liberals or woolly idealists. Nevertheless, this thorny problem is still with us and needs to be confronted. Otherwise, all talk of empowerment is misleading and, at worst, connives at new forms of control.

Notes

1. See also Deniz Kandiyoti (1988b) on the 'patriarchal bargain'.

2. *Proletarianisation* usually refers to wage labour rather than self-employment, but the principle holds.

3. With Danish International Development Assistance.

4. I was present, but not a member of either group.

5. See the experience of Urraco in Rowlands 1995b, 1997a.

Appendix: Empowerment at Tapalehui and in American 'Community Psychology'

Janet Gabriel Townsend

One disconcerting feature of writings on empowerment is the existence of two bodies of literature that almost ignore each other. Between writings of American community psychologists (CP) on empowerment, and the talk at Tapalehui (or the writings of Batliwala, Kabeer or Rowlands), there is a remarkable degree of overlap in detail but little in overall conceptualisations and less in goals.[1] The work of Paulo Freire (1973) was an inspiration to both schools. To us, it seems as if both groups have adopted Freire's concept of *conscientisation*, of the liberation of the poor through a new awareness, but only the feminists continue to expect, with Freire, the transformation of society. Jane Stein, exceptionally, seeks to draw on both schools. For her, leaning towards the CP group, 'the transformation of society is an illusive goal' (1997: 60) but, as a feminist, she writes that 'empowerment *is* about social conflict' (p. 282) although it may be about a struggle 'for *existence* rather than *resistance*' (p. 291) which may only 'just possibly facilitate deeper social change' (p. 292).

Community psychology (CP) in the United States identifies empowerment as a leading construct and as a vital process in community development. CP authors sometimes cite Paulo Freire and occasionally mention women's projects, but overall pay little attention to low income countries and even less to gender. Foucault, like Marx, is rarely, if ever, cited. For this school, expectations are limited. The empowerment of the poor would be no threat to established national or international interests, nor would it encourage radical social change. Rather, empowerment is expected to lift the poor/criminals/drug abusers/alcoholics towards the mean, improving their mental and physical health and increasing their role in decision-making in the society that presently exists. These authors see the empowerment process as humanising society by increasing inclusion and equality, not as building a new society; they have no apparent worries about capitalism. They have clearly reached their understanding of society by routes very different from those of Latin American or South Asian feminists, or the women at Tapalehui.

The community psychologists have a recurrent concern with control, far stronger than that of Batliwala (1993), Kabeer (1994), Rowlands (1997a) or Tapalehui. Themes of 'mastery and control', 'perceived control' and influence over events and 'outcomes of importance' (see below) weave through the discourse. 'Psychological empowerment is the process by which individuals gain control over their lives' (Zimmerman, 1995: 602, citing Rappaport).

We would argue that feminist concepts of empowerment have more to do with transformation than control: the transformation of individual and society. The CP school wants the poor to join the mainstream; the feminists want change in all discourse and practice.

One sharp technical difference between Tapalehui and the American psychologists lies in the recommended levels of analysis. At Tapalehui, these were (Chapters Two and Eight):

- personal empowerment;
- empowerment in close relationships (often the family); and
- collective power.

For Zimmerman (1995) and his school, and for Jane Stein, they are:

- psychological empowerment of the individual (PE)
- empowerment at the level of the organisation and
- empowerment at the level of the community.

Close relationships are not identified as significant by CP writers, perhaps because gender is rarely seen as an issue (save by Jane Stein). To us, gender transforms the whole concept of empowerment, for empowered women look at once to their close relationships, which may be their most serious difficulty. (See Chapter Seven; Rowlands 1997a.)

The similarities lie in some processes of empowerment. The emphasis of women at Tapalehui on 'the organisation' and on 'joining the organisation' (Chapter Five) is shared in the writings of the CP school. The women would agree with Brad McMillan (*et al.* 1995: 721): 'Active individual participation is a major route to achieving psychological empowerment.'

Jane Stein (1997: 40–41) reports similar effects in Costa Rica. But the CP school goes further than Tapalehui in its emphasis on organisation, which can place personal empowerment in a very limiting frame. For Jane Stein, 'dramatic transformations occur in many of the participants' because of the organisational processes, not through the 'power from within'. Other writers are more extreme:

Empowerment can *only* be realised through organisation ... Empowerment outcomes at the individual level of analysis are products of cognitive, emotional, and behavioural changes in individuals resulting from the exercise of social power ... Individuals are empowered to the extent that they understand that their own access to social power exists through organisation. (Paul W. Speer and Joseph Hughey 1995: 732, emphasis added)

People developing the power to change themselves are not in the CP picture. For Stephen B. Fawcett (Fawcett *et al.* 1995: 78), 'Empowerment refers to the process of gaining influence over events and outcomes of importance.'

For us, the notion that the empowerment of, for example, the poor, the black or the female can be achieved without major social change is a contradiction in terms. For Tapalehui, such influence is far in the future and the goal is an alternative way of being rather than a new place of influence for women in the old structures.

How, then, does PE compare with Tapalehui's personal empowerment? For Marc Zimmerman (1995: 581), PE integrates perceptions of personal control, a proactive approach to life, and a critical understanding of the socio-political environment. Perceived control, competence and efficacy are important, alongside self-esteem, the understanding people have about their community and related socio-political issues, relevant skills and actions taken to directly influence outcomes. To us, all the phrases are familiar but 'control' and 'influence' are far more important to the psychologists, as against 'self-esteem' and 'awareness' to us. At Tapalehui, peasant women and change-agents could glory in small achievements. Their awareness was largely of the structures behind adversities beyond their control, and of new possibilities for small changes through their own efforts. The new awareness itself was deeply life-enhancing. For Zimmerman (pp. 592–3):

PE also [*sic*] different from but related to power. Power suggests authority, whereas PE is a feeling of control, a critical awareness of one's environment, and an active engagement in it ... Actual power or control is not necessary for empowerment ... (in the case of) goals such as being more informed, more skilled, more healthy or more involved in decision making.

But PE for him is clearly linked to success in influencing outcomes, whereas the 'power from within' may reside more in dignity, self-esteem and awareness of choice. PE, then, is instrumental while the 'power from within' is for us a goal in itself.

Perhaps we can learn from each other. Julian Rappaport (1995), one of the leading CP theorists, is involved in work in mental health and regards narrative as a very significant resource in the empowerment process. To him, the ability to tell one's story and to have access to and influence over collective stories, is a powerful tool.

> The goals of empowerment are enhanced when people discover, or create and give voice to, a collective narrative that sustains their own personal life story in positive ways. (p. 796)

In this book, we have been presenting personal and collective narratives from women in rural Mexico who are working with issues of power. We argue that these narratives are relevant to our own discourses about power.

Note

1. Jane Stein (1997) seeks to incorporate insights from lower-income countries into the CP view; Stephanie Riger (1997), herself a psychologist, develops a critical analysis of the concept, drawing mainly on the CP literature.

References

Abelin Sas, Graciela (1996) 'La Leyenda de Scherezade en la Vida Cotidiana', in Mabel Burín and Emilce Bio Bleichmar (eds) *Género, Psicoanálisis, Subjetividad*, Buenos Aires: Editorial Paidós, pp. 31–59.

Afshar, Haleh (ed.) (1998) *Women and Empowerment: Illustrations from the Third World*, London: Macmillan.

Afshar, Haleh and Fatima Alikhan (eds) (1997) *Empowering Women for Development: Experiences from Some Third World Countries*, India: K.B. Satyanarayana Booklinks Corporation.

Albee, G.W., J.M. Joffe and L.A. Dusenbury (eds) (1988) *Prevention, Powerlessness and Politics: Readings in Social Change*, Newbury Park, CA: Sage.

Alberti Manzanares, Pilar (1997) 'La Identidad de Género y Étnia como Base de las Estrategias de Adaptación de las Mujeres Indígenas a la Crisis', in Pilar Alberti Manzanares and Emma Zapata Montero *Desarrollo Rural y Género: Estratégias de Sobrevivencia de Mujeres Campesinas e Indígenas ante la Crisis Económica*, Montecillo, Mexico: Colegio de Postgraduados, pp. 169–88.

Alberti Manzanares, Pilar, Blanca Lopez, Marta Mercado, Jo Rowlands, Janet Townsend and Emma Zapata (1995) *Informe del Taller Realizado en 'Tapalehui', Xoxocotla, Morelos en Junio de 1995*, Montecillo, Mexico: Colegio de Postgraduados.

Alberti Manzanares, Pilar and Emma Zapata Montero (eds) (1997) *Desarrollo Rural y Género: Estratégias de Sobrevivencia de Mujeres Campesinas e Indígenas ante la Crisis Económica*, Montecillo, Mexico: Colegio de Postgraduados.

Alemán, Sylvia (1997) *Sihuame e la Esperanza: Las Organizaciones Rurales en Guerrero*, Mexico: Secretaría de Desarrollo Rural, Guerrero and Universidad Autónoma de Guerrero.

Alonso R., Patricia and Roberto del Prado E. (1997) 'La Mujer Campesina en el Combate a la Pobreza: el Caso de la Red Nacional de Mujeres, UNORCA', *Estudios Agrarios*, No. 8, July–September Mexico City: Procuraduría Agraria.

Álvarez, Sonia E. (1997) 'Articulación y Transnacionalización de los Femenismos Latinoamericanos', *debate femenista* 8 (15): 146–70.

Álvarez, Sonia E. (1998) 'Latin American Feminisms "Go Global": Trends of the 1990s and Challenges for the New Millennium', in Álvarez *et al.* (1998), pp. 293–324.

Álvarez, Sonia E., Evelina Dagnino and Arturo Escobar (1998) 'The Cultural and the Political in Latin American Social Movements', in Álvarez *et al.* (1998), pp. 1–29.

Álvarez, Sonia E., Evelina Dagnino and Arturo Escobar (eds) (1998) *Cultures of Politics, Politics of Culture: Re-visioning Latin American Social Movements*, Boulder, CO: Westview Press.

Aranda, Josefina (1993) 'Politícas Públicas y Mujeres Campesinas en México', in Soledad Gonzalez (ed.) *Mujeres y Relaciones de Genéro en la Antropología Latinoamericana*, Mexico City: El Colegio de México.

Arizpe, Lourdes and Carlota Botey (1986) 'Las Políticas de Desarrollo Agrario y su Impacto sobre la Mujer Campesina en México,' in Magdalena León and Carmen Diana Deere (eds) *La Mujer y la Política Agraria en América Latina*, Bogota: Siglo XXI y ACEP.

Arizpe, Lourdes, Fanny Salinas and Margarita Velasquez (1989) 'Efectos de la Crísis Económica 1980–1985 sobre las Condiciones de Vida de las Mujeres Campesinas en México', in *El Ajuste Invisible: Los Efectos de la Crisis Económica en las Mujeres Pobres*, Colombia: UNICEF.

Bachrach, P. and M.S. Baratz (1970) *Power and Poverty: Theory and Practice*, Oxford: Oxford University Press.

Bartolomé, Miguel Alberto (1997) *Gente de Costumbre y Gente de Razón: Las Identidades Étnicas en México*, Mexico City: Siglo Veintiuno.

Basaglia, Franca (1983) *Razón, Locura y Sociedad*, Puebla, Mexico: Universidad Autónoma de Puebla.

Bassols, Barrera Marco, Iker Larrauri Prado, Teresa Marquez Martinez and Graciela Schmilchuc (1995) 'Museos AL REVES: Modalidades comunitarias y participativas en la planificación y el funcionamiento de museos', unpublished report submitted to Fideicomiso para la Cultura México/USA, Mexico City.

Batliwala, Srilatha (1993) *Empowerment of Women in South Asia: Concepts and Practices*, available from FFHC/AD Programme Officer, FAO, 55 Max Mueller Marg, New Delhi, 110 003, India.

Batliwala, Srilatha (1994) 'The Meaning of Women's Empowerment: New Concepts from Action', in Gita Sen, Adrienne Germain and Lincoln C. Chen (eds) *Population Policies Reconsidered: Health, Empowerment and Rights*, Boston, MD: Harvard University Press, pp. 127–38.

Batliwala, Srilatha (1997) 'El Significado del Empoderamiento de las Mujeres: Nuevos Conceptos desde la Acción', in León (1997), pp. 187–212.

Bebbington, Anthony and Graham Thiele with Penelope Davies, Martin Prager and Hernando Riveros (1993) *Non-Governmental Organizations and the State in Latin America: Rethinking Roles in Sustainable Agricultural Development*, London: Routledge.

Bennett, Robert J., P. Wicks and A. McCoughan (1994) *Local Empowerment and Business Services: Britain's Experiment with Training and Enterprise Councils*, London: UCL Press.

Bhasin, Kamla (1995) 'The Goal is Empowerment of Human Values', mimeo paper presented at the International Conference on Women's Empowerment and Education, New Delhi, March.

Bohman, Kristina (1984) *Women of the Barrio: Class and Gender in a Colombian City*, Stockholm: University of Stockholm Department of Anthropology.

Boltvinik, Julio (1995) 'La Pobreza Mata y la Pobreza Rural Mata Más,' *La Jornada*, 12 May.

Bonfil Sanchez, Paloma (1997) 'La Presencia de las Mujeres en los Movimientos Indígenas Contemporaneos en México', in Alberti and Zapata (1997), pp. 198–205.

Bookman, Ann and Sandra Morgen (eds) (1988) *Women and the Politics of Empowerment*, Philadelphia: Temple University Press.

Bordt, Rebecca L. (1997) 'How Alternative Ideas Become Institutions: The Case of Feminist Collectives', *Nonprofit and Voluntary Sector Quarterly* 26 (2).

Branden, Nathaniel (1997) *El Poder de la Autoestima. Cómo Potenciar este Importante Recurso Psicológico*, Mexico City: Editorial Paidós.

Brunt, Dorien (1992) *Mastering the Struggle: Gender, Actors and Agrarian Change in a Mexican Ejido*, Amsterdam: CEDLA Latin American Studies 64.

Burin, Mabel (1996) 'Género y Psicoanálisis: Subjetividades Femeninas Vulnerables', in Mabel Burin and Emilce Dio Bleichmar (eds) *Género, Psicoanálisis, Subjetividad*, Buenos Aires: Editorial Paidós, pp. 61–99.

Camara, Helder (1969) *Church and Colonialism*, London and Sydney: Sheed and Ward.

Cebotarev, Eleonora (1994) 'Las Mujeres en la Ciencia y Tecnología Agrícolas: Implicaciones para el Actual Sistema Alimentario', in Eleonora Cebotarev (ed.) *Mujer, Familia y Desarrollo*, Colombia: Manizales.

Centeño Rodríguez, Ma. del Socorro (1996) 'La Invisibilidad de la Participación de la Mujer en las Organizaciones Comunitarias (Municipio de Texcoco, Edo. de México)', unpublished master's thesis, Montecillo, Mexico: Colegio de Postgraduados.

Chambers, Robert (1984) *Rural Development: Putting the Last First*, London: Macmillan.

Cicerchia, Ricardo (1997) 'The Charm of Family Patterns: Historical and Contemporary Change in Latin America', in Dore (1997), pp. 118–33.

Claessen, Jeannette and Lillian Van Wesemal-Smit (eds) (1992) 'Women's Literacy and the Quest for Empowerment', in *Reading the World Reading the Word*, Oegstgeest: Vrouwenberaad ontwikkelingssamenwerking.

Clegg, Stuart (1989) *Frameworks of Power*, London: Sage.

Collins, Patricia Hill (1991) *Black Feminist Thought: Knowledge, Consciousness and the Politics of Empowerment*, London: Routledge.

Connell, Robert W. (1995) *Masculinities*, Oxford: Polity Press and Blackwell Publishers.

Coote, Anna and Polly Pattullo (1990) *Power and Prejudice: Women and Politics*, London: Weidenfeld and Nicolson.

Cowan, Jane K. (1996) 'Being a Feminist in Contemporary Greece: Similarity and Difference Reconsidered', in Nickie Charles and Felicia Hughes-Freeland (eds) *Practising Feminism: Identity, Difference, Power*, London: Routledge, pp. 61–85.

Cubitt, Tessa and Helen Greenslade (1997) 'Public and private spheres: The end of dichotomy', in Dore (1997), pp. 52–64.

Dagnino, Evelina (1998) 'Culture, Citizenship, and Democracy: Changing Discourses and Practices of the Latin American Left', in Álvarez *et al.* (1998).

De Barbieri, Teresita, Josefina Aranda, Celia Famomir, Rocío López, Patricia Marrero and Natacha Molina (1993) *Las Unidades Industriales para la Mujer Campesina en México: Dos Estudios de Caso, Charo (Michoacan) y Viescas (Coahuila)*, Mexico: International Labour Organization and CONAPO.

de Janvry, Alain (ed.) (1995) *State, Market and Civil Organizations: New Theories, New Practices and their Implications for Rural Development*, London: Macmillan and International Labour Organization.

Devaux, Monique (1996) 'Feminism and Empowerment: A Critical Reading of Foucault', in Hekman (1996), pp. 211–38.

Dill, Bonnie Thornton (1988) ' "Making Your Job Good Yourself": Domestic Service and the Construction of Personal Dignity', in Bookman and Morgen (1988), pp. 33–52.

Doble Jornada 1994: 8, in *La Jornada*, Mexico City.

Dore, Elizabeth (ed.) (1997) *Gender Politics in Latin America: Debates in Theory and Practice*, New York: Monthly Review Press.

Dowling, Colette (1982) *El Complejo de Cenicienta. El Miedo de las Mujeres a la Independencia*, Mexico City: Editorial Grijalbo.

Dueñas, Soledad, Carmen Gangotena and Monica Garcés (1997) *Mujeres, Poder e Identidad*, Latacunga: Plurimor.

Duffield, M. (1996) *The Symphony of the Damned: Racial Discourse, Complex Political Emergencies and Humanitarian Aid*, Birmingham: School of Public Policy, University of Birmingham, occasional paper, 2 March 1996.

Edwards, Mike and David Hulme (1992) 'Introduction' in Edwards and Hulme (eds) *Making a Difference: NGOs and Development in a Changing World*, Earthscan, London.

Edwards, Mike and David Hulme (1995) 'Introduction and Overview' in Edwards and Hulme (eds) *Non-Governmental Organisations: Performance and Accountability. Beyond the Magic Bullet*, London: Earthscan, pp. 3–16.

Escobar, Arturo (1995) *Encountering Development: The Making and Unmaking of the Third World*, Princeton, NJ: Princeton University Press.

Escobar, Arturo and Sonia Álvarez (eds) (1992) *The Making of Social Movements in Latin America. Identity, Strategy and Democracy*, Boulder, CO, San Francisco, CA, Oxford: Westview Press.

Fabra, María Luisa (1996) *Ni Resignadas ni Sumisas: Técnicas de Grupo para la Socialización de Niñas y Chicas*, Barcelona: Institut de Ciencies de Léducaci, University of Barcelona.

Faith, Karlene (1994) 'Resistance: Lessons from Foucault and Feminism', in H. Lorraine Radtke and Henderikus J. Stam (eds) *Power/Gender: Social Relations in Theory and Practice*, London: Sage, pp. 36–66.

Falk, R. (1987) 'The Global Promise of Social Movements at the Edge of Time', *Alternatives* 12 (173).

Fals Borda, Orlando (1979) *El Problema de Cómo Investigar la Realidad para Transformarla por la Praxis*, Bogota: Tercer Mundo.

Fawcett, Stephen B., Adrienne Paine-Andrews, Vincent T. Francisco, Jerry A. Schulz, Kimber P. Richter, Rhonda K. Lewis, Ella L. Williams, Kari J. Harris, Jannette Y. Berkley, Jacqueline L. Fisher and Christine M. Lopez (1995) 'Using Empowerment Theory in Collaborative Partnership for Community Health and Development', *American Journal of Community Health and Psychology* 23 (5): 677–98.

Fernández Poncela, Ana M., Guadalupe Martínez Uribe, Ma. Cristina Safa Barraza (1994) *Las Políticas Publicas y las Empresas Sociales de las Mujeres*, Mexico City: Grupo de Educación Popular con Mujeres.

Fernández Poncela, Ana M. (ed.) (1995) *Participación Política: Las Mujeres en México al Final del Milenio*, Mexico City: El Colegio de México.

Fink, Marcy (1992) 'Women and Popular Education in Latin America', in Nelly P. Stromquist *Women and Education in Latin America: Knowledge, Power and Change*, London and Boulder, CO: Lynne Reinner, pp. 171–93.

Foro de Apoyo Mutuo (1995) *Organismos No Gubernmentales. Definición, Presencia y Perspectivas*, Mexico City: Foro de Apoyo Mutuo and UNICEF.

Foucault, Michel (1980) *The History of Sexuality, Vol. 1. An Introduction*, New York: Vintage Books.

Foucault, Michel (1989) 'El sujeto y el poder', in Dreyfus and Rabinow (eds) *Más Allá del Estructuralismo y la Hermenéutica*, Mexico City: Universidad Nacional Autónoma de México, pp. 227–44.

Franco, Jean (1998) 'The Long March of Feminism', *NACLA Report on the Americas*, Special Issue on Sexual Politics, XXXI (4): 10–15.

Frazer, Elizabeth (1998) 'Feminist Political Theory', in Stevi Jackson and Jackie Jones (eds) *Contemporary Feminist Theories*, Edinburgh: Edinburgh University Press, pp. 50–61.

Freire, Paulo (1973) *Pedagogy of the Oppressed*, New York: Seabury Press.

Friedmann, John (1992) *Empowerment: The Politics of Alternative Development*, Oxford: Blackwell.

Fukuyama, Francis (1995) *Trust: The Social Virtues and the Creation of Prosperity*, London: Hamish Hamilton.

García Canclini, Néstor (1982) *Las Culturas Populares en el Capitalismo*, Mexico City: Editorial Nueva Imagen.

García Canclini, Néstor (1988) 'Culture and Power: The State of Research', *Media, Culture and Society* 10: 467–97.

Gianotten, Vera and Tom de Witt (1995) *Organización Campesina: El Objetivo Político de la Educación Popular y la Investigación Participativa*, Amsterdam: CEDLA.

Gilly, Adolfo (1997) *Chiapas: La Razón Ardiente: Ensayo sobre la Rebelión del Mundo Encantado*, Mexico City: Ediciones Era.

González de la Rocha, Mercedes (1986) *Los Recursos de la Pobreza: Familias de Bajos Ingresos de Guadalajara*, Guadalajara: El Colegio de Jalisco/CIESAS.

González de la Rocha, Mercedes (1994) *The Resources of Poverty: Women and Survival in a Mexican City*, Oxford: Blackwell.

González Montes, Soledad (1991) 'Los Ingresos No Agropecuarios, el Trabajo No Remunerado y las Transformaciones de las Relaciones Intergeneracionales de las Familias Campesinas', in Vania Salles and Elsie McPhil *Textos y Pretextos: Once Estudios sobre la Mujer*, Mexico City: El Colegio de México, Programa Interdisciplinario de Estudios de la Mujer.

Gregson, Nicky and Michelle Lowe (1994) *Servicing the Middle Classes: Class, Gender and Waged Domestic Labour in Contemporary Britain*, London: Routledge.

Guijt, Irene and Meera Kaul Shah (1998) *The Myth of Community: Gender Issues in Participatory Development*, London: Intermediate Technology Publications.

Gwynne, Robert N. and Cristobal Kay (1999a) 'Introduction to the Political Economy of Latin America', in Gwynne and Kay (1999b), pp. 1–30.

Gwynne, Robert N. and Cristobal Kay (eds) (1999b) *Latin America Transformed: Globalization and Modernity*, London: Arnold.

Hartstock, Nancy C.M. (1996) 'Postmodernism and Political Change: Issues for Feminist Theory', in Hekman (1996), pp. 39–55.

Heilbrun, Carolyn (1998) 'The End of a Long Marriage', in Ann Oakley and Juliet Mitchell (eds) *Who's Afraid of Feminism?* London: Penguin Books, pp. 111–28.

Heilborn, Maria Luiza and Angela Arruda (1995) 'Legardo Feministia e ONGs de Mulheres: Notas Preliminares', in *Genero e Desinvolvimiento Institucional em ONGs*, ed. Nucleo de Estudos Mulher e Políticas Publicas, Río de Janeiro: IBAM/Instituto de la Mujer.

Hekman, Susan J. (ed.) (1996) *Feminist Interpretations of Michel Foucault*, Pennsylvania: Pennsylvania University Press.

Hernández, Luis and Jonathan Fox (1995) 'Mexico's Difficult Democracy: Grassroots Movements, NGOs and Local Government', in Charles A. Reilly (ed.) *New Paths to Democratic Development in Latin America: The Rise of NGO–Municipal Collaboration*, pp. 179–210.

Hoogvelt, Ankie M.M. (1997) *Globalisation and the Postcolonial World: The New Political Economy of Development*, Basingstoke: Macmillan.

Howe, Florence (ed.) (1996) 'Beijing and Beyond: Towards the Twenty-First Century of Women', *Women's Studies Quarterly* XXIV (1–2).

Howell, Jude (1997) 'NGO–State Relations in China', in Hulme and Edwards (1997), pp. 202–15.

Hrdy, Sarah B. (1981) *The Woman that Never Evolved*, Cambridge, MA: Harvard University Press.

Hulme, David and Paul Mosley (1996) *Finance Against Poverty* (Vol. 1) London: Routledge.

Hulme, David and Mike Edwards (eds) (1997) *NGOs, States and Donors: Too Close for Comfort?* London: Earthscan, pp. 202–15.

Ibarolla, Maria Isabel (1991) 'Metodología de Educación Popular Femenista', mimeo, Cuernavaca: CIDHAL.

Illich, Ivan 1971 *Deschooling Society*, New York: Harper and Row.

INEGI (1990) *XI Census of Population and Housing*, Mexico City: INEGI.

Jain, Sharada (1997) 'Awareness Generation, Women's Mobilization and Gender Sensitization: Challenges for 1990s', in Afshar and Alikhan (1997).

Jeffrey, Patricia (1979) *Frogs in a Well*, London: Zed Press.

Jelin, Elizabeth (1997) 'Engendering Human Rights', in Dore (1997), pp. 52–64.

Kabeer, Naila (1994) *Reversed Realities: Gender Hierarchies in Development Thought*, London: Verso.

Kabeer, Naila (1997) 'Empoderamiento desde Abajo: ¿Qué Podemos Aprender de las Organizaciones de Base?, in León (1997), pp. 119–46.

Kabeer, Naila (1998) ' "Money Can't Buy Me Love"? Re-evaluating Gender, Credit and Empowerment in Rural Bangladesh', *IDS Discussion Paper* 363, Brighton: Institute of Development Studies.

Kandiyoti, Deniz (1988a) 'Women and Rural Development Policies: The Changing Agenda', *IDS Discussion Paper* 244, Brighton: Institute of Development Studies.

Kandiyoti, Deniz (1988b) 'Bargaining with Patriarchy', *Gender and Society* 2 (3): 274–90.

Karl, Marilee (1995) *Women and Empowerment: Participation and Decision-making*, London: Zed Books.

Korten, David C. (1990) *Getting to the 21st Century Voluntary action in the Global Agenda*, West Hartford, CT: Kumarian Press.

Lagarde, Marcela (1990) '¿Qué es el poder? in *Educación Popular y Liderazgo de las Mujeres en la Construcción de la Democracia Latinoamericana*, Mexico City: Red de Educación Popular entre Mujeres, pp. 31–42.

Lagarde, Marcela (1992) 'Las Mujeres como Sujeto Político', *FEM*, no. 48.

Lagarde, Marcela (1997) 'Rescatamos Nuestra Palabra, Usurpada por otros Discursos', *Doble Jornada*, October 6, 10–11, in *La Jornada*, Mexico City.

La Jornada, Mexico City: daily newspaper.

Lal, Deepak (1996) 'Participation, Markets and Democracy', in Mats Lundahl and Benno J. Ndulu (eds), *New Directions in Development Economics,* London: Routledge, pp. 299–322.

Lamas, Marta (1998) 'Scenes from a Mexican Battlefield', *NACLA Report on the Americas,* XXXI (4), Special Report on Sexual Politics, pp. 17–21.

Le Bot, Yvon (1997) *El Sueño Zapatista: Subcomandante Marcos,* Mexico City: Plaza & Janes.

León, Magdalena (ed.) (1994) *Mujeres y Participación Política. Avances y Desafíos en América Latina,* Bogotá, Colombia: Tercer Mundo Editores.

León, Magdalena (ed.) (1997) *Poder y Empoderamiento de las Mujeres,* Bogotá: Siglo Veintiuno.

LeVine, Sarah with Clara Sunderland Correa (1993) *Dolor y Alegría: Women and Social Change in Urban Mexico,* Madison and London: University of Wisconsin Press.

Lomnitz-Adler, Claudio (1992) *Exits from the Labyrinth: Culture and Ideology in Mexican National Space,* Berkeley: University of California Press.

Lopezllera, Luís (1995) 'Sujeto, Principios e Instancias. ONGs ante la Sociedad y Poderes', *La Otra Bolsa de Valores,* Mexico City: 32, Separata 7.

Lopezllera, Luís (ed.) (1998) *Sociedad Civil y Pueblos Emergentes: Las Organizaciones Autónomas de Promoción Social y Desarrollo en México,* Mexico City: Promoción de Desarrollo Popular A.C.

Lovenduski, Joni and Vicky Randall (1993) *Contemporary Feminist Politics: Women and Power in Britain,* Oxford: Oxford University Press.

Lovera, Sara and Nellys Palomo (eds) (1997) *Las Alzadas,* Mexico City: Centro de Información de la Mujer.

Lukes, Steven (1974) *Power: A Radical View,* London: Macmillan.

Luna G., Lola (1994) 'Estado y Participación Política de Mujeres en América Latina', in *Mujeres y Participación Política: Avances y Desafíos en América Latina,* Bogotá: Tercer Mundo.

Macdonald, L. (1997) *Supporting Civil Society: The Political Roles of Non-Governmental Organisations in Central America,* London: Macmillan.

McMillan, Brad, Paul Florin, John Stevenson, Ben Kerman and Roger E. Mitchell (1995) 'Empowerment Praxis in Community Coalitions', *American Journal of Community Psychology* 23 (5): 699–728.

Maier, Elizabeth (1994) 'Sex and Class as a Single Entity', in Gaby Küppers (ed.) *Compañeras: Voices from the Latin American Women's Movement,* London: Latin America Bureau, pp. 40–5.

Malvido, Adriana and Salvador Guerrero (1997) 'Pérez de Cuéllar: Asumir otras Formas de Pensar y Actuar, Reto en el Mundo', Informe de la Comisión Auspiciada por la UNESCO: Nuestra Diversidad Creativa, *La Jornada,* 18 September: 25.

Maton, K.A and D.A. Salem (1995) 'Organisational Characterisitics of Empowering Community Settings. A Multiple Case Study Approach', *American Journal of Community Psychology* 23 (5): 631–56.

Martínez Corona, Beatríz and Susana Mejía Flores (1997a) *Ideología y Práctica en Delitos Cometidos contra Mujeres: El Sistema Judicial y la Violencia en una Región Indígena de Puebla, México,* Puebla: Colegio de Postgraduados.

Martínez Corona, Beatriz and Susana Mejía Flores (1997b) 'La Satisfacción de Necesidades Básicas, Estrategia en las Organizaciones de Mujeres Rurales', in Alberti and Zapata (1997).

Maton, Kenneth I. And Deborah A. Salem (1995) 'Organizational Characteristics of Empowering Community Settings: A Multiple Case Study Approach', *American Journal of Community Psychology* 25 (5): 631–56.

Max-Neef, Manfred (1984) *Economía Descalza. Señales desde el Mundo Invisible*, Sweden: Dag Hammarskjold Foundation; Colombia: Fundación Fica.

Max-Neef, M., A. Alizalde and M. Hopenhayn (1989) 'Human-scale Development: An Option for the Future', *Development Dialogue*, Uppsala.

Mayoux, Linda (1998) *Women's Empowerment and Micro-Finance Pogrammes*, Milton Keynes: Open University.

Medel-Añonuevo, Carolyn (ed.) (1995) 'The Theoretical and Practical Bases of Empowerment', in *Women, Education and Empowerment: Pathways towards Autonomy*, Hamburg: UNESCO, pp. 13–22.

Melucci, Alberto 1989 'Social Movements in the Democracy of Everyday Life', in J. Deane (ed.) *Civil Society and the State: New European Perspectives*, London: Verso.

Mercado González, Marta (1997) 'Mujer y Política Agraria en México: Exclusión y Resistencia', in Alberti and Zapata (1997), pp. 81–117.

Mingo, Araceli (1997) *¿Autonomía o Sujeción? Dinámica, Instituciones y Formación en una Microempresa de Campesinas*, Mexico City: Miguel Ángel Porrúa Editores.

Montaño, Sonia (1996) 'Interlocución con el Estado: Participación en el Diseñoy Ejeución de las Politicas Públicas. Relación entre el Movimiento de Mujeres y los Organismos de la Mujer,' *Fem* 158.

Morley, David and Kevin Robins (1995): *Spaces of Identity: Global Media, Electronic Landscapes and Cultural Boundaries*, London: Routledge.

Moser, Caroline O.N. (1989) 'Gender Planning in the Third World: Meeting Practical and Strategic Gender Needs', *World Development* 17 (11): 1799–825.

Moser, Caroline O.N. (1991) 'La Planificación de Género en el Tercer Mundo: Enfrentando las Necesidades Prácticas y Estratégicas de Género', in Virginia Guzmán, Patricia Portocarrero and Virginia Vargas (eds) *Una Nueva Lectura: Género en el Desarrollo*, Lima, Peru: Flora Tristán Editores.

Moser, Caroline O.N. (1993) *Gender, Planning and Development: Theory, Practice and Training*, London: Routledge.

Nelson, Nici and Sue Wright (eds) (1994) *Power and Participatory Development: Theory and Practice*, London: Intermediate Technology Development Group.

Nelson, Paul J. (1990) *The World Bank and Non-Governmental Organizations: The Limits of Apolitical Development*, London: Macmillan.

Nerfin, Marc (1986) 'Neither Prince nor Merchant: Citizen – An Introduction to the Third System', in Krishna Ahooja-Patel *et al.* (eds) *World Economy in Transition* 47.

Neville, Spencer (1996) 'Zapatistas Work to Establish Political Front', *Green Left Weekly* 241.

Nicholson, Linda J. (ed.) (1990) *Feminism/Postmodernism*, London: Routledge.

Nuñez, Carlos (1985 *Educar para Transformar, y Transformar para Educar. Una Perspective Dialectica y Liberadora de Educación y Comunicación Popular*, Guadalajara: IMDEC.

Otto, Dianne (1996) 'Nongovernmental Organizations in the United Nations System: The Emerging Role of International Civil Society', *Human Rights Quarterly* 18: 107–41.

Oxfam (1997) 'Men and Masculinity', special issue of *Gender and Development* 5 (2).

Pain, Rachel (1991) 'Space, Sexual Violence and Social Control: Integrating Geographical and Feminist Analyses of Women's Fear of Crime', *Progress in Human Geography* 15 (4): 415–31.

Parada, Lorena (1995) *Acciones de las ONG para Promover la Participación de las Mujeres en las Estructuras de Poder y Toma de Decisiones*, paper presented at the Fourth World Conference on Women, Beijing.

Pedersen, Hee Christina (1989) *Nunca antes me Habían Ensenado eso*, Lima: Editorial Lilit.

Peralta Salazar, Ana María (1997) 'La Participación de las Mujeres Indígenas en la Producción Cafetalera del Norte de Chiapas', in Alberti and Zapata (1997), pp. 205–18.

Perkins, Douglas (1995) 'Speaking Truth to Power: Empowerment Ideology as Social Intervention and Policy', *American Journal of Community Psychology* 23 (5): 765–94.

Personal Narratives Group (1989) *Interpreting Women's Lives: Feminist Theory and Personal Narratives*, Bloomington and Indianapolis: Indiana University Press.

Peterson, Abby (1989) 'Social Movement Theory', *Acta Sociologica* 32 (4): 419–26.

Pratchett, Terry (1996) *The Hogfather*, London: Victor Gollancz.

Pratt, Mary Louise (1997) 'Where to? What next?' in Álvarez *et al.* (1998), pp. 430–36.

Ramazanoglu, Caroline (ed.) (1993) *Up against Foucault: Explorations of some Tensions between Foucault and Feminism*, London: Routledge.

Rappaport, Julian (1995) 'Empowerment Meets Narrative: Listening to Stories and Creating Settings', *American Journal of Community Psychology* 23 (5): 795–808.

Rayas, Lucia (1998) 'Criminalizing Abortion: A Crime against Women', *NACLA Report on the Americas*, Special Report on Sexual Politics XXXI (4): 22–6.

Razavi, Shahrashoub (1995) 'From WID to GAD: Conceptual Shifts in the Women and Development Discourse', *Occasional Paper for the Fourth World Conference on Women in Beijing*, Geneva: UNRISD.

Reyes, Alicia Yolanda (1994) 'Las Mujeres Solución, No Problema: Rigoberta Menchú', *La Doble Jornada*, Mexico City, 2 May: 14.

Ribeiro, Gustavo Lins (1998) 'Cybercultural Politics: Political Activism at a Distance in a Transnational World', in Álvarez *et al.* (1998), pp. 325–52.

Riger, Stephanie (1997) 'Que Está Mal con el Empoderamiento?' in León (1997), pp. 55–74.

Robles, Rosario, Josefina Aranda and Carlota Botey (1993) 'La Mujer Campesina en la Época de la Modernidad', *El Cotidiano*, March–April: 25–32.

Rojas Rosa (ed.) (1994) *Chiapas: Y las Mujeres que?* Mexico City: La Correa Femenista.

Rovira, Guiomar (1997) *Mujeres de Maíz*, Mexico City: Ediciones Era.

Rowlands, Joanna (1995a) 'Empowerment Examined', *Development in Practice* 5 (2): 101–7.

Rowlands, Joanna (1995b) 'Empowerment Examined: An Exploration of the Concept and Practice of Women's Development in Honduras', unpublished PhD thesis, Durham University, UK.

Rowlands, Joanna (1997a) *Questioning Empowerment: Working with Women in Honduras*, Oxford: Oxfam Publications.

Rowlands, Joanna (1997b) 'What is Empowerment?' in Afshar and Alikhan (1997), pp. 46–61.

Rowlands, Joanna (1997c) 'Empoderamiento y Mujeres Rurales en Honduras: Un Modelo para el Desarrollo', in León (1997), pp. 213–45.

Rowlands, Joanna (1998) 'A Word of the Times, but What Does It Mean? Empowerment in the Discourse and Practice of Development', in Afshar (1998), pp. 11–34.

Salamon, Lester M. and Helmut K. Anheier (eds) (1998) *The Nonprofit Sector in the Developing World*, Manchester and New York: Manchester University Press.

Salles, Vania (1994) 'Pobreza, Pobreza y Más Pobreza', in Javier Alatorre, Gloria Careaga, Clara Jusiman, Vania Salles, Cecilia Talamante and John Townsend, *Las Mujeres en la Pobreza*, Mexico City: El Colegio de México, pp. 47–71.

Sanday, P.R. and R.G. Goodenough (1990) *Beyond the Second Sex: New Directions in the Anthropology of Gender*, Philadelphia: University of Philadelphia Press.

Schmelkes, Sylvia (ed.) (1990) *Posalfabetización y trabajo en América Latina*, Mexico City: OREALC-CREFAL.

Schuler, Margaret (1997) 'Los Derechos de las Mujeres son Derechos Humanos', in León (1997), pp. 29–54.

Scott, James C. (1990) *Domination and the Arts of Resistance: Hidden Transcripts*, New Haven and London: Yale University Press.

Scott, Joan (1986) 'El Género: Una Categoría Útil para el Análisis Histórico', in James Amelang and Mary Nash (eds) *Historia y Género. Las Mujeres en la Europa Moderna y Contemporánea*, Valencia: Edicions Alfons El Magnanim, pp. 23–56.

Sebstadt, J. (1982) *Development and Struggle amongst Self-Employed Women: A Report on the Self-Employed Women's Association of India*, Washington: USAID.

Sen, Gita and Caren Grown (1987) *Development, Crises and Alternative Visions*, New York: Monthly Review Press.

Slater, David (1991) 'New Social Movements and Old Political Questions: Rethinking State–Society Relations in Latin American Development', *International Journal of Political Economy* 21: 32–65.

Slater, David (1994) 'Power and Social Movements in the Other Occident: Latin America in an International Context', *Latin American Perspectives* 21 (81): 11–37.

Slater, David (1998) 'Rethinking the Spatialities of Social Movements: Questions of Borders, Culture, and Politics in Global Times', in Álvarez, Dagnino and Escobar (1998), pp. 380–401.

Smith, Dorothy (1990) *The Conceptual Practices of Power: A Feminist Sociology of Knowledge*, Boston, MD: Northeastern University Press.

Speer, Paul W. and Joseph Hughey (1995) 'Community Organizing: An Ecological Route to Empowerment and Power', *American Journal of Community Psychology* 23 (5): 729–48.

Stein, Jane (1997) *Empowerment and Women's Health: Theory, Methods and Practice*, London: Zed Books.

Stephen, Lynn (1997) *Women and Social Movements in Latin America: Power from Below*, Austin: University of Texas Press.

Stern, Steve J. (1995) *The Secret History of Gender: Women, Men and Power in Late Colonial Mexico*, Chapel Hill, NJ and London: University of North Carolina Press.

Sternbach, Nancy Saporta, Marysa Navarro-Aranguren, Patricia Churchryk, Sonia E. Álvarez (1992) 'Feminisms in Latin America: From Bogotá to San Bernardo', in Escobar and Álvarez (1992), pp. 207–37.

Stromquist, Nelly (1997) 'La Busqueda del Empoderamiento: El que Puede Contribuir el Campo de la Educación', in León (1997), pp. 75–98.

Swedish Ministry for Foreign Affairs (1999) *Men's Voices, Men's Choices: How Can Men Gain from Improved Gender Equality*, available from the Ministry of Foreign Affairs, Department for Global Cooperation, S-103 39 Stockholm, Sweden.

Tarres, María Luisa (1996) 'Espacios Privados para la Participación Pública. Algunos Rasgos de las ONG Dedicadas a la Mujer', *Estudios Sociológicos* XIV (40): 7–32.

Townsend, Alan R. (1992) 'Gender at Work in the OECD Area: New Trends in Female and Part-time Employment', International Geographical Union, Study Group on Gender and Geography, Working Paper 25.

Townsend, Alan R. (1997) *Making a Living in Europe*, London: Routledge.

Townsend, Janet Gabriel (1991) 'Towards a Regional Geography of Gender?' *Geographical Journal* 157 (1): 25–35.

Townsend, Janet with Jennie Bain de Corcuera (1993) 'Feminists in the Rainforest in Mexico', *Geoforum* 24 (1): 49–54.

Townsend, Janet, Ursula Arrevillaga, Socorro Cancino, Elia Pérez, Silvana Pacheco (1994) *Voces Femeninas de las Selvas*, Montecillo, Mexico: Colegio de Postgraduados.

Townsend, Janet G. with Ursula Arrevillaga, Jennie Bain, Socorro Cancino, Susan F. Frenk, Elia Pérez and Silvana Pacheco (1995) *Women's Voices from the Rainforest*, London: Routledge.

Townsend, Janet Gabriel (1997) 'Policy Interventions for the Empowerment of Remote Rural Women in Mexico', in Afshar and Alikhan, pp. 62–88.

Tuñon, Esperanza (1997), *Mujeres en Escena: de la Tramoya al Protagonismo (1982–1994)*, Mexico City: UNAM.

Tuñon, Julia (ed.) (1992) *Familias y Mujeres en México*, Mexico City: El Colegio de México.

Valentine, Gill (1989) 'The Geography of Women's Fear', *Area* 21 (4): 385–90.

Vargas Llosa, Mario (1991) Unpublished speech made in Mexico.

Vargas Valente, Virginia, Cecilia Olea Mauleon (1997) 'El Movimiento Femenista y el Estado: Los Avatares de la Agenda Propia', *Socialismo y Participación* 80: 25–60.

Vasquez García, Verónica (1997) 'Mujeres que "Respetan su Casa": Estatus Marital de las Mujeres y Economía Doméstica en una Comunidad Nahua del Sur de Veracruz', in Soledad González Montes and Julia Tuñon (eds) *Familias y Mujeres en México: del Modelo a la Diversidad*, Mexico City: El Colegio do México, pp. 163–93.

Vélez Quero, Silvia Elena (1994) 'Sólo Socio, no Consorte: el TLC, Estados Unidos y México-Canadá', *El Cotidiano*, No. 60, January–February Mexico City: Universidad Autónoma Metropolitana.

Walby, Sylvia (1990) *Theorizing Patriarchy*, Oxford: Blackwell.

Weber, Max (1990) 'El Uso de los Tipos Ideales en Sociología', in Pierre Bourdieu (ed.) *El Oficio de Sociólogo*, Mexico City: Siglo XXI, pp. 262–9.

Wieringa, Saskia (1995) 'Introduction', in Saskia Wieringa (ed.) *Subversive Women: Women's Movements in Africa, Asia, Latin America and the Caribbean*, New Delhi: Kali for Women, pp. 1–22.

Wieringa, Saskia (1997) 'Una Reflexión sobre el Poder y la Medición del Empoderamiento de Genero del PNUD', in León (1997), pp. 147–12.

Williams, Suzanne with Janet Seed and Adelina Mwau (1994) *The Oxfam Gender Training Manual*, Oxford: Oxfam.

Wilson, Fiona (1990) *De la Casa al Taller*, Zamora: El Colegio de Michoacán.

Wilson, Fiona (1991) *Sweaters*, Basingstoke: Macmillan Education.

World Development Report (1998) Washington: World Bank.

Wrong, Dennis (1979) *Power, Its Forms, Bases and Uses*, Oxford: Blackwell.

Young, Kate (1997) 'El Potencial Transformador en las Necesidades Prácticas: Empoderamiento Colectivo y el Proceso de Planificación', in León (1997), pp. 99–118.

Yudice, George (1997) 'The Globalization of Culture and the New Civil Society', in Álvarez, Dagnino and Escobar (1997), pp. 353–79.

Yuval-Davis, Nira (1998) 'Women, Ethnicity and Empowerment', in A. Oakley and J. Mitchell (eds) *Who's Afraid of Feminism? Seeing through the Backlash*, London: Penguin, pp. 77–98.

Zapata Martelo, Emma (1997) 'Nuevas Formas de Asociación: Mujer Campesina-Iniciativa Privada. Estudio de Caso', in Alberti and Zapata (1997), pp. 117–46.

Zapata Martelo, Emma and Marta Mercado González (1996) 'Del Proyecto Productivo a la Empresa Social de Mujeres' *Cuadernos Agrarios*, Year 6, No. 13, January–June: 104–28, Mexico City: Federación Editorial Mexicana.

Zapata Martelo, Emma, Marta Mercado González and Blanca Lopez Arellano (1994) *Mujeres Rurales antes el Nuevo Milenio*, Montecillo, Mexico: Colegio de Postgraduados.

Zimmerman, Marc A. (1995) 'Psychological Empowerment: Issues and Illustrations', *American Journal of Community Psychology* 23 (5): 581–99.

Index

HUNTED

OUTRUN. OUTLAST. OUTWIT.

The Chase Is On

Edited By Kelly Reeves

First published in Great Britain in 2020 by:

Young Writers
Remus House
Coltsfoot Drive
Peterborough
PE2 9BF
Telephone: 01733 890066
Website: www.youngwriters.co.uk

Printed and bound in the UK by BookPrintingUK
Website: www.bookprintinguk.com
YB0436L

FOREWORD

IF YOU'VE BEEN SEARCHING FOR EPIC ADVENTURES, TALES OF SUSPENSE AND IMAGINATIVE WRITING THEN SEARCH NO MORE! YOUR HUNT IS AT AN END WITH THIS ANTHOLOGY OF MINI SAGAS.

We challenged secondary school students to craft a story in just 100 words. In this first installment of our SOS Sagas, their mission was to write on the theme of 'Hunted'. But they weren't restricted to just predator vs prey, oh no. They were encouraged to think beyond their first instincts and explore deeper into the theme.

The result is a variety of styles and genres and, as well as some classic cat and mouse games, inside these pages you'll find characters looking for meaning, people running from their darkest fears or maybe even death itself on the hunt.

Here at Young Writers it's our aim to inspire the next generation and instill in them a love for creative writing, and what better way than to see their work in print? The imagination and skill within these pages are proof that we might just be achieving that aim! Well done to each of these fantastic authors.

So if you're ready to find out if the hunter will become the hunted, read on!

CONTENTS

Danesgate Community PRU, Danesgate

Keaton Caygill-Robin (15)	56
Gracie Robinson (13)	57
Lara Court (12)	58
Holly Bartlett (13)	59
Karolina Wrzesinska (15)	60
Ryan Scrowston (12)	61

Eden Park High School, Beckenham

Eryk Grzegorz Rzeszowski (12)	62
Hina Kodama-Hurley (12)	63
Caitlin Elsie Lewis (12)	64
Matti Khan (13)	65
Soriyah Reid (12)	66
Charlotte Rooke-Allden	67
Louise Huynh (11)	68
Lola Bo Rolfe (11)	69
Joseph Gutierrez (11)	70
Finley Murray	71
Bryan Noumonvi (14)	72
Charlotte Fuller	73
Millie Claire Alexandra Smith (11)	74
Ella Ann Rose Watkins (11)	75
Bella Rosemary Taylor (12)	76
Cheryl Ati-Tay (11)	77
Isaac Thomas	78
Romilly Knight (12)	79

Forge Valley School, Sheffield

Gabri Squatriti Montgomery (13)	80
Martha Hunter (12)	81

Madinatul Uloom Al Islamiya School, Summerfield

Aasim Ravat (16)	82
Mujaid Islam (15)	83
Mohammed Ikramul Hoque (14)	84
Daiyan Ahmed (15)	85

Daiyan Talha (13)	86
Mohammed-Ali Shahid (11)	87
Yeasin Ahmed (15)	88
Ismail Miya (16)	89

Outwood Academy City Fields, Wakefield

Sravan Pradeep (12)	90
Stephanie Wing Yau Siow (11)	91
Caitlyn Georgina Martin (11)	92
Keta Williamson (11)	93
Maya Khurshid (13)	94
Emily Jane Brown (11)	95
Zainab Azam (12)	96
Quang Pham (11)	97
Talha Malik (12)	98
Ghulam Mustafa Asif (12)	99
Alishbah Ilyas (11)	100

The Westgate School, Slough

Abdihafeed Mustafa Osman Mohamed (11)	101
Leia Humphries (16)	102
Aleena Arif (11)	103
Lola Rose Axtell (12)	104
Aidan Payne (11)	105
Amina Maryam Achour (11)	106
Nicole Maria Krasowski (11)	107
Farina Fazeli (14)	108
Anakin Shrewsbury (14)	109
Safiyya Mukhtar (12)	110
Hamsa Pandraju (11)	111
Yasmine Biskri (11)	112
Adil Khan (11)	113
Muhammad Fareed (11)	114
Megan Duffy (12)	115
Rhys J T Dzikamunhenga (11)	116
Inaya Chaudhry (12)	117
Yasin Ahmed (12)	118
Louise Thomas (11)	119
Imaad Shaikh (11)	120
Alisha Khan (12)	121

Barween Alawie (11)	122	Adrian Fernandes (14)	161
Kamran Farooq (12)	123	Stephen Babbs (15)	162
Subayr Abdulle (12)	124	Daniel Hasan (16)	163
Ruby Louise Moore (11)	125	Ayaan Umar Sheikh (15)	164
Hansini Bellamkonda (11)	126		
Nadia Maminska (11)	127		
Norbert Tryczynski (11)	128		
Patrycja Wloczewska (15)	129		
Arham Ahmed (12)	130		
Kian Hancey (11)	131		
George Lacey (11)	132		
Tommy Fallon (12)	133		
Mackenzie Sears (12)	134		
Maia Evans (11)	135		
Kyren Charles (11)	136		

Westcliff High School For Boys, Westcliff-On-Sea

Kavin Vijaykumar (14)	137
Edwin Frederick Brown (15)	138
Sam Owens (15)	139
Hassan Mustafa Hassan Ahmed (14)	140
Eesa Khan (15)	141
Zain Bokhari (16)	142
William Brenton (15)	143
Archie Hepburn (14)	144
Christopher Butler-Cole (15)	145
Shibha Alam (16)	146
Matthew Singh (15)	147
Ben Dixon (14)	148
Harrison James (15)	149
James Holley (15)	150
Alexander Zierik (15)	151
Aston Cook (15)	152
Issac Leung (14)	153
Oscar Piggott (15)	154
Ben Wright (15)	155
Josh McCarthy (14)	156
Thomas Waters (15)	157
Ethan Tangka (16)	158
Othniel Sahay Mattukoyya (14)	159
Aran Tanseli (14)	160

THE STORIES

The Purge

The sirens echoed down the streets as people tentatively emerged out of the shadows.

Soon after came a voice, "You have ten minutes to escape before murder is legal for 24 continuous hours!"

Suddenly, the streets were flooded with hastily-packed suitcases, bundles, paper bags. I closed my curtains on my neighbours' panic-filled voices.

"Leave it! Run!"

Pouring another drink, grasping my weapon, I focused eagerly on the mobile, five more minutes. Life was going to change for the better. A knock on the door and then I knew, the hunter had become the hunted. My time was over.

Freya Olivia Evans (12)

AKS - Arnold KEQMS, Lytham St Annes

YoungWriters
Est. 1991

The Hunt

"What on earth are you doing?"
"What do you mean?" I said.
"You will be hunted if you stay in bed," he said
As I got out of my bed, I realised how loud I was squirming.
"Get up!" he screamed as I yelped out of bed.
"Arghhhhhh! Get up and deal with it!" Harold said.
Every day I was hunted, for twelve hours. People were
allowed to kill whoever they wanted, without being arrested.
From 8pm-8am, I must survive this hunt. From 8pm, the hunt
is on and before it started, I could see people, ready. Game
over.

Julian Jayaharan
AKS - Arnold KEQMS, Lytham St Annes

Police Chase

I was driving through the city of New York, police chasing, guns blazing, dogs barking and there I was, armed with a knife, still accelerating through the lamp-lit streets. I had been in this kind of situation before, but last time I didn't succeed. I was determined to get away, I had to this time. But the police were right on my tail, anticipating my every move. I could hear the police sirens bleeping and the rotors of the helicopter above my head whooshing through the air. I didn't really know what I was doing other than being hunted.

Sam Curran (11)
AKS - Arnold KEQMS, Lytham St Annes

The Safe Tree

A terrifying howl echoed through the air, ringing in my ears. I instantly identified the animal. As I dashed further into the woods, it appeared that the tree roots were getting bigger and more frequent. I heard the werewolf's paws thundering down on the soil behind me. By the light of the moon, I could see the tree where safety lay, would I make it in time? Before I knew it, I had slipped down that dark tunnel. I looked around the familiar, contorting room, the other foxes were delighted and relieved to see me back in our warm den.

Emma Yelland (11)
AKS - Arnold KEQMS, Lytham St Annes

One Night

The fairground was opening at 7pm tonight, my friend was going with me for the first time. It was 7pm and the fairground opened, my friend wanted to go to the haunted house first. Whilst we were halfway in, my friend became terrified. He heard imaginary whispers. I thought he was joking, but then I heard it too. We tried to escape as rapidly as we could. However, an old, scary, big man jumped behind my friend and murdered him with a kitchen knife. The police found out afterwards, but we still did not know why he committed the crime.

Laura Arts (11)
AKS - Arnold KEQMS, Lytham St Annes

The Mystery

The sirens echoed, the beasts were released. Chainsaws wrenched, ready for the night. Citizens sprinting for their lives while the rugged, bloodthirsty demons stalked for souls! I trudged around with ripped clothes, blood dripping off me, leaving a dark stain. My body was left hollow... Negative thoughts of myself perishing ate me up inside. Suddenly, I couldn't see anything, it was like a light switch turned off, was I in some kind of game? I could hear a sound, it started quietly, but gradually became louder... I was trapped!

Owen Reece Greenwood (11)
AKS - Arnold KEQMS, Lytham St Annes

The Forest Hunt

As I ran down the road into the deep, dark forest, I couldn't figure out what was chasing me. Something was out to get me, and they didn't want to talk. For a few moments, I started asking it questions. On the floor, there was an unnoticeable ditch where I tripped and cut my leg, I desperately needed help. My head went dizzy as I carried on walking forward. By the minute my sight was getting blurrier. By the second, I was getting dizzier, as I fell dramatically onto the floor, unconscious. I knew then I was being hunted!

Lisa Victoria Perry (11)

AKS - Arnold KEQMS, Lytham St Annes

Spy Pursuit

My identity has now been revealed. Down gloomy alleyways, I speed on my motorbike, the sound of sirens echoing behind me. I'm being hunted. I need to get to the dock. I need to escape. Left then right, then straight ahead into the darkness. As I reach the dock, I leap off my motorbike and run. My heart is pounding quicker and quicker. I find a boat full of crates, ready to leave. I clamber up the side until I find an empty one and climb into it, before slamming the crate shut and holding my breath. I'm being hunted...

Harry James Jackson (11)
AKS - Arnold KEQMS, Lytham St Annes

The Final Shot

My target lurked in the shadows. It was the dead of night and I'd been there hours, but the time had finally come. I lined up the shot through the sight, preparing to pull the trigger. It was my sixteenth assassination attempt and I had a 100% record. I didn't intend for that to alter. I took the shot and the bullet ricocheted off the brick wall and suddenly, the cards had changed. The figure spun around and aimed his gun at me. I dropped my sniper and ran for my life as the man pursued me. The gun fired...

Alfie Finn Kelly (11)
AKS - Arnold KEQMS, Lytham St Annes

Hunted

It was cold and I was being hunted. I ran through the grass, I ran around corners and darted past trees, but it was still getting closer. I could see the outline of an old house, I wondered what a house was doing in the middle of the plains of Africa, but I didn't question it. I ran as fast as I could. I was nearly at the house, it turned out that it was an old Western town. I ran into one of the houses, went up to the roof, grabbed my phone and called a camo Chinook helicopter.

Jack Peebles (12)
AKS - Arnold KEQMS, Lytham St Annes

The End Of Humanity

"It has to be here somewhere. C'mon, keep looking."
"C'mon Jay, we have to hurry or the exterminators will come soon."
Exterminators, machines that had been created to help humanity avoid extinction. But the cluster became corrupt. The cluster had command of the extermination. Soon they were killing humans, seeing them as a threat. Killing every human in sight. A whole city was brought down by them, it was a massacre. I still had nightmares. A clatter in the distance, an exterminator. I'd become the prey.
"Jay, we have to leave. Now!"
I was too close. This could help humanity...

Mary Agyemang (13)
Burlington Danes Academy, London

Frowns Of Fortune

My mum had always said we were unlucky. That fortune frowned upon us. A few days ago, I would've said she was just being morbid but now I wasn't so sure. The feeling I was being watched, stalked like prey couldn't be shaken. It haunted every aspect of my life. Soft footsteps pattered across the floor. With my heart beating faster, I came to a halt. Out of the darkness, a light shone on my frightful, bruise-ridden face.

Once the figure emerged, they asked, "What's your name?" From my frozen state, I thought, *my name, what's my name?*

Khawla Warsame (14)
Burlington Danes Academy, London

Ghoulish Apocalypse

Piercing shrieks of fear and terror echoed from the city as hundreds of civilians cried for help, dreading the zombie apocalypse. Bloodbaths surrounded me, as I scrambled in fright towards the woods. I arrived into the forest, running a fast, steady pace as I forced my lungs to breathe air in and out. With confidence, I started to slow down as I was sure that I was safe. Suddenly, a shrivelled hand grabbed me and a cold growl sent shivers down my spine. Abruptly, I assertively pushed the ghoul downhill. Without warning, the zombie lunged onto me, sending me falling...

Anais Roett (14)
Burlington Danes Academy, London

Virus H-3go

I couldn't run much longer, they knew I was weak, I couldn't run anymore. The blisters bulging, my head spinning, the sirens began.
"Oh no, if I'm caught, I'm dead."
They sped up to me.
"Stop!"
I ran into the facility to get the cure for the virus. Every day, more and more turned into monsters. I had got it and then I heard it. The creature with no eyes. If I made a sound it would be the end of me. The creature ran, I heard a bang. The monster was dead.
"Come with me now, or you'll die."

Stanley Buckingham (14)
Burlington Danes Academy, London

Chased

I still have nightmares. They haunt me 'til the day, I am on the run. Why? I once was a part of an organisation. The horrific days of the creatures tearing my limbs apart left and right. The inhalation of the toxic atmosphere was holding my breath. I felt the CCTV cameras burning my soul, then I heard footsteps. the monsters were coming. The silhouette emerged from the thick, grey smoke, intoxicating my lungs. They found me. I yelled for help, I ran, my heart burst from my chest. Today was not the day I was gonna be caught. "Arghhhhh!"

Rubayia Quashem (14)
Burlington Danes Academy, London

Hunted

My legs turned, my torso ached, every inhalation was a struggle and I couldn't run for much longer. I decided to hide myself behind a large hedge. Time had passed and it felt like it had been a while since I stopped moving so I slowly stood up. My heart was crazy due to nerves and fright. I took a deep breath and I ran.
Loud sirens went off and I heard deep voices shout, "He's over there!" and, "Get him, he went past the bush!" Unfortunately, I was too slow and they caught me, I'm now imprisoned for life.

Keyshon Annul (13)
Burlington Danes Academy, London

Getaway

At the back of the bank, Jason loaded his pistol - ready to hit the vault. He lowered his balaclava and entered calmly. Less than two minutes later, he was running to a getaway car three streets away. They drove to a secret location where a helicopter was waiting. The car had no plates, so was untraceable by ANPR. Jason changed into casual clothing and loaded two black boxes into the chopper. He set off on the flight out of the UK. Tokyo was his destination. However, his getaway was only just beginning. He still had to enter Japan unseen...

Benjamin Stanton (14)
Burlington Danes Academy, London

The Hunt Was On

Back then, when the siren wailed, I was ecstatic, yet overcome with fear. My heart was in my mouth and I was quivering. My partner, although inexperienced, was optimistic and helped suppress my doubt. We rendezvoused with our getaway driver at 12.45am. We were on the move and almost at the countryside, the ever-impending blockade had reared its head and persisted over me like a wall. Once again, I had fallen to my fear, I was paralysed but moved. I opened the door and darted towards the woods. Then felt the cold grip of the handcuff...

Markell Case-Gibbs (13)
Burlington Danes Academy, London

The Run

I couldn't run for much longer, my heart was beating like a drum, every breath I took was like a needle stabbing my throat. It wasn't safe and they knew that. Everywhere I went I could feel eyes on me. I knew they were watching. I couldn't run for much longer and they knew that. I stopped to catch my breath, then the sirens wailed. My heart stopped.

A man shouted, "524, get in here!"

I entered the van reluctantly.

Once I got in, the man whispered, "I am one of you and we need to go now."

Lena Abdelrahman (13)
Burlington Danes Academy, London

The Witch Hunter

I had 24 hours left at my house before I did Witch's Chase. When the chase happened, it felt like someone was stabbing my throat. Before I left, I made a witch power that made you disappear and no one could find me.
Until I said, "Get rid of the witch power."
In my mind, it felt like someone was driving me up the wall. I collected my witch belongings and packed them into my suitcase. My cat and I sat on the magic broomstick and escaped the danger. We went to Witch Town, on another planet called Witchoonia.

Audiea Mclean (13)
Burlington Danes Academy, London

My Last Breath

Adrenaline ran through me as I self-consciously paced through the deep, dark forest. My tormentor was coming. I knew he was. Branches whipped my shivery body and my legs could not bear it any longer. The noises in the forest gave me more company than my will desired, petrifying me. Thought whizzed through my brain as my predator caught me. This deep thought put me off of the path, my gored shoulder gave in. I couldn't keep a steady pace as I bumbled. My body had given up, I had lost and I was at the hunter's callous will.

Omar Kherkhache (13)
Burlington Danes Academy, London

Sirens

I'm so close, yet so far away from victory. The sirens wail, signalling that the hunters are close. I take a sip of my water before running again. I ignore the aching in my legs, and the cramps in my stomach, the feeling of pins being shoved down my throat. I have to keep going. Eventually, I am inside the woods. I shiver as I slowly walk through patches of crusty, dry autumn leaves. The chirps and hollers of crying birds engulf my ears, making me forget about being chased. Soon settling, I gasp. I hear the sirens... again.

Namarg Montasir (13)
Burlington Danes Academy, London

My Life Nearly Ended

I couldn't run for much longer. I was getting tired. I found a little corner and quickly got in disguise. I saw CCTV cameras everywhere. I avidly found my car and drove off to the countryside. Unluckily, they tracked my number plate, I was doomed. After twenty minutes, there were undercover police everywhere. The police shot my tyre, my car started spinning and rolling over. I thought my life had ended. I quickly jumped out and got tasered by the police. I couldn't handle it so I just gave up and let them take me in.

Adam Mansour (13)

Burlington Danes Academy, London

Infected

It was too late, I had already injected myself. It wouldn't be long until the side effects kicked in. All I could do was run. Suddenly, I heard sirens behind me and I quickly increased my speed. But then it happened, first my arms turned green and I grew. Then my legs followed by my torso and finally, my head. All of a sudden, rage started surging through my mind and I went on a rampage, stomping and eating everything in my path. Not even the strongest tanks could stop me. The world and everything in it was now mine.

Adnan Ali (14)
Burlington Danes Academy, London

The Mummies

It wasn't safe now. The mummies were after us. Their names were Ramsees Imotehp. The mummies started chasing us when they saw us stealing their treasure. My friend and I were picking their treasure. We heard a big *clang!* Their booby trap was triggered. Me and my friend fell and the mummies lost our sight. We scrambled out of the trap and started running. My heart was beating fast. Suddenly, I heard heavy breathing behind me. I turned and a hand covered with rotten toilet paper reached out for me. I screamed!

Adnan Ahmed (17)
Burlington Danes Academy, London

The Fugitives

Me and my fellow fugitives had made a plan to escape from the smart detectives. Today was the day! Me and my friend fled out of the city in a getaway vehicle. We stopped in a random forest, nobody was there. We ran deep inside and crouched and killed a bird to eat. We were beginning to get comfortable until we realised we lost our mobile phones! We searched around but not for long because we heard drones. We never moved at all. We heard a beeping sound and the drone flew away. The drone came back, followed by sirens...

Mujtaba Walid (14)
Burlington Danes Academy, London

The Witch Hunt

In the middle of the woods in 16th century England was a woman running, it seemed for her life. Her dress in tatters and her hair a bird's nest. Being a witch was what she was accused of and her punishment was what she ran from. She looked a pathetic sight, scavenging for food in the forest, running in almost all directions to get away from her village. Not far away was a team of hunters, searching for their prey. Soon enough, they found her, sleeping on the forest floor, as if she had no worries. They had her!

Barni Sodal (14)
Burlington Danes Academy, London

An Eventful End

On my quest on Hunted, to receive a massive 100,000 pounds, I had just a 29 hour period left. Little did I know how much would happen this day, I was casually walking in the city and heard some sirens. Realising those were police cars trying to get me, I zoomed away. I was followed by them, to reach a dead end. I climbed a building to escape. I was successful with five minutes left. Helicopters flying nearer and nearer, I jumped from building to building. They stopped as it was all over. The sum of money was mine.

Hersi Duhulow (13)
Burlington Danes Academy, London

Escape The Authorities

A month ago, my life changed forever as I got accepted to be part of a run. You had to run away from the authorities. If you didn't get caught, you would win a grand. I was ecstatic. My mum was my getaway driver. She first dropped me off to see my friend. We swapped clothes, went in different directions. She sat in the car with my mum, I went and got on a train to Bradford. On the train, I bumped into a group of people.

They somehow recognised me and said, "Come, we are running away like you."

Bariha Hassan (13)
Burlington Danes Academy, London

The Running Master

I couldn't run for much longer, my legs aching, my heart pounding. My body was telling me to stop, however, my mind the opposite. After all I had gone through, not now. I was one of eight chosen to play and to be able to win £200,000. It was day nineteen, I didn't know who had been caught, all I knew was that I was tired. As I was walking, a man approached me, a drip of sweat ran down my spine, my palms sweating but I acted normal.

"You won," he said.

I couldn't believe it.

Andi Duka
Burlington Danes Academy, London

Border Patrol

The sirens wailed, getting closer and closer as I lay in a bush, weeping from the agonising pain. I wasn't going back, I had made it too far. I could see the blue and red light getting closer and the sound of the police dogs barking getting more intense, when I shot up and started to sprint. The adrenaline surged through my veins and blood trickled down my leg but I didn't stop running. The police dogs were on my tail but I didn't stop. I came to the edge of a cliff when I panicked in disbelief...

Javon Richards (13)
Burlington Danes Academy, London

Escaping Back To Utopia

I was never the best runner, however, I had never felt my legs move so rapidly. My heart was in my mouth and shivers kept running up my spine, I knew that they were coming for me. After a few moments of thinking, I decided it was best to travel back to Utopia. It would be safe and no one would notice that I'd travelled to another planet. The siren started. I grabbed my stuff and travelled through the portal. There I was. Peace, quiet. They wouldn't ever find me. I was safe. But not for very long...

Jaida Corbett (14)
Burlington Danes Academy, London

The Asylum

I couldn't run for much longer, I was breathing heavily, it felt like my lungs were going to collapse! I ran away from the asylum as fast as I could. Crazy people stayed there, I wasn't crazy! As I hid, I thought, *if I hadn't gotten out, would they have killed me or hurt me?* It was dark, so it would be hard to spot me. As I calmed down and got my breath back, I started running again. It would only be a matter of time before they caught me. As I turned right, everything went black...

Maia Buitrago-Cardenas (13)
Burlington Danes Academy, London

The Bank Mission

Today, my life has changed forever. I got a new job, it is something very important. When I got into work today, something was wrong, someone had robbed the bank. The police came quickly, they asked me to come with them as I knew important information about the money that was stolen. I had put a tracker on the bag, the criminal was running away. We got in the car and sirens were wailing. We could see the criminal, he was wearing a mask. We pulled up next to him, we grabbed him and tore off the mask...

Reda Elhani (13)
Burlington Danes Academy, London

The Frantic Escape

We had twenty-four hours to escape the facility or we would be tracked down and caught. The siren was going to go off any time and we had to be out of the area then. I was close to the exit, but the unthinkable happened. The siren went off and we immediately knew our location was visible. We made it out though. We looked around the area for a red vehicle. It was not here. It was somewhere and we needed to find it. My driver remembered it was a green van and we saw it behind. We escaped!

Hamza Hassan (14)
Burlington Danes Academy, London

The Danger That Lay Ahead

The sirens wailed. They were near. My torso ached and I felt as if my body was shutting down on me. I had to keep on going as I knew the danger that was fast approaching. I then felt a presence around me, I didn't want to look so I ran as fast as I possibly could. Now fatigued and breathless, I came to a halt. There was silence... not the silence that gave you a shiver down your spine, this silence put me at ease. I had to change my disguise. All I could do now was wait...

Imman Hersi (14)
Burlington Danes Academy, London

Stalked

My legs burned, my torso ached, every inhalation felt like needles stabbing my throat but I had to keep going, I had to run for my life. I hid but I could always feel the stalker's presence, it was like a game of hide-and-seek. He was the predator and I was his prey, every drop of blood that fell, the dizzier I felt.

I knew this was the end of it so I asked, "What do you want from me?"

I was crying my eyes out when I felt a *bang* on my head...

Noor Milad (13)
Burlington Danes Academy, London

Don't Look Back

I have to leave. Now. There is no time to waste. I have a huge bombshell for the hunters. I watch as every runs as quickly as possible, I do too. As I leap into the SUV, I change my appearance and my getaway driver drives out of the city and into the country. I get my driver to pick someone very special up and leave my phone at a driveway. All of a sudden, sirens wail behind me. I am shocked. How did they find me? It is now or never. Don't look back, just keep running.

Aalaa Ahmed (13)
Burlington Danes Academy, London

The Bite

I couldn't run for much longer, my legs felt numb and the bite on my arm started to swell. Darkness flooded the forest, however, streams of moonlight illuminated my path. I only had 24 hours before I would no longer own my body. The only vaccination was across the city, I began to lose hope. Breathing started to become harder and my vision blurred. I dropped to the ground and accepted my fate, I let out one last scream and closed my eyes...

Jamire Dobbyn-Scott (14)
Burlington Danes Academy, London

Hunted

My heart was pounding, my legs were weak and my head was dizzy. I didn't know where else to go apart from the countryside. So I got out of the car and sprinted through the trees until I eventually stopped outside a cave. There was a lot of pressure on me to find my teammate before the hunters got here, so I really needed to hurry up. I ran to the next pit stop on the map and I had finally found my teammate near the lake.

Nabil Kadu (13)
Burlington Danes Academy, London

And Then...

As I ran, my legs began to feel numb. My mind was processing a lot of things at that moment. My heart was pounding so fast, I felt as though it would pop out. I couldn't run for much longer and I only had thirty minutes to reach the hide. As I was waiting for my getaway driver, sirens began to wail. At this point, I knew I was not safe.
Then I told my getaway driver, "We have to leave now."

Yusra Ali
Burlington Danes Academy, London

On The Move

The sirens wailed, the chase was on. It was not safe in the forest, I slept under bushes. It was torture. I escaped prison and was on the move. I knew they would try and catch me by all means necessary. I was in the forest and I heard a dog, I ran 'til I couldn't anymore. Had I got away?

Fidel Tesfamichael (18)
Burlington Danes Academy, London

Hospital Hallucination

My eyelids fly open as a young girl shakes my shoulder, insisting we run.

"I see it too," she whispers, dragging me from my hospital bed, stumbling down the corridor.

It's after us. We skid around the corner and the girl catches her ankle, but we still climb the stairs. We reach the rooftop, no sign of the...

"Nooooo!"

It's taking over her. She's flailing, screeching. I take a step back, losing balance from the lack of railing, falling towards traffic. In these last few seconds, I remember something, something irrelevant; now it's too late...

I haven't taken my meds.

Abigail Skerrett (14)
Cottingham High School & Sixth Form College, Cottingham

The Chase

As the clocks struck twelve, the search began. Sirens wailed. Lights beamed, illuminating the bare town streets. Eerie houses towered over the criminal imprisoning him like a caged animal. My eyes ached with pain, my fingers trembled with anxiety and the exasperating sirens defended me. As the moon glistened in the murky air, the sound of gasping drew closer to our approach. We remained silent and didn't dare move a muscle. The trap dangerously dropped down, enclosing something. Red eyes glared, legs jolted, and a fierce roar burst out. Suddenly, the bulging eyes flickered and tears began to stream.

Martha Lund (13)
Cottingham High School & Sixth Form College, Cottingham

Escape

Entangled and hemmed in by a million hate-filled words, my brain tried desperately to process exactly who I am. I would not be beaten down by others' thoughtless comments... and yet, their cruel jibes circled around me like buzzards, threatening to engulf me and gobble me up relentlessly. Trapped, isolated, broken. This would be far from a distant memory. The tears, the screams, the pain, they would stay with me forever. A hand enfolded mine and somewhere, through the dark fog of isolation and despair, I realised that I could escape this terrible torment and be no more the hunted.

Sophie Shad (13)
Cottingham High School & Sixth Form College, Cottingham

Farewell Hope

It's not safe now they know. War struck, snow-covered Russia is a dangerous place, even more so now we're on high alert. Radiation controls the mind and it certainly is here. Darkness is a gift. I tread on through the trees. Owls hooting, head throbbing. Must follow. Follow. Listen. No footsteps. He's okay... for now. Legs driving onwards. Heart breaking. Go. I am coming for him. He's my only hope. I don't want to kill him. I have to kill him. I love him. Fingers pull the trigger. I surge towards him. I clutch his face. "Goodbye, fallen angel."

Evelyn Rona Higgins (14)
Cottingham High School & Sixth Form College, Cottingham

Incapable

We can't escape! There, there's a man deliriously darting around the mall. I can hear gunshots constantly ringing in my ears. Although, I don't think the insane man is harming anyone, yet at least. I can see the corridor and shops opposite. I think the psychotic man is running away from something, someone. The police, maybe. I hear sirens. Are they here to save us? But why would they put us on lockdown? Surely they would help evacuate?
"Over here!"
The police are rescuing a group of teenage girls. *Bang!*
What was that? The man? He went the other way...

Leone Hill (13)
Cottingham High School & Sixth Form College, Cottingham

The Day We Found Them

The creature convulsed in the corner, spewing its grimy compound. Yet it felt different. It seemed more human than the others. Human extremities poured from its mangled head and occasionally, human skin showed from the mauled mess of oozing pustules. Yet still, I must finish the job. I took the shot, it lurched forward until the bullet hit. I heard a piercing chorus of screams from below. I peered through a hole and I saw them. The hive hummed beneath me, their shrill cry mirroring my silenced pest. Then slowly, all their eyes turned to me. And then, they came...

Alfie Sibary (13)
Cottingham High School & Sixth Form College, Cottingham

Hunt

The hunter oiled his gun, an instrument of death waiting to be tuned. Torches lit up the camp in the distance and soldiers staggered about, clutching beer bottles. Something caught the hunter's eye, there he was, the commander. The one he had come for. As the hunter lay in the mud, he heard something behind him. He slashed with his knife blindly, narrowly missing the doe's neck which scuttled away quickly. He needed to get back to his gun. Any second now the shot would come, and it did. He pulled the trigger, killing the attacker and saving the commander.

Oliver Horsfield (13)
Cottingham High School & Sixth Form College, Cottingham

Lost Blood

Lying on the cold concrete, completely paralysed, neck weeping with blood, I only had a few minutes. I should've stayed home. Walking along the street alone, with a stranger behind me, tracking me. Not looking, but hearing him creeping faster, coming closer. In a moment of panic, I turned a corner, then I felt a powerful grasp. He dragged me back and slashed my neck, no not slashed, bitten. I fell hard and he fled, but I was alive. I felt an agonising surge of pain, then nothing. The shiver, the ache, gone. Was this death? Then came the thirst...

Frances Eileen Mary Kirby (13)
Cottingham High School & Sixth Form College, Cottingham

Him

She was running, no, sprinting, through the forest, her breath heavy and her face flushed. Sweat dripped from her forehead. She'd gone days without her medication and her ears began to ring and eyes flicker with pictures of him. He was there. His face was shadowed but she knew he was there, pale and blood streaming down his head, just like the last time she had seen him. There was nowhere for her to run, he caught up, panting and she teetered over the edge of the ravine.

"Revenge," he said in a husky voice.

Then darkness...

Eliza Hinchliffe (14)
Cottingham High School & Sixth Form College, Cottingham

Alone

I had nightmares, fearing for this day to come. I couldn't run for much longer. My heart pounding out of my chest. The moon illuminating the emptiness surrounding me. As I was staggering up and down the hills, hearing the robotic voice drawing closer and closer, I was in an isolated universe. Nowhere to go, nowhere to hide, no one to help. I was trapped. They knew I couldn't go on for much longer. They stalked my every move. Exhaustion took over me, I could feel my legs tiring. It was over.
"That's it, done. We have won."

Holly Hines (13)
Cottingham High School & Sixth Form College, Cottingham

The Creator

My legs were burning, every breath felt like an extra needle going into my stomach. A dark shape whizzed past me and pinged into a tree. I couldn't see what it was, but I didn't have time to look. Ever since a massive electro pulse went off called the 'Ware', no electronics were working anywhere. No guns, no phones, no cars, no help, no rules. People had just turned into savages. I got to the fence, marking territory and jumped over. I was safe. I would like to say I was innocent, but I created this mess, created the 'Ware'.

Alex Horsfield (13)
Cottingham High School & Sixth Form College, Cottingham

They Said

They said it was safer not to know how nor why. Our world was a wasteland, why? Sprinting towards the only form of life left on this dreaded Earth, I thrashed through leafless bushes, staggering up and down the hills. I didn't think I could run for much longer, but I needed answers. I hadn't had water nor food for days, only time would tell how long I had left. I could see bright lights getting closer, closer until I was standing right in front of them. They said it was safer not to know why, I wanted to know...

Ashlynne Downie (13)
Cottingham High School & Sixth Form College, Cottingham

Jungle Hunt

The night was drawing in. The beasts were closing in on me. The pride was gaining distance. I tried to make one last burst but I was running on empty. Already I had reached the forest, escaped a net and sheltered behind a tree. But now, the beasts circled around me. I had no idea why they wanted me or why they carried sharpened weapons but I hopelessly stumbled on. It seemed like I was no longer king of the jungle. I was alone and weak.

Leah Price (13)
Cottingham High School & Sixth Form College, Cottingham

Virus

Sunny day. Big, heavy clouds out of nowhere. A bulky man on a screen, demanding his virus. A bomb timer. Ten minutes. *Tick-tock!* The hunt is on... We start on 34th Street, Greenwich. Heart is going 100mph. Searching the building, *tick-tock!* Cutting 2nd Avenue and onto 14th. Heart racing going from gear one to gear six, now we're on 20th. An old, crooked building. This is where it is. Ragged stairs. We have five minutes. *Tick-tock!* There's two minutes. We're in an isolated room. Found the virus. Neutralise the virus? Virus released. Break out! There's a door...

Keaton Caygill-Robin (15)
Danesgate Community PRU, Danesgate

The Glarer

It all began two months ago when I was walking, I saw a man in the shadows. As I walked closer, he was gone.
As time went by, he started whispering, "There's no escaping."
What does that mean? I panicked so started running but every time I thought I was alone, he was there.
I packed my things and I said, "This is the end."
He said, "As long as you're here, I am too."
He whispered, "I'm the Glarer."
I started running, then fell. It was all a dream, but he was still there. He is the Glarer.

Gracie Robinson (13)
Danesgate Community PRU, Danesgate

Tick, Tock

I was astounded; we'd been gone for two years but only now had been found. It started when Mona heard the wailing sirens from outside. She quickly realised we weren't safe. We packed what we could and headed for the roof. As I looked down, the situation became apparent. Meanwhile, footsteps could be heard from the stairwell. Panic-stricken, we found a nearby apartment window left open. As we dove through, a large thud could be heard. As we searched, me and Mona jumped under the bed. All that could be heard was the clock's slow *tick. Tick... tock!*

Lara Court (12)
Danesgate Community PRU, Danesgate

Bath Bombshell

Soaking my cares away, enjoying a gorgeous bath full of bubbles, I watched the candles flickering as the lovely Christmas smell drifted up my nostrils. Suddenly, a gentle buzz interrupted the silence and took me by surprise. I reached to the side and picked up my phone.

Holding the phone up to my wet ear, a calm voice murmured, "You will die soon, traitor!"

What had I done? Who was that? Why did they want to kill me? The buzzing phone told me nothing. The creaking steps told me the end would be sooner rather than later...

Holly Bartlett (13)

Danesgate Community PRU, Danesgate

Fear: Such A Pretty Thing

Fear: noun, an emotion caused by the threat of danger, pain or harm. Fear is such a pretty thing, the feeling of cold dread and adrenaline coursing through the body. Oh so, so tasty... I love chasing them, seeing their terrified eyes brimming with tears, or their pained screeches as I tear their flesh apart. I love when they run, run as fast as their legs can carry them, until they collapse and scramble backwards, trying to hide as if I can't smell their sweet fear. Fear is such a pretty thing, the only thing they feel when falling asleep...

Karolina Wrzesinska (15)
Danesgate Community PRU, Danesgate

Alien Containment

We had to leave now, the alien had escaped from its containment cell. We ran for our lives, each blink displayed more fear. Steam scattered from the cell. Rapidly we ran, the alien was coming, searching everywhere. We hid from the alien. Its green eyes, as green as neon lamps, glared at us. Its long-fingered claws reaching out to snatch us and take us to the plane. I felt such extreme fear, I could not move. This was the end. It was all over... The alien was standing in front of us. There was no escape...

Ryan Scrowston (12)
Danesgate Community PRU, Danesgate

Hunted

Mistakes were made, now I'm here. Through the forest, up the hill, sombre clouds darkened the sun. Blood dripping, I'm limping, my life flashed before me. Why did a relationship ruin my life? Footsteps thumping, my heart's pumping, men shouting. I can't run for long, I'm getting colder, my eyes are sullen, my feet are swollen. They're behind me, the darkness surrounds me. There's a house with no lights, the place I'll go they'll never know. Stalked upon night, a kiss ruined my life. Upon the hill, water beneath. They're behind me. What do I do? Jump...

Eryk Grzegorz Rzeszowski (12)
Eden Park High School, Beckenham

Hunted

"Go, go! Check every room completely! Don't let her get away!" shouted a familiar, cold voice.

Silently, I dashed under the table and analysed the room. I heard the guards creeping around and my panic became overwhelming. Staring around the room I tried to find a better place to hide, even better to escape. That was when I saw the vent, this was my perfect escape. After I climbed onto the marble table, I reached for the vent and concentrated, the tingling feeling came to my hand. Lightning sparked out of my fingers electrocuting the vent. This was my escape.

Hina Kodama-Hurley (12)
Eden Park High School, Beckenham

Hunted

Sat. Nothing. A crisp touch of peace. One second. A thousand hours, infinite words. *Tick! Tock!* The clock inside of me pounded. Silence. I know they're out there. I can feel it. The sirens. Darkness of the mind. Empty. My time is over. Sat. Nothing. Thoughts crashed against the walls of my mind. Disasters within myself. Tears. Falling through. I knew they would come for me. Banging on the walls. It's time. Time for whatever was going to happen. To wake up from the endless dream. Time. The alarm rang. The awakening. Sitting up, I reach to end the pain.

Caitlin Elsie Lewis (12)
Eden Park High School, Beckenham

Running From Death

The euphoric atmosphere which had hung upon the group diminished into the night air, like a flame blown out. The slow tempo of boots squelching into the waterlogged field transitioned into a rapid urgency of escape. Everyone absconded, the presence of death, strong. Those who were the slowest were audibly crunched underfoot. A dozen turned to half of what was present just a minute ago. Mist formed in front of the remaining captives as they exhaled, running to witness a tomorrow. Individuals were abstruse, unable to comprehend their misfortune. The inevitable... death.

Matti Khan (13)
Eden Park High School, Beckenham

Mother Monster

"What kind of daughter leaves her mother?"
It was coming closer and closer, every step. Eveleigh was getting tired, anxious. Her legs grew weaker every second she continued, deep down she knew that it would come back to find her. Desperate to find a place to hide, she stopped at the nearest tree and climbed up. Her fingers sank into the thick bark of the tree. Time was running out. She sat up there for what felt like hours. She heard police sirens wailed. She was safe.
Now the monster said, "You can't take me away from my daughter!"

Soriyah Reid (12)
Eden Park High School, Beckenham

Hunted

Running. Running past blurs of objects, maybe doll boxes, maybe dangling dead bodies, I wouldn't know. That voice. The voice was in my head.

The voice was rattling in my ears speaking, "I see you."

My hairs stood straight up. Turning around, but only an empty corridor stood. I turned around, a large shadow was standing over me.

"You think you can escape?" he laughed.

He struck. I watched as a knife out of nowhere sliced clean through my heart. Hot blood erupted all over me. My scream had never been so silent. I was another victim.

Charlotte Rooke-Allden
Eden Park High School, Beckenham

Hunted

And there it was... Its coal-black fur, large feathered wings and blinking yellow eyes caught my curious-self. It flashed brightly before my eyes. A creature so speedy yet so incomprehensible such as it couldn't be real, could it? *I need to catch it,* I thought immediately. A creature such as this must definitely be caught, it'll grant me wealth, popularity and the dream life I've been waiting for.
So I chased it. Suddenly, there was a sharp pain in my chest. Blood dripped down my body, I screamed but no one heard...

Louise Huynh (11)
Eden Park High School, Beckenham

Hunted

Walking. The sound of crunchy autumn leaves beneath my feet. Being scared of death. Panting heavily, I heard voices as I plummeted to the cold, wet ground. Bottling my breath up inside of me, I got back up and hastily sped up to the top of the hill where no one could find me. Dr Gyroskov, he was hunting me. Why? Slowly but surely, my head was as heavy as a ginormous boulder and I started to slow down.
"Stop!"
I froze. Dr Gyroskov was right there, studying me like a scientist scrutinises his newest specimen.
Bang...

Lola Bo Rolfe (11)
Eden Park High School, Beckenham

Hunted

How did this happen? One left burnt. Forward, bitten by tarantulas. I went right to see a key for the end.
"Come boy."
He was coming. How did he get past the life-ending booby-traps? I dashed to a mirror maze with millions of me. One right a lion. Forwards, knife floor. I went left to see a knife with dried blood. He was here. I chose the knife floor. *Slice!* I finally woke up, wanting to go for a walk. *Ding!* I got a key out of my pocket instead of my phone. I was still in 'The Hunted'...

Joseph Gutierrez (11)
Eden Park High School, Beckenham

Gone

A bad choice. The darkest night the archipelago had ever seen. The sea was an inky blue. The sands under my feet were like grainy quicksand and thunder rumbled with rage. It was after me. No, there were more. They wanted me dead. My life depended on my stamina. Unexpectedly, a hideous smell struck my nose and a howling monster leapt out! I could taste blood. Metallic, disgusting. I felt four freezing, clammy paws over my back. I was a goner. A goner. A goner. However, the trees whacked it out of the way. A miracle. Time to go onwards.

Finley Murray
Eden Park High School, Beckenham

Delectable

The atmosphere was tenebrous. I ran swiftly and hungrily to peel the flesh off his skin. I ran to taste the delicious blood that poured from his leg. He knew he was finished. Fiercely, I threw my spear at him, plunging right through his heart. Panting for breath, burning with fury, thirsty for revenge, I ambled towards him as he lay dead on the ground. I grabbed my spear, eager to taste sweet blood and fresh meat. Fiercely, I cut open my friend's stomach and feasted on his delectable insides. I enjoyed a feast and it was glorious.

Bryan Noumonvi (14)
Eden Park High School, Beckenham

Hunted

Everything went quiet, it was time to start the hunt. The clicks of doors, the adrenaline pumping, it all fuelled my thirst for blood. Trampling into the school with an axe in my hand. I was hungry. Something was different. There was a child out of class. My first victim, my starter, my lunch. Following the stench, I found the child standing at the end of the corridor not knowing the hell that would befall him. Axe held up, I feasted.

Picking the hair out of my teeth in my cell. It was all worth it. Finally, I was full.

Charlotte Fuller
Eden Park High School, Beckenham

Howl

Panting. My paws ache. I can't run for much longer. My fur is covered in crimson twigs and bloody thorns. But the hunters are catching up. I need to move and fast. *Bang!* A shot in the darkness. They miss but my tail is warm and sticky. Pain. I slump to the floor. I can't go back or forward; God, take me to Heaven already! Light. They're closing in. Those blinding beams will be my death sentence. Move! Just kill me, I can't go on. Voices shouting. Shots shattering the silence. No one can hear me howl.

Millie Claire Alexandra Smith (11)
Eden Park High School, Beckenham

Hunted

There I was, running for my life. It was dark in the forest. I was just taking in the plants but it all changed. It's coming. Where should I go? The venomous, yellow eyes were drawing close. I was being lashed by the branches. Blood was flowing down my face, clothes were being torn. Vines, trees and ivy were closing in. Oh no! Footsteps drew nearer. The path was ending. I was done for. There were more devilish eyes. I was trapped. They were getting closer and closer and closer. There was howling. The sound of death.

Ella Ann Rose Watkins (11)
Eden Park High School, Beckenham

Hunted

I had 24 hours but time had run out. I could feel my heart pounding in my chest. My hands began to shake, the world began to spin, the same thought ran through my head like a broken record: *they won't find you, you're okay.* The world disappeared and I blacked out... My eyes fluttered open, my head ringing. I could hear foreign voices and footsteps that echoed tauntingly across the room. What they did to those people was wrong. What if they did the same to me? One instinct, one impulse... run.

Bella Rosemary Taylor (12)
Eden Park High School, Beckenham

Hunted

It was a calm day. I was on a relaxing holiday in the Caribbean. The weather was very warm and I could feel the breeze brush against me. As I sat in the sun, I could feel the eyes of someone watching me from behind. However, I decided to leave it and go into the water. The cool waves of the aquamarine sea washed up onto my feet. Suddenly, something tapped me. I turned around but nothing was there. Not even a family. I felt scared but I was certain someone was there. Or was there?

Cheryl Ati-Tay (11)
Eden Park High School, Beckenham

Survivor

We drew first blood in the war. And they will take their revenge. I found the first two weeks ago. She was a rotting corpse. Dead, like many of them we killed. I found the second two weeks later, maggots crawling out of the large clotted bite marks all over his body. The third, I found yesterday. Just a skeleton. I am number four, I know I am next. I hear a guttural scream over the hill and a thousand icy daggers dig into my skin. I will not fall. I will survive.

Isaac Thomas
Eden Park High School, Beckenham

Hunted

It was an extremely stormy day. The wind was lashing at the back of my bitterly cold legs. Night was calling and I knew I would have to take refuge for the night sometime soon. All this running away, all for the fact my time had run out. They were coming for me and they were coming for me at a scarcely quick rate. Soon, I would become too tired for any more running. I knew I didn't have much life left in me! I had stopped for a rest. They caught up...

Romilly Knight (12)
Eden Park High School, Beckenham

Hunted

The beast was coming. Sent by the power to put us in line. When they are disobeyed, the beast comes. Every day, their grip on us tightens. Refusal to work, inability to work, leads to death. Only the elderly can remember a time without the power. Only the elderly can remember a time when you weren't killed for having an opinion. The power cannot be stopped. Prophecies state that only one will rise and one will succeed. They will liberate the land and make us all free from this life of misery. But you can only prolong the inevitable. *Snap!*

Gabri Squatriti Montgomery (13)
Forge Valley School, Sheffield

Hunted

Hunted. Hunted for your life, belongings and freedom. I'm fleeing from the country. Away from my family and life but I have to do it for my safety. But it isn't easy and never was going to be. I am being hunted by the government, the police and the police we call 'The Chasers' and that's where I am now. Behind me is a car full of armed Chasers. My heart is pounding and I am starting to get tired. I don't know if I will make it out alive. I am a refugee and I am being hunted.

Martha Hunter (12)
Forge Valley School, Sheffield

The Cage!

"Fight! Fight! Fight!"
The chant echoed through the Colosseum. Hundreds and thousands of people sat, eager on their seats, preparing themselves for the battle ahead of them. In the centre, a cage moulded out of glistening black metal, entrapping its inhabitants. A courageous warrior stood shaking in the middle! Waiting for him patiently, a monstrous savage! Its fiery eyes blazed through the bars of its cage, visualising the scene of its release and the moment where it brutally mutilates the body in front of it! The bars came up and... blood splattered everywhere! The crowd went wild. I was next...

Aasim Ravat (16)
Madinatul Uloom Al Islamiya School, Summerfield

The Betrayed

Enveloped by civilisations of historic pain, paralysed in a state of awe, stood the hunted. The hunter, the hunted, our eyes instantly interlocked. No introduction was required. Its bloodthirsty figure dazzling from the once innocent moon, like a pirate's sapphire. Any spark of hope that may have resided within me had been thoroughly extinguished. The silhouette had begun his imminent descent, down the podium it once was. His eminence seemed to teleport from grave to grave. A sense of familiarity ran through my veins. Privileged enough to send me to my eternal fate, until I realised... it was my brother.

Mujaid Islam (15)
Madinatul Uloom Al Islamiya School, Summerfield

Untitled

Incandescent. Pure, brilliant light saturates the former dismal oblivion. I wrestle against my fastened bonds. Footsteps echo across the bare room. Everything is white. Except the man. Bent double, eyes bloodshot, he paces the room. My eyes freeze white with fear, sweat trickles down my spine in anticipation. It agonisingly morphs as I sit helpless and still. Suddenly, my ropes are slashed! Behind me, the creature battles itself, ramming the fist it used to free me against the wall. Unhampered by my daze, I flit towards the door. My head passed first. Carnage after, my blood blemishing the white walls.

Mohammed Ikramul Hoque (14)
Madinatul Uloom Al Islamiya School, Summerfield

Murderous Intent

The door smashed open as a bullet poured through. Two guards hurried into the room. Panic striking, one guard shot a bullet at the window. He had escaped. No trace could be found. Was he hiding? Guards were confused. Police were ordered to investigate, this was horrific! A serial killer? A threat, a fugitive was one the run. Two hours had passed. One important call came through. A man had called. He had reported seeing him at the graveyard. The police quickly reacted. They hurried to the destination, they heard a cry as they entered. Had he killed once again?

Daiyan Ahmed (15)
Madinatul Uloom Al Islamiya School, Summerfield

The Abandoned Forest

Jack, Ibrahim and Max were at home. They planned to play football later, but Jack kicked the ball strongly and it went into the forest. The forest was abandoned, however, they still went in. They went in the direction that the ball went in and eventually found the ball. However, they saw a silver, thick chain stuck to the ground. Straight in front of them, they saw a figure approaching, it had blood running down the side of its face and arm and his eyes were completely white. All three of the boys were running until they heard Jack scream...

Daiyan Talha (13)
Madinatul Uloom Al Islamiya School, Summerfield

Demon Or Demons?

There was no time to run longer, the demon's legs were energised with energy and I was coming to an end. The demon would have eyes like a predator and had the power of stealth, like no other. I didn't know if I was experiencing a dream or was I running of my own will? All I could remember was buying a few groceries from a supermarket and the shopkeeper had decisive eyes, tattoos all around, added with a few piercings that would show off his true colours. I had only very little energy left in me. Would I survive?

Mohammed-Ali Shahid (11)
Madinatul Uloom Al Islamiya School, Summerfield

100 Seconds Left

There was 100 seconds left, now 93 left. My life depending on the 86 seconds remaining. I saw my life flashing in front of me like it does to someone about to die. The end hunting me. Like I'm prey, not letting me forget that I have 51 seconds until my end. Was it possible? Could I make it? I hunted my memory for the answers I needed to live for so I could escape from all of this chaos! I was scared and lonely and I didn't know what to do. Seven seconds left, waiting for my death...

Yeasin Ahmed (15)

Madinatul Uloom Al Islamiya School, Summerfield

The Gravestone Hunt

Creeping through the dark wasteland of the dead, hunting for what would get me my reward. I really needed the money, even if I had to dig up a dead body just to get it. And if I didn't, I would end up back here but six-foot under! I was too young to die. I was thinking for too long, I tripped over a stone and hurt my ankle. My heart and head were arguing about what to do. But a silhouette appeared and asked me what it was I hunted! Was I hunting, or... was I the hunted?

Ismail Miya (16)
Madinatul Uloom Al Islamiya School, Summerfield

The City Boy

Theo just woke up. He was at the city before 'he' was... it was painful. It hurt like a cut that never closed.

"Mary..." he started, then he remembered.

'He' took her away from him. 'He' took everyone he cared about. His mixed emotions: anger, fear, hate; rose up inside of him like a volcano about to explode.

"Arghhhhh!" he began to roar.

Bang! His chest suddenly popped. He looked down to see a gashing river of blood. It was 'him'. 'He' came for Theo. Theo's head throbbed.

"Goodbye," he said with sarcasm and everything around him faded to darkness.

Sravan Pradeep (12)
Outwood Academy City Fields, Wakefield

The Chase

I couldn't run for much longer, the police were on the hunt for me. Panic and desperation were suffocating me. *Boom!* An explosion of bullets was ringing behind me. I was in danger. I could hear a familiar voice screaming. It was me! I tripped over and pain started to invade me. Quick footsteps were eagerly coming. I couldn't let them catch me. I was in prison for nothing. I was innocent. I stood up and ran for my life. My heart ferociously pounded and I couldn't hear sirens around me. I was safe but where could I go next?

Stephanie Wing Yau Siow (11)
Outwood Academy City Fields, Wakefield

The Caterpillar... Wait, What?

I had 24 hours; to run, to hide. Why 24 hours and not minutes? Well, you see... I'm being chased by a caterpillar. Yes. You heard right. It's not any caterpillar though, and yes I'm sure it's a caterpillar, it's a gigantic, alien caterpillar. I stopped in a dark alley, it seemed to go on and on and on, it was like there was no end to it until... I bumped into the monster! How did it find me? I guess this is it! I had a few last words,
"Bye Mum, Bye Dad, Bye little sister, goodbye."
Thud!

Caitlyn Georgina Martin (11)
Outwood Academy City Fields, Wakefield

The Dead Of Night

It's the dead of night. There are footsteps getting louder every second. The next thing I know, my mum's coming in, telling me to go into the kitchen. The police were there. Someone was after us. My mum was bringing suitcases filled to the brim with clothes. I was clueless about what was happening. We went to my grandma's cabin. Two weeks later, there was thumping on the door. Nobody was there, we called the police. They stayed with us. The police got a call and the person that was stalking us got sent off to another area, far away!

Keta Williamson (11)
Outwood Academy City Fields, Wakefield

I Am The Hunter

They had to be here somewhere. Months I have been searching, waiting for this day to come. Anger and frustration eating me up inside, I was ready to kill. It was time to catch my prey. Mother died nine months ago, heart attack, that's what the doctors said but I knew it was him. Running away like that after Mum died, thinking no one would notice, I noticed. All of a sudden, I saw him. There he was, my heart was pounding. I sprinted across the deserted grasslands. Fury was all I felt. There he was. I was the hunter...

Maya Khurshid (13)
Outwood Academy City Fields, Wakefield

The Kill

I was running through the forest, the trees weren't moving and were dripping in cold blood, the bushes were trembling in fear. Sticks and stones moved towards me. The howl of a creature roared in the distance but was creeping towards me. Slowly. What was it? It was a werewolf! I ran and ran. Police sirens were getting closer and closer with each step I took. I daren't look behind me just in case. Its big paws were coming closer, it was coming, its mouth drooling with saliva. It was coming in for the kill...

Emily Jane Brown (11)
Outwood Academy City Fields, Wakefield

Run For Your Life

I couldn't run for much longer. The slow and steady footsteps were getting closer by the second. All of a sudden, the footsteps stopped. I felt like my legs were going to give way. My eyelids were getting heavier and my brain wasn't as quick as before. I was tired of carrying this heavy weight on my shoulders wherever I went. I felt like hiding away from the world. If there was only a way for me to be free. I glanced at all the buildings around me and decided that it was my time to leave this scary world.

Zainab Azam (12)
Outwood Academy City Fields, Wakefield

Undead

The determined soldiers lost the battle. Who was the enemy do you ask? Zombies. The civilians were extremely vulnerable. I was one of them. It was a month since the zombies started their invasion, I didn't think much about it until they came to my hometown. I started running but I felt something, I felt a cold, bloodied hand being placed on my shoulder. All of a sudden, a shot was fired. I saw a soldier with his AK-47, he saved me but he had to save several more. Should I help him or run away? What should I do?

Quang Pham (11)
Outwood Academy City Fields, Wakefield

Desperation

He was curled up in a ball, clutching his maggot-infested wound, lying on the freezing stone floor. He was in prison for a crime he didn't even commit. He had allegedly killed the Ukranian President on a business trip and was now locked up. His cell was minuscule with tall, smooth walls so that he couldn't climb out. On the top of his cell, there were bars, so that he had some sunlight. He had to escape. It all started one night, it was bitterly cold, so nobody patrolled the outside. Would he escape from hell?

Talha Malik (12)
Outwood Academy City Fields, Wakefield

Prison Break

I collapsed, mud smudged all over me from head to toe. I had no time, they were coming... and I was lost. My friends had vanished and my phone was lifeless. I was now running for my life, who was chasing me? The cops, why? The queen abducted my brother and I tried to get him back... If you get in my way like she did, let's just say you'd end up in her position. I heard a loud *bang* and soon enough, they found me and that was the last thing I remembered before waking, locked in a cell.

Ghulam Mustafa Asif (12)
Outwood Academy City Fields, Wakefield

Hunted

I couldn't run for much longer, my heart was jumping out of my chest. They were just a second behind. I wasn't sure my legs could take it. My bones were aching now. I kept telling myself just a few more steps. My mind went blank and in a matter of seconds, I lay flat on the floor. I got up and started running. I was nearly there. I was finally there! I was so exhausted but so overwhelming, happy to have arrived first! I saw it shining, my Pandora ring! And now it was mine to keep forever.

Alishbah Ilyas (11)
Outwood Academy City Fields, Wakefield

Moon Beast

"Where are the others?"

Harper only shook his head.

"What happened?"

"The last moonquake opened a chasm. Garcia and Sanders dropped straight down."

"And the creature?"

Harper started to spasm wildly before his rusty helmet exploded into tiny pieces, dispersed around the cold, icy floor. The gloom behind them was ominous and the shadows hid the hideous creatures lurking in the distance. All of a sudden, everything went quiet. The distant screams that echoed through the murky, volatile forests and all you could hear was the lone howl of a wolf and then at that moment, the sinister monster came.

Abdihafeed Mustafa Osman Mohamed (11)

The Westgate School, Slough

![YoungWriters Est. 1991]

Prey

She shook uncontrollably. Her heart slammed against her meatless ribs, trying to escape. She wound herself tightly into a ball like wool, receding deeper into the shrubbery, wishing she'd never been born, wishing she'd been thrown into the river as an infant. She'd held in her tears for far too long, but now Eloise had stopped running, they fell out of her like rain. She prayed. That's what you do when death comes knocking... Or walking in heavy black boots. If she shut her eyes, maybe they'd disappear. But they'd spotted her now. After they'd finished, the shaking would stop...

Leia Humphries (16)
The Westgate School, Slough

The Graveyard

Heart pounding, head banging, palms getting sweatier by the minute. I could feel the darkness of the room closing in on me as it got tighter and tighter. Suddenly, I heard the sound of feet shuffling, moving closer towards me. I bolted! As fast as the wind could carry me. At that moment, my blood turned cold and I could feel fear trembling all over. I looked behind me, scanning the area, nothing! Then wandering through the graveyard, the air suddenly turned black all around! Icy cold fingers gripped my arm in the distance.

"Help!" I screamed.

But nobody heard...

Aleena Arif (11)
The Westgate School, Slough

Hunted

Sprinting towards the tree, panting and exhausted. I leant on it, giving my heart a break as sweat dripped down my forehead. Unexpectedly, a bullet whistled through the leaves, taking my breath away,
"He has a gun?"
Suddenly, an ice-cold hand gripped my arm, digging their fingernails into my skin. Instantly, I picked up the large log at my feet and struck them across the face. All I remembered was the endless stream of blood flowing out of their head. Silence and relief filled the air but the nightmare of the lifeless body staring at me would haunt me forever.

Lola Rose Axtell (12)
The Westgate School, Slough

Innocents

It's been twelve days since the virus started to spread, turning innocent people into mindless, rampaging beings, covered in oozing black boils and disfigured limbs. Luckily, the 'plague' or virus hasn't managed to infect me yet, but I'm sure it's only a matter of time. You see, it's not difficult to become infected. The 'innocents' as I've named them, don't have to touch you. I could be infected by breathing the wrong air... After thinking about my parents and wondering their whereabouts, it begins. I can feel my blood freezing in my veins, my breath leaving me. I am changing...

Aidan Payne (11)
The Westgate School, Slough

Adrenaline

The sinister chill of the night gave me shivers. I regretted immensely entering this murky part of this humongous forest. The sapphire stars and lapis moon faded as I got deeper and deeper into this forest. Then, a shotgun fired and bellowed throughout this forest. The gigantic bang got quieter and quieter. A chill ran down my spine. My heart was pounding. the chase was on. I sprinted as fast as I could and I didn't look back. Suddenly, loud stomps were getting closer, and I didn't feel anything. The freezing wind covered me and then... nothing. Nothing at all.

Amina Maryam Achour (11)
The Westgate School, Slough

Faint Memories

The hunting began two minutes ago. Everyone was scared. The rations were small. I would say it could last only three days. I felt a presence around us, it was not welcoming. I heard five shots and screams in the distance. I sat there, terrified... Suddenly, I heard footsteps, I stared at the door with eyes full of terror. There was another shot but no scream. This was unusual. I stood up and hid. After a while, every object disappeared, everything disappeared. I didn't remember any detail but I thought I fainted or I was too scared, I didn't know...

Nicole Maria Krasowski (11)
The Westgate School, Slough

You Or Me?

Only echoes of my footsteps could be heard. Unforgiving emptiness enveloped the place. All of a sudden, a spotlight focused on me. I found myself running, to flee, to forget. "Tick-tock goes the clock, tick-tock..."

My head swivelled from side to side. The lights flickered on and off. On and off. On and off. Unable to stand it, I ran. There was no goal, no aim, just an endless pathway of darkness. I closed my eyes and opened them again. The place was illuminated now. In front of me stood my reflection. My captor. My prisoner. My hunter.

Farina Fazeli (14)
The Westgate School, Slough

The Pack Hunter

They chased me. The beasts, only metres behind me, its saliva in puddles on the ground. Sweat oozed down my face. My legs were clawed by thorns, but it was the lesser of two evils. I could see the haven at the mountain's peak. But suddenly, the steps behind became more frequent. As if it was multiplying. Or regrouping! This urged my body to battle bravely against my pain, knowing that the malicious monsters behind me were ready to claw me to shreds, only leaving my skull as evidence of their feast. Suddenly, I was knocked down. I was doomed!

Anakin Shrewsbury (14)
The Westgate School, Slough

Witches For Life

It is no longer safe for us now that they know. I don't want to leave Chattam but for me and my sisters, we have to. They will blow the horn soon to signal that they have arrested witches. When they do, we have to run or die. There it is, loud and clear, over the cries of, "Burn them!" I tell Loria to get ready and then tell Ishida the same. The second horn blows and their chase for us begins. "Diapparato!" all three of us yell and we disappear across the country to a place called Nottingham! Safe.

Safiyya Mukhtar (12)
The Westgate School, Slough

Lana... The Ferocious Hunter

A baby girl named Lana, was born in 1847 to a brave hunter in a small village surrounded by deep forests. Lana's dad was not only a hunter, but also the head of the village army, to protect villagers from wild animals. From the age of nine, Lana also started hunting, getting stronger and braver as she grew. She became a great fighter by the age of fourteen, but sadly, her father passed away. No one stepped forward to lead, saving the villagers. Fierce Lana had to step forward to protect everyone by killing wild animals. So she did so.

Hamsa Pandraju (11)
The Westgate School, Slough

The Haunted House

It was a dark day, that was when the lady heard her back door open. She ran as quickly as she could but when she arrived, she saw a phantom. She closed her eyes for a few seconds and when she opened them, she couldn't believe herself, there was nothing there. Terrified, she locked every possible entrance to the house. After thirty minutes, her security alarm started ringing. It sounded like a siren, she knew she had to escape but she was trapped inside. That's when she saw the creature her mother told her about. A child...

Yasmine Biskri (11)
The Westgate School, Slough

The Hunt

I wanted to try and discover a new species, so I went to wander the forest. As I explored the depths of the forest, I caught a glimpse of a figure. Excitement, but also a bit of worry, filled my head. Suddenly, I heard a noise behind me. *Whoosh!* I gasped. It caught me by surprise. My heart started beating faster. I ran... I ran through the forest, adrenaline coursing through my veins. No exit could be seen. A thud came from behind me. Panting, I ran towards the direction of the light. I looked to my right and screamed...

Adil Khan (11)
The Westgate School, Slough

Preyed

As I ventured in the eerie forest for some shelter, I kept looking back because of my tickly feeling up my back. Was there someone watching me? I moved on.

"Arghhhhh!" I bellowed.

To my relief, it was just an owl. Wait! I could see a fire! Should I go towards it or should I leave? I could hear voices. I was going to go to it. As I blindly walked on, it seemed further and further onward. Eventually, I was worn out and needed some rest but it was right here. As I came to a clearing...

"Arghhhhh!"

Muhammad Fareed (11)
The Westgate School, Slough

Hunted By Wolves

My heart was pumping from head to toe, my feet felt like tons of bricks. The howling of the wolves seemed to be following us. The trees took my breath away. We had to leave. Now! If I didn't know that being hunted felt like this, I did now. Sirens wailed, wolves howled. My dream was coming true! Suddenly, a loud bang occurred, the sirens stopped. Completely stopped. My heart fell back into position, and the bricks almost cracked. I still felt like a spider without a web but I knew my web would be winding up again very soon...

Megan Duffy (12)
The Westgate School, Slough

The Chase

I wandered around the deep, dreary sky. The woods wept and shrieked constantly. For a minute, I stood there shuddering. But a thought appeared. That thought built up my courage, and there I trudged, into the bewildering woods. In the blink of an eye, my mysterious figure-like target was loitering within the darkness. I took my sword out and pursued it. The creature made a great stop. It glared at me. As soon as I could, I swung my sword with all my strength and slew it rapidly. It lay on the floor in shame. I was victorious.

Rhys J T Dzikamunhenga (11)
The Westgate School, Slough

The Cat Hunt

We have to leave. Now.

"Don't you understand, we have lost Coco."

Coco is my pet cat, she went missing a few weeks ago. We put posters up everywhere. Every time I went back to the posters, they were being taken down. I saw a car which had been following me, every time he kept changing cars, but it was the same driver all the time. What would they want me to do? I looked at the other place where I had put the other poster. I had noticed it said, 'Stop!' I realised later on, I was being hunted.

Inaya Chaudhry (12)
The Westgate School, Slough

The Prison Escape

After the murder I committed of Donald Trump, I was sentenced to life in prison. However, I was not going to take that sentence. I screamed while being taken to the world's most secure prison. As I arrived, many gates were open which was strange. Suddenly, I was there at my cell as my life rotted away. My inmate was kind and had been digging a hole to escape for fifty years. It was nearly complete. Suddenly, *boom!* It was open, we ran. However, my inmate was fat and slow. "Go on without me." I ran...

Yasin Ahmed (12)

The Westgate School, Slough

Hunted!

Sprinting faster and faster as I could hear the crunch of leaves getting louder and louder. I was being hunted. I was getting more scared as every minute went past. It felt like forever. I was so deep into the forest that I could hear the howls of the wolves like they were right next to me. I was lost in the depths of the forest, not knowing where to go. I was thinking, *I am going to die today!* I was petrified. Suddenly, out of nowhere, I heard sirens. My legs were getting tired. I couldn't run any longer...

Louise Thomas (11)

The Westgate School, Slough

Hide-And-Seek

I had 24 hours. The night got quieter and quieter. The adrenaline pumped through me faster than I could think. I had no time to think but run. I had to find a nearby house. Whoever was hunting me was still following me. I realised it was here. I found blood-covered bodies everywhere in the house. Knives and corpses everywhere. Then I heard noises above. I ran to the basement, hoping it wouldn't come. On the wall it said, 'Hide or seek?' I checked my watch, it was nearly dawn. It was there. I ran backwards and it got me.

Imaad Shaikh (11)
The Westgate School, Slough

The Chase

A tear ran straight down my cheek, my heart racing as fast as a lightning bolt. The zombies were gaining. Claire held my hand tighter than ever. All I could hear was the screams of millions of innocent people. Guilt rushed through my brain. I could've saved them but I had to run for my life. I was so scared, it felt like the trees were surrounding us, yet that was all I could see, trees and trees. I could hear the zombies, gaining on us. I rushed into an abandoned bunker, leaving Claire... She screamed, my heart sank.

Alisha Khan (12)
The Westgate School, Slough

Death Of Freedom

My heart was pounding as the sirens spoke loudly. I dared to ignore everything around me. From the day I was a criminal, I wanted to be free. As the police warned me not to move, without regret, I disobeyed their orders. I would do anything for freedom, nothing could stop me. As I grabbed a gun for protection and threat, I rushed into the courtyard of the prison where all that stopped me was a fence and... barbed wire. I was blinded as the searchlight struck fear in my eyes. This could be the end. I was being hunted.

Barween Alawie (11)
The Westgate School, Slough

Being Framed

There I was, in the middle of the forest - my head spinning. All I heard were sirens surrounding me. I ran further into the woods, the dogs barking, footsteps coming closer and closer. I tripped. I couldn't see anything, I was going blind. I was hurting, I tried to run but couldn't, it seemed like I had no bones. My eyes started to close but I didn't let them. My head was spinning with mixed emotions. I was wondering why I was being chased. I was with my friends, then they disappeared. Now, I knew I was being hunted.

Kamran Farooq (12)
The Westgate School, Slough

Sweet Dreams

My heart was pounding as I could detect screams from all directions. It was probably... no, it was a werewolf. The werewolf was far away, so I had nothing to worry about. So, why was I shaking so much? Something was calling me. I lifted my head up and gazed at the moon.

"Come to me and I will secure your safety and keep you away from this vulgar beast!"

I was hypnotised by its elegance. It dragged me towards it. I didn't know what to do but it kept its promise. I was safe. Or... that's what I thought.

Subayr Abdulle (12)
The Westgate School, Slough

Time Is Ticking

Grab the bag and leave, I keep thinking, *I need to get the money, Anne took it off me. It's mine, fair and square.* One hour later... they are chasing me. The army have knives and guns. I am just putting one foot in front of the other, quicker and quicker each time. I make a musical beat with my feet. *Bang, bang!* I hear the gunshots. I see blood dripping onto my feet and I hear a ringing in my ear. It is the red residue. I am losing my own life slowly but surely. Time is running out.

Ruby Louise Moore (11)
The Westgate School, Slough

Frightened

One day, my parents went for a vacation and me and my cousin were staying together. But my cousin had an important job and left. I went to bed. It was exactly twelve o'clock, midnight, and I could hear somebody breaking into our house. I knew we had some valuable things in the house. I put all the things in the nearest bag I could grab. I opened the door and started running. It was pitch-black outside and was raining heavily. I could hear somebody chasing me. I was out of breath. For once, I-I-I was hunted.

Hansini Bellamkonda (11)
The Westgate School, Slough

The Wolf Surprise

I went down the scary, dark woods and was trying to achieve my goal of hunting down an animal. I had all my gear ready for something to happen to me. I searched for a few minutes and still hadn't found anything but I wasn't giving up, not just yet. I searched and searched but I found my victim, a wolf! We had eye contact for five seconds, was it good? Was it bad? Something came in and interrupted our 'staring contest' and the wolf began to attack. The wolf was attacking but I stabbed it. I was very scared.

Nadia Maminska (11)
The Westgate School, Slough

Unknown Voices

I heard a strange voice from the distance. A voice that I couldn't recognise. I started to walk in the direction of it. I realised that there was only me. The sound was louder and louder, like many voices speaking faintly at the same time. I looked behind me and I was frozen with fear. I knew I had to run. Now. Suddenly, a familiar voice started to call me. I ran towards it as fast as I could. Then I saw my brother. He wanted me to hide in the bunker but it was too late. More zombies released...

Norbert Tryczynski (11)
The Westgate School, Slough

Him

When I found out my boyfriend was insane, I had no intention of running. I thought I was able to control him, or at least get him the help he deserved, until he brought that knife up to my throat and threatened to sluggishly slice it, making me agonise longer. He had no mercy. His hefty, russet eyes made that obvious. Regardless of how I would shriek and wail, he wouldn't let go, and now I could feel his breath on the back of my neck. He was out to get me. He wanted me lifeless, I knew too much.

Patrycja Wloczewska (15)
The Westgate School, Slough

The Forest Figure

It went dark. All of a sudden, a black figure appeared from under the moonlight. As fast as a cheetah, I ran until the figure was out of sight. Then I tripped. I fell on cold and white snow which froze my bones. A wolf howled, as if it had been stabbed, then I got up and dashed towards the forest. I hid under a bark log, so I would be invisible but it was the only hiding spot there. It would be the first place it would search.

It approached the log and whispered, "I know you're there..."

Arham Ahmed (12)
The Westgate School, Slough

The Hunted

It was now 4:30pm, the sun was starting to go down. The trees swayed in the dim light. I saw a shadow in the distance and then it disappeared into thin air... Then I heard my name called behind me. They said they were looking for me. I wanted to scream but they were around the corner so I could not. It sounded like three men, I just wanted to get home. I could see figures moving in the leaves. I was so scared. I didn't know what to do. At this point, I knew I was being hunted. Hunted!

Kian Hancey (11)
The Westgate School, Slough

The Life

I was running faster and faster, trying to establish some distance between me and the monster behind. The Godzilla-like creature edged ever so closer as my speed was waning down. After that, I managed to hide from the monster, to gain my breath back and my energy back. I waited there for ten minutes and after that, I set up camp. I collected leaves for a bed and put them under a tree, then made a fire. I was very tired so I went to sleep. Then I woke up and saw the last thing in my life.

George Lacey (11)
The Westgate School, Slough

The Hunting Crow

I had 24 minutes to get my mum her cake, as my dad set me a timer for her surprise party. As I was walking back, I decided to go through a narrow path. It was then I realised I was being followed, not by a person though. I looked behind me to see just a little black crow, I thought nothing of it and kept walking. I looked at the time, I still had fifteen minutes to get back home but then I felt something behind me again. It was different this time. I then saw *him* behind me...

Tommy Fallon (12)
The Westgate School, Slough

The Creepy Man

There was once a creepy man who had been haunting me. I woke up in the middle of the night and saw him there, outside of my house, waiting for me to come outside to him. I stared at him, I looked away for one second and he was gone. I did not know where he went. He had vanished somewhere else. I was shaking with fear as a shiver ran down my spine. I was shocked that he could have vanished away that quickly. I shut my curtains and got back into my bed, wrapped up all warm.

Mackenzie Sears (12)
The Westgate School, Slough

The Chase Is On...

It all started one midnight when it glimmered on my face and I heard the sirens go off. It started... I ran, this was probably the scariest time of my life. I grabbed my bag. I hid, we had to gather sticks and build a den or a place to stay in. It was getting dark. This was the part I wasn't ready for... As I was building my den, I felt a gush of wind pass me, it shot shivers down my spine. *What was that?* I wondered. I decided maybe I should go back in the den...

Maia Evans (11)
The Westgate School, Slough

A Fugitive

I am hunting someone for some time, he is wanted by the police for many different things. He had a flat on his own, somewhere in France. Police are raiding each house to see if he's there. People have said they have seen him around. The police are on it, wrong man. The last time they saw him, it was at the shopping centre and now he is a long way away from there. We can't let him go because he is a danger to the hometown, we have to find him.

Kyren Charles (11)
The Westgate School, Slough

The Man In The Crimson Jacket

As the shutters slowly lowered, a wrinkled hand brought it to a stop. My drowsy eyes pivoted to the man's tender mouth. He wore a thick, crimson jacket and begged me that the pill was his mother's last hope. I strolled back through the counter and entered the medicine cabinet, my hands rummaged through antiseptics. His pill was perched on the top shelf. My foot searched for balance and slipped on a rusty remote.

"Breaking news! Twelve pharmacies have closed down following footage of a man, wearing a crimson jacket, butchering pharmacists to death."

The cabinet door shut behind me...

Kavin Vijaykumar (14)
Westcliff High School For Boys, Westcliff-On-Sea

Redbone

Cold frost pierced my fingertips, my brain screams at me, *stay warm!* I don't want to. This is me. Drifting in the emptiness. No confines, shackles. I am boundless, yet frozen. I won't close my eyes, it's too late for that. The cold creeps up and bites. So sharp, yet it doesn't leave me bitter. This is my end. Yet I don't feel remorse, regret, pain. These things mean nothing to me. Nothing means anything. Existence is a coincidence. We are all drifting. Never from place to place. From thoughts to feelings. From feelings to null, nothingness. The answer: Redbone.

Edwin Frederick Brown (15)
Westcliff High School For Boys, Westcliff-On-Sea

Dead Rotting Flesh

Dead rotting flesh. Arms limp, stumbling legs. A watching mind in an uncontrolled body. The lifeless corpse trundling on amidst an apocalyptic wasteland. The body smells human but the mind thinks *run*. A shrill scream emits from a nearby derelict home and the legs pick up speed. A horde of dead rotting flesh surrounding a youth's mutilated body. Identity is unimportant to the masses. The mind watches on as the body is devoured. No control. No influence. No stopping the body. The smell of putrid flesh filling the air like a sunflower dispersing its seeds. The deed was done now.

Sam Owens (15)
Westcliff High School For Boys, Westcliff-On-Sea

Pursuit

Petrified and alone, I had nobody to turn to. The loud crunch of snow filled my ears as I looked back, witnessing once more the creatures pursuing me, vicious snarls rang, abundant with primitive intent. Suddenly, I stumbled. Time seemed to slow down. Panic clouded my head like mist. They surrounded me. Their breath puffs of savage desire crystallised in the air. Like Genesis laid the first stone of the Bible, they had surely sown the seeds of my demise. The jaws of death encompassed me, yet bringing not torment but despair. Bleak emotions eroded my sanity. Inevitable death awaited...

Hassan Mustafa Hassan Ahmed (14)

Westcliff High School For Boys, Westcliff-On-Sea

Gun

I aimed. I shot. I killed. Gun was my name, it was my life. *Click!* Bullet in the chamber. *Click!* I held it down. Everything was in place. Adrenaline soared, the metal still icy. The trigger was pulled, no aim required. Slicing through the exterior, their death was inevitable. Blood emerged from the tomb, it was trapped in. Awakened, it now ran free against the wet, moist air. Mist condensed rapidly upon the exterior of my burning surface. The tension released. I cooled down. The hunt had finished. The hunted killed. Gun had done well. Gun had completed the hunt.

Eesa Khan (15)
Westcliff High School For Boys, Westcliff-On-Sea

Survival Tactics

Veins popped out of his forehead like an inflatable ring. His scrunched-up face radiated a red aura, steam escaping from every hole in his body. We skated for our lives. Wind rushing past our skin, each hair stood on end. Goosebumps. But the freedom felt better than breathing. Trifling tasers almost connected with us. By the skin of our teeth, Manhattan Station filled to the brim at rush hour, each of us leapt over the barriers. We ploughed through crowds of sheep fixated on their phones. Police cars blocked the street to our certain freedom. Roughest night this year...

Zain Bokhari (16)
Westcliff High School For Boys, Westcliff-On-Sea

Hunted

I was close. Not close enough. Leaves cracked beneath my feet, trying to give me away. Hushed voices echoed through the air, taunting me, deceiving me. I stopped. They were closer now. I could sense it. Adrenaline erupted throughout my body, swirling around like a torpedo. I collapsed to the ground, trying to stifle my trembling breath. Littered with anticipation, I kept on moving, and with each step, I was closer and closer. Suddenly, a cluster of sound exploded behind me and a knife was plunged deep into my back. It did scar, but at least I had found them.

William Brenton (15)
Westcliff High School For Boys, Westcliff-On-Sea

Outbreak

They slowly multiplied until the desolate, white room was occupied by ten of them. Each one hunched over, their yellowish skin pulled taut over dark sinews and tendons. Like clockwork, automatons came to life just as the next pair materialised in the centre of the room, their sunken eye sockets glanced around the room with milky eyes that gave off a melancholy aura. Almost as if ordered, they started to lurch forward towards the thick glass screen that divided them and us. The lead member was starting to pick up pace and he reached the glass. It had begun.

Archie Hepburn (14)
Westcliff High School For Boys, Westcliff-On-Sea

Are You The Hunter Or The Hunted?

Unsuspecting and innocent, it peered through the trees. I knew its mind wasn't clear, I supposed it was my job to... sharpen it. My heart pounded like a kettledrum, my nose moistened at the seducing scent of blood. The poor thing must've been cold and scared. Its hands quivered as it erratically pointed its gun in all directions. It was paralysed, yet I'd never felt so alive! The thrill... it boiled over. I leapt. Delicious red sauce oozed from its organs as I pierced every limb. The best thing they did was beg for mercy, another piece for my collection.

Christopher Butler-Cole (15)
Westcliff High School For Boys, Westcliff-On-Sea

The Last Meal

Slowly they crawled out of their secluded cabins. Abandoned by the parents that once loved them, they had nothing left. Stripped from their security of the homes and ditched into a farm for slaughter. They were to be slaughtered, eaten and never to be seen again. Acceptance had filled the air as they all lined up slowly approaching their death. They were dead inside. Nothing could save them for there was no purpose left in their life. Blood burst out the weak vessel of the children as they were squeezed by the claws of the demons. They were only food.

Shibha Alam (16)
Westcliff High School For Boys, Westcliff-On-Sea

The Door

Through years of running, I had crossed continents, hemispheres and everything in-between. There was a knock at the door. It opened and it was simply the local mailman. Granted, I couldn't understand what he was saying, he handed me a letter and with a smile, he took off. I slumped back into the chair with relief. As I did so, there was some sort of commotion outside. It could have been anything but this time, it was different. In the space of ten seconds, curiosity turned to paralysing fear. I could only watch on as the darkness began to turn...

Matthew Singh (15)
Westcliff High School For Boys, Westcliff-On-Sea

My Sixth Sense

At first, it was just a feeling, a sixth sense I couldn't really explain. But then it changed like there was someone behind me, on my path. A cold hand trying to break into the veracity of my reality. The sense grew stronger, I could feel the hand now as it cemented itself inside my brain, caging itself in, refusing to let itself out. I was slowly being destroyed from the inside, running wouldn't help. When I screamed, only they could hear. My fiction was their reality, I was powerless, having no control, just a sixth sense I couldn't understand.

Ben Dixon (14)
Westcliff High School For Boys, Westcliff-On-Sea

The Noise

I woke up in a shady, humid corridor where water dribbled and pooled around me. I sprang to my feet, dazed and confused. Then, I heard it. A demonic screech, so high-pitched and loud that I froze with terror. So I ran. I darted away to my right, dodging puddles and dancing through vines. The row followed me, seemingly getting closer and closer. A corner approached, I swung around it and into a cramped room, containing a cupboard. I slipped inside and held the door closed with my foot. Then it entered the room and steadily opened the door...

Harrison James (15)
Westcliff High School For Boys, Westcliff-On-Sea

My Hunt

It was a very different time when I first saw you. Innocent. Elegant. Impossible. I gave chase. You disappeared. I grew paranoid. I called you a traitor. I called you dangerous. Yet, I saw your face in everything. I grew hateful, of you, of everything. I turned myself into a fortress, I eradicated any amicable thoughts of you and let the hunt begin. It took years before I saw you again. Again, I gave chase but this time, you did not run. You were ready. You were prepared. There was nothing more that I could do and you were free.

James Holley (15)
Westcliff High School For Boys, Westcliff-On-Sea

The Chase

"We have to leave!" Steve said. "Now!"
At that moment, a bag was thrown over his head as he fell
on the floor, screaming for his life.
As I watched, I felt guilty about leaving him but I knew I did
not have much time. I sprinted to the boat, past all the
menacing buildings, as I wondered what Steve's fate would
be. I thought about all the fun times we'd had together and
that it had all come to an end. I was cornered, men all
around me. All I felt was regret, I could've helped Steve...

Alexander Zierik (15)
Westcliff High School For Boys, Westcliff-On-Sea

Darkness

I was scared. He was coming. I was nearing the end of the alley. It was getting darker as I ran further away from the murky, yellow lights from the distant street. I looked back, all I could see was the man's silhouette getting closer to me. It was getting darker, darker. The man started shouting. He was shouting louder and louder. I didn't dare look back. I could hear his footsteps. He was getting closer by the second. I kept running as fast as I could but suddenly, I felt his arm on my back. I looked back. Darkness!

Aston Cook (15)
Westcliff High School For Boys, Westcliff-On-Sea

Escape

I had little to work with, the chase was on. I had to leave now if I was to escape. They were here already. How did they know? Only a week had passed, I thought I was free. I ran round the back. Only the woods filled my eyeline. I looked back, red and blue lights filled the night sky. The sirens screamed through the silence, wheels screeched across the tarmac. The hounds of hell were loose, their barks yelled to surrender. Leaves crunched on every step and flashlights flickered through the trees. I ran and ran, I was hunted.

Issac Leung (14)
Westcliff High School For Boys, Westcliff-On-Sea

Observer

Scared. Another butcher marched past, their whispers muffled by the yells of those in uniform. He turned away from the march, knowing too well what was coming. Shouting. Motion. A scuffle of feet, an emergence from the pack. Running. The mere souls ran towards him, panic etched in their face. He panicked, the stripe-robed figure got closer and closer. He could hear the agony in their breath, adrenaline. They dropped. The bullets ripped through their remaining flesh as a butcher would carve the meat. Terrified, he ran.

Oscar Piggott (15)
Westcliff High School For Boys, Westcliff-On-Sea

HUNTED - THE CHASE IS ON

Patience

I need to wait. I lie down, calming my breaths. The bushes cover my position, keeping me hidden from the wolves in the encampment below. I can't move, if I do, I'll be heard. The rainforest around me echoes with the cries of its wildlife alongside the cheers of the men beneath me. It's almost peaceful, I can't rest yet, I must focus. A winding serpent coils up my leg. Then, the roar of a Jeep disturbs the peace. He is here. I ready my weapon and take aim. Dead, still, I aim for the head and I fire...

Ben Wright (15)
Westcliff High School For Boys, Westcliff-On-Sea

Followed

I didn't look back. I couldn't. The fear that rushed through me was too overwhelming, I knew I couldn't run for much longer but there was nowhere I would go where I would feel safe. Soon, I started to lose all feeling in my body, every part of me went numb as I heard the choir of blood-curdling screams that followed me in every step. That's when I heard it, I didn't see it but with that one sound, every single hair on my body stood up. I thought about just giving up. I was given no choice.

Josh McCarthy (14)
Westcliff High School For Boys, Westcliff-On-Sea

Cross Country

"Run! I heard him say.
So that's what I did. I lost my footing, went spiralling down.
From the floor, I rolled, coming face-to-face with the floor.
Great start, I thought to myself before scrambling up and
starting up again. Closer now, I heard that voice again. My
time was nearly up, I could feel it. A new personal best
today, or I would be running all year long. With two laps left,
panic started to set in. I didn't make it, I was done for but I
glanced back. I had to finish. I had to.

Thomas Waters (15)
Westcliff High School For Boys, Westcliff-On-Sea

Demons

It wasn't supposed to end this way. I didn't mean it, they would not leave me alone. They shout, scream and jest at my every action. They hunt for me wherever I go. Even when there is no one, they still follow. My silent screams suspended in space. The dead body at the side of the room brought me back to my senses. He was evidence as was I. Evidence must be destroyed. As the flames engulfed me, I came to a stop and so did my hunters.
"A local man was burnt alive in the fire he started himself."

Ethan Tangka (16)
Westcliff High School For Boys, Westcliff-On-Sea

Being Caught

I gasped for breath as I stumbled down the stairs that were now starting to look like a mane. Had I lost him? This question resounded in my mind, but I did not look back as I feared my predator would catch up to me. If only I could reach the police station. Seconds later, that felt like minutes, flashed before my eyes. Before I knew it, the man had caught up to me. There was only some time before he would be running next to me. I looked at everything for the last time. This was the end!

Othniel Sahay Mattukoyya (14)
Westcliff High School For Boys, Westcliff-On-Sea

The Last Resort

It's not safe now they know we're here. We have to leave, now. I run for my life, not even looking back, as I see the people I love get swallowed by the evil darkness that surrounds us. We are being hunted and we are on the run. Is there anywhere safe anymore? There's only one option I have left, to run to the last safe place on Earth, Base 43. I run for my life, alongside my brother, the last person around I can trust. Then, as we run from the horde, I see my brother die before me.

Aran Tanseli (14)
Westcliff High School For Boys, Westcliff-On-Sea

Forced

As the bell tolled, it had begun. The hunt, the chase, the game. Whatever it was, it had begun. I ran into the abyss of the unknown, desperate not to be caught. Finally, I had found it, it shouldn't exist but it did. A way out, a path. Or was it? A trap or miracle? A beacon of hope or a death wish? The only way to know was to go forward. Farther or closer? How could I ever know? Who do I trust? My brain or my gut? My mind or my heart? Who? Pure knowledge or pure instinct?

Adrian Fernandes (14)
Westcliff High School For Boys, Westcliff-On-Sea

Fear

The thing hunts me. It breathes down my neck and it whispers in my ears. It's in my nightmares and it's in my dreams. It burns through my soul and ruptures my thoughts. Everywhere I go, it is following me, tracking, tracing my footsteps. I want it off me, I want it out of me but yet, I can't get rid of it. I can't work it off. I can't run for much longer. Soon it will end. Everything will end. I will be free. Finally free from the hunt. Fear, fear has hunted me.

Stephen Babbs (15)
Westcliff High School For Boys, Westcliff-On-Sea

The Blue Monster

We have to leave. Now. Our aquatic enemy is approaching with menace. If we don't run now, we are walking dead humans. A cacophony of noises circulate my ear; Above it all, is the howl of a childless mother, whose child has likely, very likely, been engulfed by the mouth of the flood. Moments later, I find myself running from a towering gush of blue. At this point, I can't distinguish between reality and fantasy.

Daniel Hasan (16)
Westcliff High School For Boys, Westcliff-On-Sea

On The Run

I am on the run. The police are after me. No time to think. No time to stop. I left it at home. But now it is too late. My soul quenched for some companionship. Very frightening it is, for one to acquire freedom solely. Loneliness is my biggest fear. I pull my hoodie over my head, concealing my face, exiting society as the tempestuous wind hit my cold, red cheeks.

Ayaan Umar Sheikh (15)
Westcliff High School For Boys, Westcliff-On-Sea

YOUNG WRITERS INFORMATION

We hope you have enjoyed reading this book – and that you will continue to in the coming years.

If you're a young writer who enjoys reading and creative writing, or the parent of an enthusiastic poet or story writer, do visit our website **www.youngwriters.co.uk**. Here you will find free competitions, workshops and games, as well as recommended reads, a poetry glossary and our blog. There's lots to keep budding writers motivated to write!

If you would like to order further copies of this book, or any of our other titles, then please give us a call or order via your online account.

Young Writers
Remus House
Coltsfoot Drive
Peterborough
PE2 9BF
(01733) 890066
info@youngwriters.co.uk

Join in the conversation!
Tips, news, giveaways and much more!

YoungWritersUK   @YoungWritersCW